POLICY CHALLENGES AND POLITICAL RESPONSES

POLICY CHALLENGES AND POLITICAL RESPONSES

PUBLIC CHOICE PERSPECTIVES ON THE POST-9/11 WORLD

Edited by

William F. Shughart II
Department of Economics
The University of Mississippi
Mississippi, MS, USA

And

Robert D. Tollison
Department of Economics
Clemson University
Clemson, SC, USA

Reprinted from *Public Choice*, Volume 124, Nos. 1–2, 2005

Springer

A.C.I.P. Catalogue record for this book is available from the Library of Congress

ISBN: 978-1-4419-3918-0 e-ISBN: 978-0-387-28038-7

Published by Springer
P.O. Box 990, 3300 AZ Dordrecht, The Netherlands

Sold and distributed in North, Central and South America
by Springer,
101 Philip Drive, Norwell, MA 02061, U.S.A.

In all other countries, sold and distributed
by Springer,
P.O. Box 322, 3300 AH Dordrecht, The Netherlands

Printed on acid-free paper

Printed in the Netherlands

Table of Contents

Articles

Public Choice (2005) **124:** 1–18
DOI: 10.1007/s11127-005-4740-5

Public choice in the new century

WILLIAM F. SHUGHART II[1,*] and ROBERT D. TOLLISON[2]
[1]*Department of Economics, The University of Mississippi, P.O. Box 1848, University, MS 38677-1848, USA;* [2]*John E. Walker Department of Economics, Clemson University, 222 Sirrine Hall, Clemson, SC 29634, USA (*Author for correspondence: E-mail: shughart@olemiss.edu)*

Accepted March 2005

Abstract. This special issue of *Public Choice* was designed to afford leading scholars the opportunity to summarize the current state of the public choice literature in key areas of public policy concern and to offer their thoughts about future directions of research. By laying out public choice frameworks for analyzing some of the major challenges confronting democratic governments at the dawn of the 21st century, the issue's overarching goal is to demonstrate the vibrancy and continuing relevance of the public choice research program.

1. Introduction

No, we are not posing as a two-headed Nostradamus here. We do not pretend to know what the future holds for the public choice research program in general. Neither can we forecast the particular problems and analytical methods that will engage the field's attention in the new century.

Our goal in assembling this special issue was much more modest: public choice is just beyond celebrating its fiftieth birthday. In a burst of creative activity that spanned the two decades beginning circa 1950, the discipline's acknowledged founders, Black (1948a,b, [1958] 1987), Arrow ([1951] 1963), Downs (1957), Buchanan and Tullock (1962), Riker (1962), Olson (1965) and Niskanen (1971), launched a revolution in the study of *Homo politicus*.[1] They did so by applying the rational-actor model of economics to problems of collective decision-making by voters, legislatures and bureaucracies. Orthodox faith in the benevolence of political man (and woman) was displaced by hard-nosed analyses of how the behavior of self-interested individuals adapts to changes in incentives and constraints as they move from the realm of ordinary markets to the realm of politics. As a result, public choices are now seen to differ from private choices, not because people are motivated differently in the two settings, but rather because the institutions of collective decision-making differ fundamentally from the institutions of private decision-making.

Fifty years on seemed to us a propitious time for reassessment. The revolution launched by the field's founders and carried on by their students is nearly complete in the professional journals of economics, political science and sociology. Rational choice models and methods have become such commonplace tools of academic research that the time is quickly fading from memory when mere descriptions of political institutions and public policy processes were the scholar's modus operandi. The methodologies of positive economic science, including rigorous theorizing and statistical testing, have come to underpin nearly all accepted explanations of the many and varied "unintended", frequently perverse consequences of democratic policymaking – outcomes once excused as the lamentable but correctable errors of well-intentioned human beings.

Public Choice, which began life as samizdat circulated by Gordon Tullock in Blacksburg, Virginia, under the title *Papers on Non-Market Decision-Making*, is now ranked among the top 30 journals in the social sciences and has spawned several imitators. Dennis Mueller's survey of the theories and methods of public choice, which started as a 39-page article in the *Journal of Economic Literature* (Mueller, 1976), has grown, in its third edition as a book, to nearly 800 pages (Mueller, 2003). The field has its own specialized handbooks (Mueller, 1997; Shughart & Razzolini, 2001), a two-volume encyclopedia (Rowley & Schneider, 2004) and a roster of distinguished critics (Kelman, 1987; Green & Shapiro, 1994).[2]

One might be tempted to conclude that public choice scholars have nothing left to say; that, paradoxically, public choice has become a victim of its own success. Such a conclusion would be premature, however, as this special issue hopes to show. World events continually present new problems for analysis, perhaps none more important than the rise of Islamist terrorism, whose bloody intentions were revealed on September 11, 2001. That same event brought some old questions back to the surface: a decade after President Bill Clinton proclaimed the era of big government to be over, the run-up in military spending appropriated to defeat the Taliban, to topple Saddam Hussein and to wage a global "War on Terror" combined with equally massive increases in domestic spending (for public education, for homeland security and for regulating corporate accounting practices, among others), with post-9/11 economic recession and with deficit-financed income-tax cuts to produce unprecedented growth in the size of the federal government during President George W. Bush's first term. Government's scope too has been expanded by passage of the USA Patriot Act, the creation of a cabinet-level Department of Homeland Security and congressional adoption of the recommendations of the 9/11 Commission for reorganizing the American intelligence community under a new Director of National Intelligence. Europe, meanwhile, introduced a new currency and began the process of writing and ratifying a new constitution designed to integrate the continent more fully politically as well as economically.

The new century brought with it a number of other policy challenges, perhaps less momentous than 9/11, but no less interesting from a public choice perspective. President Bush's defeat of Al Gore on Election Day 2000, marred by doubts about the outcome in Florida, raised concerns about the accuracy of vote counts and generated calls for replacing the winner-takes-all Electoral

College with a more democratic method of selecting presidents. Popular democracy was in full cry as the 21st century began. California's voters succeeded in recalling Governor Gray Davis and electing Arnold Schwarzenegger in his stead. Initiatives and referendums placed on ballots there and in many other US states, both "red" and "blue", asked Americans to express their opinions on controversial policy issues ranging from gay marriage to taxpayer funding of stem-cell research. The financing of political campaigns, the extent of liability for "pain and suffering" damages under the tort laws and the merits of vouchers for promoting school choice continued to engage public debate.

The old and new policy challenges of the century just begun are problems of collective decision-making, to which public choice scholars can bring their unique perspective. That is the task we set for the contributors to this special issue. They were invited to assess the state of the public choice literature in key policy areas and to offer their thoughts about future directions of research in light of current events. We, as editors, did not ask all of the important questions, nor did we expect our colleagues to say the final word on the topics they were assigned. Indeed, as we will emphasize in the volume's concluding article, a great deal of unfinished business remains on the agenda of public choice. Public choice scholars have not yet resolved some of the field's most fundamental questions, such as what motivates a free people to vote in the first place. However, by laying out public choice frameworks for analyzing some of the policy challenges of the post-9/11 world, our contributors demonstrate the energy and continuing relevance of the public choice research program.

2. A Roadmap to the Special Issue

This special issue of *Public Choice* contains eleven substantive chapters by some of the field's leading scholars. The first two authors set problems of contemporary democracy in broad context by assessing the present state of the social contract that separates the objects of collective choice from those reserved to private individuals.[3] Subsequent contributors turn the reader's attention to more specific policy issues of current interest, ranging from constitution-making in the European Union to tort reform. The editors conclude the volume by briefly summarizing what has gone before and speculating on the future of public choice.

One of the ironies of the new world order that emerged following the collapse of the Soviet Union is that, except perhaps in the isolation of the academy, the intellectual foundations of collectivism are everywhere in retreat. Unfettered markets are widely acknowledged to be superior to government planning as engines of economic prosperity. Supplanting totalitarianism with democracy has become a key foreign policy goal of the major western powers. Yet, in many of these nations, including the United States, governments continue inexorably to expand both in size and scope. The era of Ronald Reagan and Margaret Thatcher seemingly has been consigned to the dustbin of history. New domestic spending initiatives to provide prescription drug benefits for senior citizens, to "leave no child behind" in the public schools, and to strengthen homeland security against the threat of terrorism have, under an ostensibly "conservative" Republican president, triggered rates of governmental growth in the United States not seen since Franklin Delano Roosevelt's New Deal (Shughart, 2004).

In "Afraid to be Free: Dependency as Desideratum", James Buchanan argues that collectivist impulses are alive and well in the polity, not because the ideas of Karl Marx remain intellectually respectable as guides to managing the macroeconomy, but rather because of the seductions of what he calls "parental socialism". Preferring security to liberty, people are afraid to be free. Demanding protection from the many vagaries of modern life, they readily cede the freedom to make their own choices to others, thereby evading responsibility for deciding how much money to set aside for their retirement years or how to pay their own health care expenses. Although self-interested political elites, still in thrall to socialism's "fatal conceit" and smug in their father-knows-best attitude toward the great unwashed masses, do not hesitate for their own narrow purposes to exploit the polity's yearning for safety and predictability, Buchanan's overarching point is that the growth of government is more a matter of "bottoms-up" demands than of "top-down" dictates. As such, socialism will survive and be extended in the new century until and unless the polity's addiction to state subvention is palliated, perhaps in realization that cravings for more government cannot continue to be met in the absence of confiscatory tax rates or the adoption of political-support eroding reforms, such as raising the age at which retirees can begin drawing their promised public pensions or limiting participation in welfare programs through means-testing.

The next contribution to this volume, by Charles Rowley, brings historical perspective to bear in evaluating the soundness of the US Constitution circa 2005. Opening the discussion with an overview of the political philosophies of Thomas Hobbes and John Locke, he argues forcefully that, in 1776, and again in 1787, the Founding Fathers of the American republic resolved those two competing visions of the origins and functions of the state decisively in favor of Lockeian principles. In that view, governments are instituted among men not to establish order – to end the war of all against all Hobbes thought to be man's fate in the state of nature – and to confer rights on a grateful citizenry, but rather to safeguard humankind's natural rights to life, liberty and property – rights emanating from the Creator and antecedent to government – from the sovereign's depredations. Quoting liberally from the Declaration of Independence, the writings of James Madison and the language of the

Constitution itself, Rowley catalogues the breadth and depth with which a Lockeian spirit infuses American political institutions.

"Fragmenting Parchment and the Winds of War" then takes on a darker color. Beginning with the Civil War (1861–1865), the very institutions of government crafted at Philadelphia to secure the rights of a free people were turned against them. Resolving to save the Union rather than to fulfill the oath of office requiring him to preserve, to protect and to defend the Constitution against all enemies, foreign and domestic, Rowley describes how Abraham Lincoln exploited the acts of secession by eleven southern states to claim extraordinary emergency powers for the presidency, powers which he used liberally to suppress opposition to his war policies. Lincoln trampled on individual liberties by suspending the writ of habeas corpus, freeing him to arrest and detain civilian critics without benefit of trial. Included in the administration's dragnet were 31 Maryland state legislators sympathetic to the Confederate cause, the mayor of Baltimore, a Maryland congressman, and leading local newspaper editors and publishers, the jailing of all of whom was rationalized as necessary to keep that state in the Union fold. In what Rowley views as an impeachable offense, the president went so far as to threaten to jail Roger Taney, the Chief Justice of the Supreme Court, after Taney sustained a constitutional challenge to his actions.

America continued down the slippery slope of eroding constitutional protections during the First World War, after unrestricted German submarine warfare finally provoked Woodrow Wilson into requesting congressional authority to send an American Expeditionary Force to the mud of France. Rowley recites the many constitutional violations committed by the Wilson administration, violations that, like Lincoln before him, he justified on the basis of wartime emergency. The chief executive who had campaigned for reelection on an isolationist platform became a jingoistic warrior who sought decisive victory, no matter the cost in blood, in treasure, or in civil liberties. Wilson reinstituted the draft, orchestrated a centrally directed command economy, badgered citizens into buying "Liberty Bonds" to help finance the war effort, censored the press, and quashed dissention.

That same theme is struck in the remainder of Rowley's essay, which moves forward in time to the Second World War, to the Cold War and to the post-9/11 War on Terror. As before, Rowley maintains that the executive and legislative branches of government repeatedly took advantage of threats to national security, most recently under the authority of the hastily passed USA Patriot Act, to undermine the civil and economic liberties the Founding Fathers sought to secure for posterity at Philadelphia. And, moreover, as Rowley also contends, constitutional safeguards have been overridden with the active cooperation of a judicial branch all too willing to cede emergency war powers to the president and the Congress. Rowley's pessimistically concludes from the historical record that Lockeian principles simply cannot withstand

Hobbesian impulses for order when freedom is under external assault and, arguably, internal limits on government power are most vital.

As the old century ended and the new century began, constitutional issues took center stage on the European continent. The drafting of a new constitution for the European Union (EU) and the commencement of the process for ratifying it represent the most ambitious steps taken along the road to economic and political integration initiated by the Treaty of Rome in 1957, which established the European Economic Community (later the European Community), and subsequently carried forward by the treaties on European Union in 1992 (Maastricht), of Amsterdam in 1997 and of Nice in 2001. Russia and the former Soviet republics embarked contemporaneously on a parallel path of constitution-making as they transitioned away from communist rule toward more western-style political systems. These events, many of which are still underway, supply significant opportunities for scholarly research in the field of study launched in modern form by Buchanan and Tullock (1962) in the *Calculus of Consent* and now known as constitutional economics or constitutional political economy.

Mueller summarizes the growing literature that explores, within a public choice framework, the many crucial issues raised by the constitutional changes occurring in Europe, both East and West, at the beginning of the twenty-first century. "Constitutional Political Economy in the European Union" is organized around studies of political institutions that, while certainly not unique to Europe, tend to be more prevalent there. That institutional orientation allows Mueller to range widely across the European political landscape, moving his discussion from the consequences of multiparty systems and direct democracy to comparisons of parliamentary versus presidential systems, of unicameral versus bicameral legislatures, and of federations versus confederations.

Mueller then applies the insights gleaned from the literature of constitutional political economy to evaluate recent events in the EU and in the nations emerging from Soviet hegemony. As they have evolved thus far, Mueller sees the opportunities for constitutional reform presented in Eastern and Western Europe to be golden opportunities that have by and large been missed. The knowledge gained by public choice scholars over the past 40 years that could have been applied in practice has not been applied and on the few occasions when scholarly advice in drafting constitutions has been solicited, it has fallen on deaf ears. The post-Soviet Russian constitution and the EU's draft constitution both ignore what Mueller calls the "first law of constitution writing": the people who are likely to hold office under the new constitution should not be involved in its drafting. If so, as he concludes the modern experience shows, the constitutional rules of the game will tend to serve the interests of the prospective officeholders rather than the interests of the ordinary citizenry.

Todd Sandler next turns our attention to perhaps the most significant policy challenge of the new century, namely, formulating responses to the threat of terrorism. Although terrorism is ages old, the events of September 11, 2001, placed it at the top of the list of policymaking concerns of western democratic societies, which have been the main targets of the wave of recent attacks launched by Islamist extremists, beginning with the first bombing of the World Trade Center in 1993. The challenges of dealing with terrorism raise issues both of domestic policymaking – striking the appropriate balance between homeland security measures and the protection of civil liberties – and of foreign policymaking – coordinating multinational responses to terrorist threats, which increasingly are transnational in character, originating in one country and targeting another. Each dimension of the terrorism policymaking agenda requires solving problems of collective action, problems which are the meat and bread of public choice scholarship.

Professor Sandler has been at the forefront of the students of terrorism who bring a rational choice perspective to their studies of the problem. His earlier collaborative work with Walter Enders (Enders & Sandler, 1993, 1995) modeled terrorists as rational actors who allocate their limited resources both across targets and over time so as to maximize the expected net benefits of terrorist action. Among other things, the rational-actor model predicts that terrorists will alter their behavior in predictable ways in response to antiterrorist measures, by, for example, substituting assassinations of foreign-service personal for embassy bombings when steps are taken to protect embassies against bomb threats, and by reducing commercial aircraft hijackings and shifting to softer targets in response to tighter airport security. Reporting empirical evidence supporting these and other predictions of the theory, Enders and Sandler have shed important light on the behavior of terrorist groups and on the effectiveness of various policies designed to counter them.

In the essay contributed to the present volume, Sandler applies the tools of noncooperative game theory to analyze the collective action problems involved in dealing with transnational terrorism. He situates multinational responses to terrorism in the context of the familiar prisoners' dilemma and assurance games and shows how coordinating collective action, be it military retaliation, freezing terrorists' assets, or abiding by non-negotiation pledges, can be expected to be plagued by free-riding, the more so the larger is the number of nations whose participation is required to ensure an effective response. The prisoners' dilemma faced by nations attempting to coordinate their antiterrorism policies is magnified, as Sandler points out, by the rationality of the opposing side: cooperation creates incentives for terrorists to undermine multinational coalitions by attacking soft targets in coalition member-states, as they succeeded in doing by bombing the train station in Madrid, Spain, on March 11, 2004. Although Sandler's analysis suggests that unilateral responses to terrorism are more likely to be pursued than multilateral ones, the collective action problem is not thereby laid to rest, since effective counterterrorism measures by a single nation will simply cause terrorists to shift their attacks to less secure venues in other parts of the globe. The only light at the end of the tunnel, in Sandler's view, is that escalation of terrorist activities in the years to come may, by increasing the perceived gains from multinational cooperation, increase the chances of coordination success.

The rapid expansion in the size and scope of government would rank second in importance to the terrorist threat on many of the lists of the critical policy challenges of the new century composed by public choice scholars. Insofar as it produced significant increases in spending to support military incursions in Afghanistan and Iraq, to fortify homeland security, and to wage the "War on Terror", the growth of government has in part been a predictable response to the tragedy of 9/11. But, in the United States at least, domestic spending has risen since 9/11 at nearly the same pace as defense spending. Taken together with the mild economic recession that followed the attacks on the World Trade Center and the Pentagon, which hit the travel and tourism industries especially hard, and with the reductions in income tax rates enacted as economic stimulus during the second President Bush's first term in office, the run-up in federal government expenditures fueled a return to the era of chronic budget deficits that, except for a brief hiatus during the late 1990s, has been the US fiscal norm since about 1960. Somewhat surprisingly, the budgetary red ink now being forecast as far as the eye can see was, for all practical purposes, a non-issue in the presidential election campaign of 2004.

In an essay entitled "Government Growth in the Twenty-First Century", Randall Holcombe probes the strengths and weaknesses of public choice theories of governmental growth in order to lay a foundation for conjecturing about the trajectory likely to be followed in the new century. He focuses on three theories that have been developed to explain past expansions in the size and scope of the public sector. The first is budget-maximization, which models government growth as primarily driven by the ongoing demands for resources on the part of self-interested public officials, who benefit personally from expanding their bureaucratic fiefdoms. Government in this theory is a Hobbesian Leviathan whose size is limited only by the constitutional constraints that control its insatiable appetite for revenue. Rational-choice reasoning supplies a second approach to modeling governmental growth. Here, the public sector expands in response to the demands of the median voter for redistributive wealth transfers or, alternatively, in consequence of competitive rent-seeking into the public budget by various special-interest groups. Individuals and groups register their preferences at the polls for programs and policies that benefit them personally, and since reelection-minded politicians have strong incentives to cater to those preferences, the public sector expands. Owing to the fact that the public budget is something of a fiscal commons, that expansion may well go beyond the social optimum. But in the end, the growth of government is a result of democratic choice. The so-called ratchet hypothesis is the third theory of government growth Holcombe addresses in detail. In terms of that theory, government leaps in size during periods of crisis, such as war, both real and manufactured (e.g., the "War on Poverty", the "War on Drugs"), recession, and depression. Echoing Charles Rowley's analysis, constraints, even constitutional ones, are weakened as the polity clamors for government to "do something" to alleviate the crisis conditions. Government size ratchets up during times of trouble, but does not return to pre-crisis levels once the emergency has passed. There is, in other words, a path dependency in government's growth trajectory that moves it inexorably upward.

Holcombe examines each of these theories in turn, testing their explanatory powers against the facts of US government growth at the local, state and national levels in the nineteenth and twentieth centuries. Providing some support for the budget-maximizing/Leviathan model, he concludes that government growth has been driven in large part by its ability to raise additional revenue by expanding the tax base. Hence, whether government will continue to grow in the new century depends, in Holcombe's view, on the effectiveness of constraints that limit the share of the private sector's wealth to which the public sector has taxable access. If so, the old saw of containing government expansion by "starving the beast" seems to have some validity, and renewed interest is warranted in constitutional amendments that impose upper bounds on the fraction of GDP that can absorbed by taxes.

A standard lesson taught in high-school civics classes is that democracy delivers the governmental programs and policies the majority of the citizenry wants. Elections register the "will of the people", which is in turn faithfully executed by the political leaders the voters have chosen to hold public office. But public choice scholars have long recognized that the people's will is mythical; it can only be discovered reliably in a very restrictive set of circumstances, namely, when the domain of collective choice is unidimensional (there are only two candidates on the ballot or preferred policy outcomes can be arrayed along a simple linear scale, left-right, for example) and voters' preferences are single-peaked (every voter has a unique, most-preferred candidate or outcome).

If one of both of these assumptions do not hold, as they do not in many, perhaps nearly all actual electoral settings, characterized as they are by multi-candidate races and multiple issues on the ballot, simple majority rule can be indecisive (i.e., fail to select a winner at all), be prone to vote "cycles" subject to manipulation by agenda-setters who control the order of voting and by voters who cast ballots strategically for less preferred candidates or issues in order to avoid even worse outcomes, or select options that are not in fact preferred by the majority. The results of democratic decision-making processes, in other words, are a function both of the dimensions of the public choice domain – the constitutional rules that determine the types of decisions that will be made collectively versus those that will be made privately – and of the institutional framework that governs such matters as the extent and distribution of the franchise (suffrage), how candidates and issues gain eligibility to appear on the ballot, and how elections are decided, be it by plurality rule, majority rule, or some more inclusive vote requirement. Moreover, even if the people's will were somehow registered without error, self-interested politicians could not be relied upon to carry it out faithfully owing, among other things, to institutional barriers to entry into politics, including the well-known advantages of incumbency, their incentives to respond to the demands of well-organized pressure groups, and rational voter ignorance.

The basic insights of public choice reasoning into democratic decision-making process, emphasizing the importance of domain restrictions and voting rules, are summarized by Michael Munger in his lively contribution to this special issue. He then discusses another, frequently neglected feature of the institutions that govern how voters' preferences are registered: the technologies of ballot counting. The near debacle of the 2000 US presidential election, whose outcome was in doubt for weeks, arguably was caused by the continued reliance, in some of Florida's counties, on an outmoded system of punch cards, an early twentieth-century technology that produced hundreds of "spoiled ballots", "hanging chads", "over-votes" and "under-votes". Failure to adopt more modern ballot-counting methods threatens to undermine public confidence in the legitimacy of democratic processes, making election results seem arbitrary or giving rise to perceptions that elections can been "stolen". As Munger emphasizes, however, the public choice view is that *all* election outcomes are arbitrary, in the sense that they turn on the particular political institutions and voting rules in place.

Munger also contributes a public choice analysis of the Electoral College, the institution adopted by the Founding Fathers of the American constitutional republic for selecting presidents and vice presidents. He evaluates recent proposals for either abandoning the Electoral College altogether or reforming the winner-takes-all rule for electoral vote counting, and finds them to be flawed in several respects. The overall public choice lesson of Munger's contribution is that, while it may be desirable to upgrade archaic ballot-counting systems in the new century, no one should expect new technologies to provide a more accurate assessment of the people's will. There is no such thing.

By all accounts, American politics is awash in money. Every election cycle seems to set records for campaign contributions and campaign spending. If the people's will can be thwarted by electoral fraud, it also can be subverted by candidates for public office whose positions on important public issues are bought and paid for by special interests. Indeed, the rising costs of US elections, along with candidates' growing dependency on contributions from fat-cat donors and numerous political action committees (PACs), frequently is seen as a cause of voter alienation and low rates of participation in democratic processes.

"Some Talk: Money in Politics. A (Partial) Review of the Literature", by Thomas Stratmann, looks deeply into the extensive scholarly work that examines the causes and consequences of campaign finance. Stratmann's detailed review covers five important areas of study. He begins by summarizing research on the impact of campaign contributions and campaign spending in two types of elections, involving candidates for political office, on the one hand, and ballot propositions on the other. In both cases, early research tended to raise more questions than it answered. Money sometimes was found to have little, if any, effect on election outcomes, sometimes was found to have perverse effects (lowering the vote shares of incumbents, for instance), and almost always was found to have markedly different effects in races for the US House of Representatives than in races for the US Senate. Although the conflicting results have not yet been fully reconciled, Stratmann chronicles the progress made recently by taking the simultaneous determination of vote shares and campaign expenditures into account. Controlling for previously omitted variables – candidate quality and voter partisanship, in particular – has proven fruitful in helping sort out the marginal productivities of spending by incumbents and challengers and by supporters and opponents of ballot propositions. Much work remains to be done, however.

Stratmann next turns attention to two related issues, namely, the impact of money on politicians' policy decisions and the determinants of campaign contributions. Do contributions to successful candidates buy their votes? Do contributors give money to their friends, to their opponents, or simply to buy "access", the opportunity to present their points of view? After reviewing the relevant literature on the first issue, Stratmann presents the results of an original meta-analysis of 265 existing empirical studies that report estimates of the impact of campaign contributions on legislative voting behavior. On the basis of this analysis, he concludes that the weight of the evidence supports the hypothesis that political contributions do in fact influence how legislators vote. Money's salience in politics is reinforced by research on the determinants of campaign contributions, which shows that dollars tend to flow to incumbents in close races, that individuals and groups tend to donate to their ideological soulmates in the legislature, and that legislators holding party leadership positions or serving on powerful legislative committees enjoy considerable fund-raising advantages.

Stratmann's essay ends with a survey of the comparatively small literature on campaign finance reform. As attempts to control the influx of money into politics are mostly of recent vintage, scholars have to date explored only a few of the many interesting questions raised by the adoption of regulations imposing limits on contributions or by proposals to shift the financing of political campaigns from private parties to the general taxpayer. The available evidence, in large part exploiting variations in campaign finance laws across the US states, seems to be somewhat ambiguous. Spending caps can entrench incumbents or they can make races more competitive; public financing of political campaigns likewise can raise or lower candidates' margins of victory. Ambiguity enters the picture because we do not fully understand what motivates campaign contributions in the first place, how voters respond to political advertising and how they evaluate information about the amounts and sources of the funds candidates receive. Efforts to correct the ills perceived to be endemic in the financing of modern political campaigns call for a return to first principles, and for more careful study by public choice scholars.

The institutions of direct democracy – the New England town meeting, evoked affectionately in a famous Norman Rockwell painting, and the decision rights exercised by the polities of Swiss cantons – have long been the neglected stepchildren of public choice scholarship. It was thought, largely correctly, that the costs of collective decision-making faced by assemblies of the citizenry render direct democracy impractical in large numbers settings. Students of public choice processes accordingly focused their attention on legislatures, political parties and other institutions of representative democracy, the much more common system of democratic governance that takes advantage of the cost savings made possible when voters delegate authority to make policy decisions on their behalf to smaller bodies of elected public officials.

In his contribution to this special issue, John Matsusaka restores balance to the public choice literature by tracing the development of two increasingly important forms of direct democracy – the ballot initiative and the referendum. "The Eclipse of Legislatures: Direct Democracy in the 21st Century" documents the extraordinary growth of these methods of collective decision-making in the United States and elsewhere. Matsusaka explains the rise of direct democracy in modern times, which began in 1978 with voter approval of a state constitutional amendment limiting property tax increases in California (Proposition 13), as being propelled by three trends: rising educational attainment, enabling voters to become better informed about public policy issues, falling costs of voter access to policy-relevant information, mainly driven by the revolution in communications technologies, and a meltdown of public confidence in elected officials. The advance of initiatives and referendums, which Matsusaka expects to continue unabated in the new century, has been so remarkable that one might be tempted to think that legislatures will cease to be significant actors in the democratic process.

However, Matsusaka does not view direct democracy, as do many students of politics, as a substitute for legislatures in the sense that citizens take control of decisions as a last resort, after their elected representatives fail to deliver the policies the majority wants. Because he sees more of a complementary relationship between direct democracy and representative democracy, legislatures will continue to function as institutions for making public choices in policy areas, such as public finance, where they enjoy a comparative advantage in knowledge or technical expertise. Matsusaka argues that direct democracy will flourish for the most part on questions of social policy, such as capital punishment, abortion rights, and gay marriage, where the opinions of elected representatives are no better informed than those of their constituents.

"The Eclipse of Legislatures" reviews the public choice literature reporting evidence on the effects of direct democracy on political outcomes, including government spending, taxes and public budgeting. In general, that literature finds policy outcomes to be consistent with majoritarian values. Matsusaka also asks how well direct democracy performs in terms of protecting the rights of the minority, and concludes that minorities fare no worse under direct democracy than they do under representative democracy. Lest one think that direct democracy is a panacea, Matsusaka discusses circumstances in which the threat of a citizen initiative can push legislative policy choices away from the median voter's ideal point. Indeed, as he observes, the impact of direct democracy on the behavior of the legislative and executive branches of government is an important area for future public choice research. To this point, however, Matsusaka sees no cause for alarm – and, indeed, much to applaud – in direct democracy's continued proliferation in the coming century.

As the twentieth century wound down, television news watchers were treated almost daily to scenes of corporate executives doing "perp walks" toward waiting police vehicles or climbing courthouse steps with legal counsel in tow to answer before a federal judge the felony charges filed against them. While the twenty-first century was still in diapers, the accounting irregularities at firms such as WorldCom, Enron, Global Crossing, and Tyco, had transformed these previously obscure companies – and people like Bernie Ebbers, Kenneth Lay, Jeffrey Skilling, Gary Winnick and Dennis Kozlowski – into household names. Ensuing high-profile investigations of the institutions of corporate governance by several committees of Congress and by the US Securities and Exchange Commission generated stories of cozy relationships between corporate executives, their boards of directors and the big-name accounting firms retained to audit their financial statements. The media frenzy surrounding these investigations ultimately prompted Congress to pass the Sarbanes-Oxley Act in 2002, a law intended, among other things, to increase the independence of corporate boards and to tighten existing federal financial reporting requirements, to all appearances promoting fuller disclosure of the fiscal conditions of publicly traded companies.

Like political decision-making, corporate governance is a collective action problem. Just as voters delegate authority to the legislative and executive branches of government to formulate and execute policies on their behalf, shareholders delegate responsibility for overseeing the business activities of the companies they own to corporate boards of directors, which in turn hire and supervise the executives charged with managing firms in the shareholders' interest on a day-to-day basis. Just as the individual, rationally ignorant voter exercises little or no control over the actions of his or her elected political representatives, the logic of collective action endows corporate executives with a great deal of discretion in pursuing policies that benefit themselves personally at the owners' expense. In consequence, much of the existing literature on corporate governance is devoted to studies of the mechanisms of control adopted by modern corporations to help align the interests of management more closely with those of the owners of the firm.

Harold Mulherin contributes a wide-ranging survey of this literature to the present volume in an essay entitled "Corporations, Collective Action and Corporate Governance: One Size Does Not Fit All". Mulherin's paper is a cautionary tale, in the end warning against the adoption of reforms that apply equally across the corporate sector, regardless of company size, industry, or internal control mechanisms already in place. He buttresses his conclusion by presenting new empirical evidence, drawn from the Value Line Investment Survey in the first quarter of 2000, on several features of corporate governance, such as board size, ownership concentration and capital structure, across a sample of 1,235 firms in 40 industries. This new evidence documents the substantial variation in the institutions of governance that exists within corporate America at the dawn of the new century, suggesting that a "one-size-fits-all" approach to reform will impose heavier compliance costs on some firms than on others and, hence, redistribute wealth among the shareholding public. Future research that identifies the likely "winners" and "losers" from Sarbanes-Oxley and similar regulatory initiatives will, as Mulherin notes, provide the key to understanding the forces now shaping political responses to corporate governance's perceived defects.

America's public schools have been in steep decline for decades. Average scores on standardized achievement tests have fallen steadily since the mid 1960s. US public school students fare poorly in international comparisons of academic competency, especially so in math and science, and college professors routinely complain of the poor reading, writing and study skills their students bring to the classroom. Ignorance of history is rampant, even among the cream of the public-high-school-graduate crop. Home-schooling is on the rise. The evidence of failure is indisputable, and one does not have to look far for plausible explanations. One is monopoly. Because children are required to attend the public school in the local district where their parents reside, competition between schools is muted. True, school choice can be exercised in Tiebout-like ways at the time a family first moves to a new city, but exit becomes more difficult once a house has been purchased: the house must be sold and moving costs incurred in order to transfer to another school district. A family that decides to live in a district with good public schools becomes a hostage to the local monopolist. If the quality of the schools subsequently deteriorates, they may be locked into their original choice because failing schools reduce property values, imposing capital losses on homeowners. Teachers' unions supply a second explanation for public school failure. Among the most powerful special-interest groups in the nation, these unions thwart entry into the teaching profession through teacher-certification requirements, oppose output-based evaluations of teacher competency and merit-pay schemes in favor of compensation based on seniority and on college credits earned in Schools of Education, and support work rules, including generous staffing of classrooms with teachers' aides, that make their jobs easier.

The ongoing decline of American public education has created interest in programs intended to introduce competition between public and private schools by providing parents with "vouchers" that would defray some or all of the costs of enrolling their children in private schools. US public schools are in large part financed by taxes levied on property owners in the local school district and parents are not relieved of this tax burden when they transfer their children from public to private school. They must continue to pay their property tax bill plus the full cost of attending the private school. By granting the parents of school-age children implicit reductions in their property taxes, vouchers lower the cost of switching. Threatened with the loss of students to private schools – and a reduction in the property tax revenues available for funding their operations – public schools face incentives to improve their performances, or at least that is the argument of the supporters of voucher programs.

In "The Public Choice of Educational Choice", Lawrence Kenny surveys the literature that attempts to explain the political forces underlying the adoption of voucher programs in the United States. Despite the arguments of voucher proponents, such programs have in fact been enacted heretofore in only a handful of American cities and states. Why is this so? Kenny contributes important new empirical evidence to help answer this question. Studying a wide range of voucher initiatives, including measures introduced at both the state and federal levels (the latter to create a voucher program for the DC public schools), Kenny finds that successful adoption hinges on specific features of the voucher proposal itself, the demographic characteristics of the state, and political ideology. In particular, he reports the results of estimating linear probability models suggesting that voucher programs are more likely to be enacted when participation is limited to low-income households, when they are targeted at failing schools in large metropolitan areas, and when the Republican Party controls the executive branch and both chambers of the state legislature, especially so when the Republicans in power are ideologically conservative, as measured by the index assigned to senatorial voting records by the Americans for Democratic Action.

There are many questions yet unanswered in the school choice debate, as Kenny observes, supplying fodder for future public choice research. His summary of the existing literature and the new evidence he reports shows that the political process leading to the adoption or defeat of voucher proposals is amenable to systematic empirical explanation. Well-organized special interests, such as those of homeowners and teachers' unions, play key roles in determining political outcomes here as they do in public choice processes more generally. In the end, Kenny's contribution demonstrates the power public choice reasoning brings to bear in illuminating the constellation of forces that shape the political responses to contemporary policy challenges.

In the final essay invited for this special issue, Paul Rubin engages the contentious issues surrounding the tort reform debate. Everyone has a favorite horror story about the "jackpot justice" being handed down by judges and juries around the country nowadays in lawsuits alleging harm caused by defective products and negligent corporations. Although frequently overturned on appeal, multimillion-dollar damage awards for a spilled cup of coffee, a scratched BMW hood, or a fall from a ladder have become commonplace. The citizens of many states have seen obstetricians and anesthesiologists move their practices elsewhere to avoid astronomical medical malpractice insurance premiums. The print and electronic media are flooded by ads placed by law firms seeking clients who may have been harmed by taking either an over-the-counter or a prescription drug discovered possibly to have serious side-effects.

"Public Choice and Tort Reform" documents the expansion in tort liability faced by manufacturers and health-care professionals that has occurred in the United States since the 1950s. Rubin discusses the "innovations" that set the law of torts on a growth path that, at the beginning of the new century, absorbs 2.2% of US GDP. The most important of these innovations substituted tort liability for voluntary contract, eliminating opportunities for buyers and sellers to determine for themselves how claims of injury will be resolved in the event of an accident and what types and amounts of compensation will be paid. Other factors underlying the expansion of tort liability discussed by Rubin include extension of strict liability from manufacturing defects to design defects, growth in the damages awarded by juries for highly subjective "pain and suffering", and "jurisdiction-shopping" by lawyers on the lookout for plaintiff-friendly venues.

Rubin's main contribution, however, is to situate the tort reform debate within a public choice framework. In doing so, he identifies the organized special interests that are active in pushing reform – business organizations and, to a lesser extent, medical doctors – and in resisting it – primarily the American Trial Lawyers Association and various consumer activists. Rubin then goes on to describe in detail the strategies that have been used by the partisans on both sides of the debate to push their respective policy positions. After reviewing the small number of existing studies of the political economy of tort reform, Rubin ends his essay by laying out a lengthy agenda for future research that should whet the appetites of public choice scholars.

3. Conclusion

The contributors to this special issue of *Public Choice* have brought the field's theories and methods to bear on a wide range of policy challenges that face western democratic governments at the start of the twenty-first century. Our authors have shown that public choice scholars still have much to say both about new public policy issues – such as constitution-making in the European Union, the rise of transnational terrorism, corporate governance and tort law reform – and old ones like the growth of government, the boundaries of the collective choice domain, direct versus representative democracy, and the financing of political campaigns. Public choice evidently has not yet reached the end of its history. Indeed, in a theme we return to in the volume's concluding essay, a great deal of unfinished business remains on the public choice research agenda.

It is time, however, to let the contributors speak for themselves. The reader can judge whether we have met our goal of demonstrating the vibrancy and continuing relevance of the public choice research program.

Notes

1. Given the interest-group theory of government's centrality to the public choice literature, George Stigler's (1971) name may well belong on the list.
2. For more general criticisms of the rational actor model of economics, grounded in notions of "commitment", see Sen (1977).
3. Hardin (1999, pp. vii–viii; his emphasis) argues on Hobbesian grounds that liberal democratic constitutions work, *when they do*, by coordinating the society's politically effective groups on a particular political (and sometimes economic) order, to those groups' mutual advantage.

References

Arrow, K. J. ([1951] 1963). *Social Choice and Individual Values* (2nd ed.) New York: Wiley.

Black, D. (1948a). On the rationale of group decision making. *Journal of Political Economy*, *56*(1), 23–34.

Black, D. (1948b). The decisions of a committee using a special majority. *Econometrica*, *16*(3), 245–261.

Black, D. ([1958] 1987). *The Theory of Committees and Elections*. Dordrecht: Kluwer Academic Publishers.

Buchanan, J. M., & Tullock, G. (1962). *The Calculus of Consent: Logical Foundations of Constitutional Democracy*. Ann Arbor: University of Michigan Press.

Downs, A. (1957). *An Economic Theory of Democracy*. New York: Harper & Row.

Enders, W., & Sandler, T. (1993). The effectiveness of antiterrorism policies: A vector-autoregression-intervention analysis. *American Political Science Review*, *87*(4), 829–844.

Enders, W., & Sandler, T. (1995). Terrorism: theory and applications. In Hartley K. & Sandler T. (Eds.), *Handbook of Defense Economics*, Vol. 1 (pp. 213–249). Amsterdam: North-Holland.

Green, D. P., & Shapiro, I. (1994). *Pathologies of Rational Choice Theory*. New Haven: Yale University Press.

Hardin, R. (1999). *Liberalism, Constitutionalism, and Democracy*. Oxford: Oxford University Press.

Kelman, S. (1987). "Public choice" and public spirit. *Public Interest*, *87*(Spring), 80–94.

Mueller, D. C. (1976). Public choice: A survey. *Journal of Economic Literature*, *14*(2), 395–433.

Mueller, D. C. (Ed.) (1997). *Perspectives on Public Choice: A Handbook*. Cambridge: Cambridge University Press.

Mueller, D. C. (2003). *Public Choice III*. Cambridge and New York: Cambridge University Press.

Niskanen, W. A. (1971). *Bureaucracy and Representative Government*. Chicago: Aldine-Atherton.

Olson, M. (1965). *The Logic of Collective Action: Public Goods and the Theory of Groups*. Cambridge: Harvard University Press.

Riker, W. H. (1962). *The Theory of Political Coalitions*. New Haven: Yale University Press.

Rowley, C. K., & Schneider, F. (Eds.) (2004). *The Encyclopedia of Public Choice*, 2 Vols. Kluwer Academic Publishers: Dordrecht, Boston and London.

Sen, A. K. (1977). Rational fools: A critique of the behavioral foundations of economic theory. *Philosophy and Public Affairs*, *6*(4), 317–344.

Shughart, W. F. II. (2004). George W. Bush and the return to deficit finance. *Public Choice*, *118* (March), 223-234.

Shughart, W. F. II., & Razzolini, L. (Eds.) (2001). *The Elgar Companion to Public Choice*. Edward Elgar: Cheltenham, UK and Northampton, MA, USA.

Stigler, G. J. (1971). The theory of economic regulation. *Bell Journal of Economics and Management Science*, *2*(1), 3–21.

Public Choice (2005) **124:** 19–31
DOI: 10.1007/s11127-005-4743-2

Afraid to be free: Dependency as desideratum

JAMES M. BUCHANAN
Center for Study of Public Choice, Buchanan House, MSN 1E6, George Mason University, Fairfax, VA 22030 USA
(E-mail: jburgess@gmu.edu)

Accepted March 2005

Abstract. Although collectivist ideas have everywhere fallen into disrepute, this essay argues that socialism nevertheless will survive and be extended in the new century. That gloomy prospect looms, not because socialism is more efficient or more just, but because ceding control over their actions to others allows individuals to escape, evade and even deny personal responsibilities. People are afraid to be free; the state stands in loco parentis. The breaching of plausibly acceptable fiscal limits in the first half of the new century will determine how the basic conflict between welfare dependency and liberal principles will be resolved.

1. Introduction

For this special issue, the editors asked me specifically to submit an essay under the general title, "Capitalism, Socialism and Democracy in the Twenty-First Century". In this solicitation, they were encouraging me to think in grandiose terms – to offer a public choice–constitutional political economy perspective on the larger organizational-ideological alternatives that may emerge. We do not, of course, either collectively or privately, make choices as among the grand organizational alternatives. For the most part, and most of the time, we make choices on the various margins that present themselves, with the result that all societies are more or less capitalistic, more or less socialistic, more or less democratic. Nonetheless, these Schumpeterian terms may be helpful in organizing my general argument.

This argument can be succinctly summarized. If we loosely describe socialism in terms of the range and scope of collectivized controls over individual liberty of actions, then "socialism" will survive and be extended. This result will emerge not because collectivization is judged to be more efficient, in some meaningful economic sense, or even because collectivization more adequately meets agreed upon criteria for distributive justice, but rather because only under the aegis of collective control, under "the state", can individuals escape, evade and even deny personal responsibilities. In short, persons are afraid to be free. As subsequent discussion will suggest, socialism, as a coherent ideology, has lost most of its appeal. But in a broader and more comprehensive historical perspective, during the course of two centuries, the state has replaced God as the father-mother of last resort, and persons will demand that this protectorate role be satisfied and amplified.

"Capitalism", an unfortunate but widely used term again loosely described in terms of the range and scope for individual liberty of action outside collectivized direction and control, must remain vulnerable to continuing marginal encroachments, and this thrust of change will remain despite possible analytical and empirical evidence that such encroachments signal retrogression along widely recognized success indicators.

"Democracy", defined broadly enough to include its many institutional variants, will reflect the preferences of the citizenry, who remain largely immune from the findings of science, and the increasing corruption that must necessarily accompany any expanding range of collective-political control will simply be tolerated and ignored. An overarching theme of the whole paper is that the thrust of development will be dictated by "bottoms up" demands rather than by "top down" dictates of an elite.

I shall flesh out this general argument in later sections. Only in the final section of the paper shall I offer a more hopeful alternative to the pessimistic scenario sketched out above. Such an alternative emerges, however, as much from a sense of moral obligation to believe that constructive reform is within the possible as it does from any realistic prognosis of elements which are discernible beneath the surface of that which may be now observed.

2. The Sources of Socialism

There are at least four sources or wellsprings of ideas that motivate extensions in the range and scope of collective controls over the freedom of persons to act as they might independently choose. In the political dialogue these sources are, of course, intermingled, but in philosophical discourse it seems useful to make distinctions. I shall label these four sources as (1) managerial, (2) paternalistic, (3) distributionist and (4) parental. I shall discuss the first three of these four categories in this section. I shall treat the fourth source, that of the parental motivation, separately in Section 3, because I suggest that this source has been relatively neglected by analysts and, more importantly, that it is likely to swamp the other three in influence during the early decades of this new century.

2.1. *Managerial socialism*

This is the form of socialism that is now dead and buried, both in ideas and in practice, having been "done in" during the last decades of the twentieth century. This is the socialism that is defined as the collective ownership and control of the means of production, and which involves efforts at centralized command and direction of a national economy as institutionalized through a central planning authority. It is now almost universally acknowledged that the motivating ideas here were based on scientific-intellectual errors of major proportions – errors summarized under Hayek's (1988) rubric of "fatal conceit". Even in its idealized form, the construction involved an ubiquity of perverse incentives and ignored the impossibility of ascertaining knowledge from widely dispersed and dynamic relationships. The scientific flaws now seem evident, but the cautionary lesson to be learned is that, for a whole century, among the best and the brightest economists and philosophers, indeed among the intelligentsia and academics generally, discussion was carried on in what now seems a setting of amazing ignorance.

And with tragic consequences. Efforts to implement the idealized and basically flawed construction, whether piecemeal or in total, ran up against the limits imposed by the necessity that ordinary mortals rather than idealized automatons must operate the system. The gross inefficiency that should have been minimally predicted emerged; corruption itself became the only lubricant for otherwise rigid structures of interaction; rewards disproportionately favored opportunistic behavior; personalized favoritism was matched by unalloyed cruelty in the absence of effective exit options.

The economy allegedly organized on the command-control principles of managerial socialism simply cannot, and demonstrably could not, deliver the goods in any manner even remotely comparable to those economies organized under the principles derivative from Adam Smith's system of natural liberty. This variant of socialism, which found much of its origin in the highly successful Marxist ideological thrust, will not soon resurface. The first half of this new century will not witness demands for collectivized planning for planning's sake.

2.2. *Paternalistic socialism*

The demise of managerial socialism has not, however, substantially lessened the demands for collectivization that stem from the alternative sources, including recognition by self-anointed elites that only by collectivization can the choices and actions of the masses be directed toward those patterns that "should be wanted if these masses only knew what was in their own best interest". This attitude, or set of attitudes, was importantly present in the imposition of managerial socialism, but, conceptually at least, it can be separately examined and analyzed. The ultimate motivation here need not stem from any argument to the effect that collective control is, in any sense, more "efficient", as defined in some neutral aggregative value dimension. The motivation is located in the value scalar itself; that which persons privately express is not that which the elite prefer. Preferences need to be shifted in more acceptable directions. The French term, *dirigisme*, is actually more descriptive of this mind-set than any comparable English term.

The persons who adopt this stance do not necessarily object to capitalism, or, rather, the market process, as the allocative means of implementing their objectives. Indeed, the market may be left to do the heavy lifting, so long as the incentives are collectively adjusted so as to guarantee results dictated by the normative ideals of the elite. Much of the current political dialogue is imbued with this set of attitudes, notably much of the environmental emphasis, along with the impassioned crusades against tobacco and obesity.

This source of support for a widened collective control over liberty of choice will not fade away. It seems unlikely, however, that it will come to exert a major force toward further socialization. The limits of such efforts are exemplified, historically, by the failed experiment with prohibition of alcohol in the United States in the first third of the twentieth century and by Hillary Clinton's aborted effort in the early 1990s to remake the medical care industry. In this case, "democracy", howsoever its complex processes may actually work, becomes a conservative bastion against efforts by any elite to impose its own value structure through collectivized coercion.

2.3. *Distributionist socialism*

"Socialism is about equality" – this short statement moved quickly onto the center stage of discussion after the apparent demise of central planning and control. The advocates of centrally managed economies moved with surprising alacrity to align themselves with the welfare state – social democrats. The gross scientific errors that had produced the fatal conceit were swept aside as if they had never been promulgated with the argument that, all along, distributional equality is and had remained the primary value for socialists of all stripes. Nor is the distributionist thrust absent from the arguments of the paternalists, whose attention may be focused on in-kind transfers of defined goods and services to designated recipients, but always aimed in the direction of more equality in the final access to such goods.

In its unadulterated form, however, the distributionist argument is exclusively about equality, or rather inequality, in the distribution of goods and services, without concern for the makeup of the bundle. The allocative function may be left exclusively to the market (capitalism), as it responds to the preference patterns of persons as consumers and producers within the post-tax, post-transfer redistributional limits. The focus here is not upon what the market generates, or even on how it operates, but rather on the distributional outcomes that would emerge in the absence of the specifically directed and collectivized tax-transfer structure.

At the level of abstract political philosophy, and notably as brought into modern attention through the work of Rawls (1971), this source for collective action is the only one that is at all consistent with the precepts of classical liberalism. Even the hard-core libertarians find it difficult to defend the unconstrained distributional outcomes of the market process, of unrestricted capitalism, as embodying widely shared norms for fairness. Even when the perverse incentives that arise on both the tax and transfer sides of the fiscal account are fully recognized, and even if the shortfalls between the stylized distributional adjustments that may be imagined and the actual adjustments that are possible through democratic politics are also taken into account, widespread support for some distributional correction may be evidenced. And, to the extent that the socialized sector of activity is measured so as to include the tax-transfer budget, "socialism" seems unlikely to disappear from observed political reality.

Support for extending this tax-transfer budget, as motivated by strictly redistributionist objectives, may, however, be much less than implied by the oft-encountered class warfare demagoguery of electoral politics. The poor, the distributionally disadvantaged, are not observed to be using the majoritarian processes of democracy to exploit the rich, at least beyond relatively narrow limits. And, indeed, much of the class warfare rhetoric seems to reflect the ranting of the elitists who call on the distributionist motivation to advance their basic *dirigisme*.

3. Parental Socialism

To my knowledge, the term "parental" has never been explicitly discussed as being descriptive of the motivation behind the collectivization-socialization of human activity. I introduce this term here for want of a better one to describe a source that is difficult to encapsulate even if easy to treat in more extended discussion. In one sense, the attitude is paternalism flipped over, so to speak. With paternalism, we refer to the attitudes of elitists who seek to impose their own preferred values on others. With *parentalism*, in contrast, we refer to the attitudes of persons who seek *to have values imposed upon them* by other persons, by the state or by transcendental forces. This source of support for expanded collectivization has been relatively neglected by both socialist and liberal philosophers, perhaps because the philosophers, in both camps, remain methodological individualists.

As the title for this paper indicates, and as I have noted earlier, this ultimate motivation for maintenance and extension of control over the activities of persons through collective institutions will, in my assessment, be more important in shaping the patterns of development during the first half of the new century than any of the other, and more familiar, sources discussed in the previous section. Almost subconsciously, those scientists-scholars-academicians who have tried to look at the "big picture" have assumed that, other things being equal, persons want to be at liberty to make their own choices, to be free from coercion by others, including indirect coercion through means of persuasion. They have failed to emphasize sufficiently, and to examine the implications of, the fact that liberty carries with it *responsibility*. And it seems evident that many persons do not want to shoulder the final responsibility for their own actions. Many persons are, indeed, afraid to be free.

The term "parental" becomes quite descriptive in its inference that the attitude here is akin to that of the child who seeks the cocoon-like protection of its parents, and who may enjoy its liberty, but only within the limits defined by the range of such protection. The mother or father will catch the child if it falls, will bandage its cuts, will excuse its behavioral excesses along all dimensions. Knowledge that these things will be done provides the child with a sense of order in its universe, with elements of predictability in uncertain aspects of the environment.

This cozy setting is dramatically disturbed when the child becomes an adult, when responsibility must be shouldered independently from the family bounds. Relatively few persons are sufficiently strong, as individuals, to take on the full range of liberties and their accompanying responsibilities without seeking some substitute or replacement of the parental shelter. Religion, or God as the transcendent force that exemplifies fatherhood or motherhood, has and does serve this purpose (more on this below). Organized community is a less satisfactory but nonetheless partial parental replacement for some persons. More importantly, and specifically for purposes of the discussion here, the collectivity – the state – steps in and relieves the individual of his responsibility as an independently choosing and acting adult. In exchange, of course, the state reduces the liberty of the individual to act as he might choose. But the order that the state, as parent, provides may be, for many persons, well worth the sacrifice in liberty.

Note that, as mentioned earlier, the source for extension in collective or state control here is "bottom up" rather than "top down", as with paternalism. Persons who are afraid to take on independent responsibility that necessarily goes with liberty demand that the state fill the parental role in their lives. They *want* to be told what to do and when to do it; they seek order rather than uncertainty, and order comes at an opportunity cost they seem willing to bear.

The thirst or desire for freedom, and responsibility, is perhaps not nearly so universal as so many post-Enlightenment philosophers have assumed. What share of persons in varying degrees of bondage, from slavery to ordinary wage-salary contracts, really want to be free, with the accompanying responsibility for their own choices? The disastrous failure of "forty acres and a mule" was followed by the lapse into renewed dependency status for emancipated former slaves in the American south. And the surprising strength of Communist parties in the politics of post-Cold War central and eastern Europe attests to the thirst on the part of many persons "to be controlled".

4. God Is Dead; Long Live the State

Prior to the eighteenth century, to the Enlightenment, and particularly in the West, God, as institutionally embodied in the church (and churches), fulfilled what seemed to be a natural role as the overarching "parent" who assumed ultimate responsibility for the individual in a last-resort sense, as biological linkages were necessarily lost in the aging profile. Manifestations abound. "We Are All God's Children", "God Will Take Care of You" – these familiar hymnal assertions are merely illustrative of the near-universal attitude. Psychologically, persons went about their ordinary lives secure in the feeling that God would clear up any mess they might make, analogous to parents' behavior toward children. Of course, transgressions might be followed by punishment, in this or another life, but predictability characterized both the rules themselves and the prospect for both reward and punishment. God, as institutionally embodied, provided order in the lives of all.

But what if Nietzsche is right? What if God is dead? What happens to the person who is forced to recognize that the ordering presence of God is no longer real? What if God cannot be depended on to clean up the mess, even in some last resort sense? Who and/or what can fulfill the surrogate parent role? Who and what is there beyond the individual that can meet the yearning for family-like protectiveness? Who and what will pick us up when and if we fall? Who and what can provide the predictability that God and his agency structures seemed to offer?

In the more extensive idealizations, as imagined by some medieval scholastics, secular politics, or the state, is an unnecessary appendage to God's embodiment in the church. Nascent efforts in post-medieval centuries to establish secular authority independent of church control were opposed throughout the European realm. But the monopoly of the Catholic church was broken, by Luther and his followers, well before the onset of the Enlightenment. God was no longer monolithic in the image of one institution. Competing interpretations emerged, and the conflicts among churches came to be intermingled with conflicts among states as representatives of those churches. In the process, secular authority came to be divorced from ecclesiastical authority and to assume independent stature.

By the time of the Enlightenment, the secular nation-state had almost reached its maturity, and nationalism, the sense of nationhood, was a more or less natural repository for the sentiments of those persons for whom God had died. For many, the state, as the collectivity, moved into the gap left by the demise of the church's parental role. The individual who sought family-like protection, but who no longer sensed the presence of such protection in the church, or in God so embodied, found a substitute in the collectivity. The individual could feel that he or she "belonged" to the larger community and was necessarily dependent on that community. The death of God and the birth of the national state, and especially in its latter-day welfare state form, are the two sides of the coin of history in this respect.

The transposition through which the state replaced God in the parental role, for many persons, was aided and abetted by two historically parallel developments. First, the Enlightenment, in itself, did not contain justification for the burgeoning of the state, as such. From the Enlightenment, classical liberalism rather than collectivism emerged. But, as the next section will indicate, classical liberalism singularly failed to offer persons any psychological security coincident with the loss of religious faith. Almost immediately following the Enlightenment, however, arguments for socialism, as treated above, were advanced. And all arguments for socialist organization depend critically on the expansion of the collectivized or politicized sector of activities.

Implementation of the socialist proposals for change, in whole or in part, was accomplished through the combination of Marxist ideology, paternalism of the intelligentsia, distributionist argument and the residually desperate search for a parental replacement for God. Socialist collectivism promised the order that seemed absent in post-Enlightenment liberalism. Persons more or less readily accepted the dependency status that socialism carried with it because, by becoming dependents of the collectivity, they were able, at the same time, to share in the communal project that collectivism seemed to represent.

The state did, indeed, become God. This transposition was, of course, most evident in the Soviet Union and other Communist regimes. But essentially the same psychological shift in public attitudes took place in Western democratic societies. Persons accepted the dependence on the state as normal; even those who at the same time railed against the increasing collective-governmental intrusiveness. It came to be increasingly rare to find persons and groups who supported releasing the shackles of dependency. The collapse of the Communist regimes in the last decades of the century did little or nothing toward slowing down the growth of the welfare state; this, in itself, demonstrates that the parental motivation for collectivization remains perhaps the strongest of those identified above.

5. The Lacuna of Classical Liberalism

The central organizing idea of classical liberalism emerged from the Enlightenment, notably from its Scottish variants. This idea, best enunciated by Adam Smith, is that extensive collective direction and control over activity is not required at all; that, with minimally invasive institutions that guarantee person, property and contract, persons can be left at liberty to make their own choices and, in so doing, generate maximal value. The spontaneous order of the market, emergent as persons are allowed to make their own choices in a "simple system of natural liberty", implies that there is only a limited role for the sovereign state.

Modern socialism, at least in the first three variants noted above, was born as a reaction against classical liberalism, and especially against the limited successes of classical political economy during the first half of the nineteenth century. As indicated, managerial or command-control socialism was based on intellectual error, on a failure to understand the basic principles of market order. Paternalistic socialism rejects the democratic features of market outcomes, and, by inference, also rejects small-d democracy in governance. Distributional socialism can, as noted, be accommodated within classical liberalism by appropriate adjustments imposed on market outcomes.

The lacuna in classical liberalism lies in its failure to offer a satisfactory alternative to the socialist-collectivist thrust that reflects the pervasive desire for the parental role of the state. For persons who seek, even if unconsciously, dependence on the collectivity, the classical liberal argument for independence amounts to negation. Classical liberals have not involved themselves in the psychological elements of public support for or against the market order.

"The spontaneous order of the market" – this is an intellectual idea that is not naturally understood by those who have not been exposed to the teachings of economists. And economists themselves in their sometimes zeal for working out the intricacies of complex models have neglected their primary didactic purpose. They have assumed that, like the ideas in the natural sciences, once an idea is accepted by the scientific community, it will become a part of the conventional wisdom of the public, as implemented in institutional reforms. Economists, as the putative repositories of the principles of classical liberalism, have not sensed the categorical differences in public reception of their scientific findings and those of their fellow natural scientists. In a very real sense, every person is his or her own economist, who pays little or no respect for the truths of economic science.

For far too many members of the body politic, the market order requires that persons subject themselves to "the blind forces of the market", as if the independence so offered carries no offsetting gains. There is a widespread failure to understand that the independence offered by the entry and exit options of the market offsets the *dependence* on others when markets are closed or displaced. And such dependence, importantly, includes dependence on the state, and on its bureaucratic agents. The individual can readily walk away from a market relationship. He cannot walk away from the taxing authority.

The entry and exit options provided by the market serve as the omnipresent frontier open to all participants. And economists could well have done more to exploit the familiar frontier experience by instancing the analogue here. Their failure to do so illustrates the point made above, that adherents of classical liberalism, and especially economists, have not been sufficiently concerned with preaching the gospel of independence. Classical liberalism, properly understood, demonstrates that persons can stand alone, that they need neither God nor the state to serve as surrogate parents. But this lesson has not been learned.

6. Capitalism and Its Contradictions

Capitalism ("free enterprise" would be a much better term here) is the institutionalized embodiment of classical liberalism. As idealized, it is best described as a system in which values are set; resources are allocated; goods and services are produced and distributed through a network of voluntary exchanges among freely choosing-acting persons and groups – a network that functions within a collectively imposed legal structure that protects persons and property and enforces contracts while at the same time financing those goods and services that are most efficiently shared among many users. Such an idealized capitalistic system would, at most, command collectively up to 15% of national value product.

During the half-century since World War II, we have observed that, even in Western countries outside the nominally socialized Communist bloc, the collectivized sector has extended its allocative-distributive reach to estimates ranging from 40% to 60% of total value generated. What are such systems to be called? Half capitalist and half socialist?

Contradictions become apparent once we recognize that the principles upon which the whole organizational structure allegedly rests are those derived from classical liberalism rather than from socialism in any form. It is as if these principles carry the politicized or socialist half of value on their backs, as it were, as a deadweight burden. Such principles include the rule of law, which requires that all persons, regardless of dependency status, be subjected to the same law, including, importantly, those who become agents for the collectivity. In addition, democracy, as a political form, requires open and universal franchise, with eligibility for agency roles being open to all. Within the appropriately defined jurisdiction, all persons are guaranteed freedom of entry and exit to and from occupational and geographical opportunities, subject only to the respect dictated by the legal protections noted above. All persons in the organized polity are insured that personal rights are protected – rights to speak, to practice religion, to associate with whom they may choose.

The listing might be extended, but the point made should be clear. There is no discrimination among persons in the implementation of the basic principles of classical liberalism. The implication also is clear. To the extent that the burgeoning tax-transfer element in the budgets of modern democracies is motivated by demands that the state take on a parental role, this element must be characterized by *generality*. Persons become subject to tax on the one hand and eligible for transfer payments on the other by their membership in the polity and not by their identification as a member of this or that group, as defined in nongeneral terms (see Buchanan & Congleton, 1998). Any departure from the generality norm, any discrimination, must introduce classification among persons, which violates the classical liberal presupposition of equality.

Major programs in the welfare-state budgets are, at least nominally, organized on generality principles. Tax financed or pay-as-we-go pension schemes are general in coverage, although with built-in redistributive elements. Tax-financed medical services are open to all members of the community, although here, too, there are built-in redistributive features. Contradictions emerge, however, as the fiscal demands placed on these programs increase, almost explosively, in the face of changing age profiles and rapid advances in medical technology. Pressures will increase, and indeed are already observed, to contain such demands in part by explicitly introducing departures from generality, by imposing means-tests as criteria for eligibility for transfers. To the extent that changes are made in this direction, public support for the programs that stem from the parental motivation must decline. As increasing numbers of persons come to recognize that, with the changes, the state will no longer take care of them, even in some remote residual sense, their image of these programs is dramatically modified. The transfers will come to be viewed as discriminatory payments to politically selected groups, rather than transfers to an inclusive class of eligibles.

On the other hand, if the generality principle is preserved, even if not fully honored, the predictable demands on the fiscal capacities of the welfare states are simply not sustainable. Efforts to meet the commitments under the various programs, most notably the pension and medical services systems, would require that the extraction of taxes from pretax market returns goes well beyond the limits that are behaviorally feasible, quite apart from public choice questions about political will. After all, the Laffer curve relationship is a very real constraint in any polity.

Almost without exception, the welfare-state democracies are being, and will be, increasingly confronted with the disjuncture in the two-pronged decision structure, which, ultimately, reflects the clash between classical liberalism and socialism. As their preferences are expressed through the political process, citizens may genuinely want to extend the parental role of the welfare state, to allow the state to replace God. At the same time, however, citizens may, at their private choice margins, seek to minimize their tax obligations. The liberal principle that persons are to be free to create taxable capacity as and if they so choose is not consistent with the socialist principle that the welfare dependency be expanded beyond plausibly acceptable fiscal limits. The first half of the new century will determine how this basic conflict may be resolved.

7. Prediction and Prospect

Straightforward prediction, based on an assessment of the workings of democratic processes, as observed, would suggest that the budgetary pressures will provoke increasing departures from generality norms in various welfare programs. Means testing or targeting will be extended well beyond current levels. The ranks of those who are explicitly classified as dependents of the nanny state will be reduced, perhaps substantially. As noted, such a breakdown in the generality norm will be accompanied by withdrawal of political support as claimant groups come to be seen as net parasites on those who create taxable capacity. Western welfare democracies may well approach the model for "the churning state", described by de Jasay (1985), in which differing groups compete among themselves for claims against each other.

Of course, such predictions need not be fulfilled. As an example, consider predictions that might have been made, say, from the early 1970s. Who might have predicted that Margaret Thatcher's reforms would move Britain dramatically up in the European league tables; that Ronald Reagan would restore the American spirit; that the Soviet Union would collapse? Western welfare democracies have not yet passed the point of no return. Public attitudes, as reflected through political leaders, may come to embody the recognition that the collectively generated demands on the fisc cannot be met from revenues produced from tax structures that remain plausibly acceptable. The principle of generality in welfare programs may be maintained, more or less, as the demands are scaled back within reasonable limits. As such reforms are implemented, increasing numbers of the citizenry may actually shed off, at least in part, the sense of dependency on the state.

The legacy of Marx is a spent force. The legacy of Bismarck is alive and well. It can, however, be contained with leadership and understanding, as Bismarck himself thought possible.

8. Postscript

This paper has been written on the presumption that terrorism, through the damage inflicted, the reaction and response, along with preventive measures, will not permanently change the basic institutions of Western democracies. If this presumption is invalid, the effects can only be to reinforce the central argument advanced. Terror, in actuality or in threat, almost necessarily places the individual citizen in a more enveloping dependency relation with the state. Events may dictate that the range and scope of collectivized controls be extended. And, along this dimension, even the ardent classical liberal finds difficulty in mounting effective opposition.

In such extension, a comparable tension to that instanced above will arise. Pressures will emerge for departures from the institutions of generality and toward the introduction of discrimination with consequences that are perhaps worse than those involved under the welfare umbrella, narrowly defined.

References

Buchanan, J. M., & Congleton, R. D. (1998). *Politics by Principle, Not Interest: Toward Nondiscriminatory Democracy*. Cambridge University Press: New York and Cambridge.

Hayek, F. A. (1988). *The Fatal Conceit: The Errors of Socialism.* University of Chicago Press: Chicago.

de Jasay, A. (1985). *The State*. Basil Blackwell: Oxford.

Rawls, J. (1971). *A Theory of Justice*. Harvard University Press: Cambridge.

Public Choice (2005) **124:** 33–56
DOI: 10.1007/s11127-005-4744-1

Fragmenting parchment and the winds of war: The Constitution of the United States, 1860–2004

CHARLES K. ROWLEY
Program in Economics, Politics and the Law, James M. Buchanan Center for Political Economy, 5188 Dungannon Road, Fairfax, VA 22030, USA
(E-mail: crowley@gmu.edu)

Accepted March 2005

Abstract. The tension between Hobbesian and Lockeian perspectives on the origins and functions of the state was resolved decisively at Philadelphia in favor of the latter. Fourscore and seven years on from 1787, however, Abraham Lincoln's resolve to save the Union rather than to preserve the Constitution launched a series of attacks by the executive and legislative branches, sustained by a complaisant judiciary, on the parchment so carefully crafted by the republic's Founders. This essay documents the federal government's exploitation of security threats, from the Civil War to the War on Terror, to dismantle constitutional rights to life, liberty and property.

1. Introduction

The United States Constitution was a social contract, completed in 1787, and designed to establish a minimalist federal government, authorized to protect the lives, liberties and properties of individual Americans from internal and external aggression. In this paper, I shall demonstrate that both the Constitution and its revolutionary forerunner, the Declaration of Independence, reflected the political philosophy of John Locke, as enunciated most relevantly in his 1690 book, *Two Treatises of Government.*

I shall also demonstrate that the federal government, in all its branches, has invaded the constitutional rights of American citizens during each major episode of war, as presidents, legislators and judges vie with each other to breach their oaths of office to preserve, to protect and to defend the Constitution. The Lockeian Constitution, seemingly, is defenseless against the Hobbesian winds of war that periodically blow across the nation. In consequence, the parchment of the Constitution is now fragmented to such an extent that it may well be beyond repair.

2. Anarchy Versus Order: The Political Philosophy of Thomas Hobbes

Political philosophy has always been dominated by controversies falling along two great spectra: anarchy versus order and oppression versus freedom (Bobbio, 1993, p. 29). It is difficult, if not impossible, to straddle these two spectra. Ultimately, a political philosopher must choose between the two (Rowley, 1996).

Thomas Hobbes (1588–1679) is the world's leading philosopher whose political philosophy was strictly focused on the former spectrum. The ideal that he resolutely defends is order against anarchy (Rowley, 1998b, pp. 517–518). Fundamentally, Hobbes is obsessed by the threat of anarchy, which he considers to be the return of mankind to the state of nature. The evil that he most fears is not oppression, which derives from an excess of power, but insecurity, which derives from a lack of power. Therefore, he feels called upon to erect a philosophical system as the supreme and insuperable defense against insecurity: insecurity, first of all, of one's life; second of material goods; and last, of that small or great liberty that an individual may enjoy while living in society (Bobbio, 1993, p. 29).

Hobbes's three main political works, *Elements* (1650), *De Cive* (1651), and *Leviathan* (1651), provide descriptions of the state of nature that, in all essentials, are identical. The principal objective condition is that individuals are equal, *de facto*, in nature. Being equal, they are capable of perpetrating the greatest of evils upon each other, namely death. The second objective condition is the scarcity of commodities that, together with equality, generates a permanent state of reciprocal lack of trust. This lack of trust causes each individual to prepare for war and to make war, if necessary, rather than to sue for peace.

The third objective condition is the *ius in omnia*, the right to all things, given by Nature to any individual living outside civil society. Since there is no criterion to distinguish between 'mine and thine', each individual has the right to appropriate all that falls into his power, or, at least, that is useful to his own preservation. The combination of these three conditions inevitably generates 'a situation of merciless competition, which always threatens to turn into a violent struggle' (Bobbio, 1993, p. 39). This situation is made worse by the fact that nature has placed in this predicament individuals dominated by passions that incline them to unsociability.

Hobbes does not have a favorable view of his fellow men. For example, in *Leviathan*, he divides men into those devoted to covetousness and those devoted to sloth, remarking that these 'two sorts of men take up the greatest part of mankind' (*Leviathan*, Ch. XXX, p. 224). Furthermore, a description of the state of nature in *Elements* stresses vainglory as the passion 'which proceedeth from the imagination or conception of our *own power*, above the power of him that contendeth with us' (*Elements*, Ch. 1, ¶9).

In *Leviathan*, Hobbes identifies three causes of conflict: competition, which makes men fight for gain; diffidence, which makes them fight for security; and glory, which makes them fight for reputation (*Leviathan*, Ch. XIII, p. 81). The fundamental problem, therefore, is that of power: 'So that in the first place, I put for a general inclination of all mankind, a perpetual and restless desire of power after power, that ceaseth only in death' (*Leviathan*, Ch. XI, p. 64).

The state of nature as defined by Hobbes is terrifying because the desire for power creates a situation that is a state of war. Indeed, the state of nature is a state of war of all against all: 'Hereby it is manifest, that during the time men live without a common power to keep them all in awe, they are in that condition which is called war; and such a war, as is of every man against every man' (*Leviathan*, Ch. XIII, p. 82). This is an intolerable condition, one that fearful individuals sooner or later must abandon if they wish to save what is most precious to them, their lives.

Hobbes believed in natural law. The dilemma of man in the state of nature is constituted not by the absence of morality, but by the total frustration of that morality as a consequence of insecurity (Warrender, 1957, p. 103). According to Hobbes, right reason comes to the rescue of men who wish to leave this precarious state of affairs, suggesting to them a set of rules, the laws of nature, that aim to secure peaceful cohabitation. These rules are subordinate, however, to a first, fundamental rule that prescribes the seeking of peace, since the laws of nature cannot be upheld in the absence of this condition (Bobbio, 1993, p. 46).

There is only one way to make the laws of nature effective, to force individuals to act according to their reason and not according to their passions, namely to establish an irresistible power in the form of the state. To achieve peace, individuals must enter into a permanent covenant of union (*pactum subiectionis*) that creates the state, thus exiting the state of nature and entering into civil society. The only way to constitute a shared power is for all to consent to sacrifice their own power and to transfer it to a single individual (or body). The recipient of power is not party to this covenant – if he were he would shred it at will – but rather is the recipient of the supreme economic power (*dominium*) and the supreme coercive power (*imperium*). 'There is no power on earth' says the verse in the Book of Job that describes the sea monster, *Leviathan*, 'which is equal to it' (Job 41:24).

3. Oppression Versus Liberty: The Political Philosophy of John Locke

John Locke (1632–1704) is the world's leading philosopher whose political philosophy was strictly focused on the second spectrum, oppression versus liberty. The ideal that he resolutely defends is liberty against oppression. In order to understand Locke's philosophy, it is necessary to return to the concept of the state of nature, which is the starting point in Locke's genetic account of the emergence of civil society (Rowley, 1996, pp. 18–20; Rowley, 1998a, pp. 596–597).

Locke's characterization of the state of nature is much less bleak than that of Hobbes. In *Two Treatises of Government* (1690), Locke asserts that 'Want of a common judge with authority, puts all persons in the state of nature' (*Second Treatise*, ¶19) and 'Men living together according to reason, without a common superior on earth, with authority to judge between them, is properly the state of nature' (*ibid.*). Locke further defines the state of nature as incorporating moral elements. Individuals are endowed with full-blown moral rights and obligations, defined by the eternal and immutable law of nature (*ibid.*, ¶135).

The law of nature provides for the natural right of each individual to life, liberty and property, and the corresponding duty of each individual to refrain from invading the natural rights of others. Whether or not individuals honor these rights depends on the social characterization of the state of nature, which ranges from a 'state of peace, good will, mutual assistance and preservation' at one extreme (*ibid.*, ¶19) to a 'state of enmity, malice, violence and mutual destruction' at the other (*ibid.*). In Locke's judgment, the state of nature typically is one of limited safety and considerable uncertainty, and of significant but not desperate inconveniences.

Locke recognizes three imperfections in the state of nature, namely partial judgments, inadequate force for the execution of judgments, and a variety of judgments made by different individuals in similar circumstances. Three things are necessary to remedy these imperfections, namely a judiciary to administer law impartially, an executive to enforce the decisions of the judiciary, and a legislature to lay down a uniform rule of judgment (Barker, 1960, p. xxi).

In order to secure these remedies, individuals must enter into civil society and thereby must 'give up every one his single power of punishing to be exercised by such alone as shall be appointed to it amongst them; and by such rules as the community, or those authorised by them to that purpose shall agree on' (*ibid.*, ¶127). Artifacts in the form of civil society cannot possess rights naturally. Only by consent can individuals subject themselves to the authority of the state: 'For no government can have a right to obedience from a people who have not freely consented to it' (*ibid.*, ¶192).

According to Locke, '[T]he great and *chief end*. . .of men uniting into commonwealths, and putting themselves under government, *is the preservation of their property*' (*ibid.*, ¶124; emphasis added). The natural right to property is not an inalienable right, in the sense of life and liberty, at least if we define an inalienable right as a right that cannot be lost in any way. Property can be given away or exchanged voluntarily (alienated) and it can be lost involuntarily through negligence or wrongdoing (forfeited). The natural right to property does imply, however, that property cannot be taken away by some other party, including government (prescribed). In this sense, Locke would denote the natural right to property as an imprescriptible right that severely limits the powers delegated by property-owning individuals to civil society:

> The *supream power cannot take* from any man part of his *property* without his own consent. For the preservation of property being the end of

> government, and that for which men enter into society, it necessarily supposes and requires, that the people should *have property*, without which they must be suppos'd to lose that by entring into society, which was the end for which they entered into it, too gross an absurdity for any man to own. (*ibid.*, ¶138; emphasis added)

In a number of places in the *Second Treatise*, Locke declares that the legislature is the supreme power in government: 'This *legislative* is not only the *supream power* of the commonwealth, but sacred and unalterable in the hands where the community have once placed it' (*ibid.*, ¶134). Yet, he argues, there are limits to its powers: 'the legislative being only a fiduciary power to act for certain ends, there remains still *in the people a supream power* to remove or *alter the legislative*, when they find the *legislative* act contrary to the trust reposed in them' (*ibid.*, ¶149).

Locke recognizes the right of individuals to join in resisting oppressive government, most especially where the legislature and/or the executive endeavors to take away or to destroy the property of the people (*ibid.*, ¶222). Whenever government behaves in such a fashion, it puts itself into a state of war with the people, who are then absolved from any further obedience, and who are returned to their former liberties. The people are then free to return a new legislature. Those who have abused their authority, forfeit all rights under the law of nature and may be killed, or used at will, by any person.

4. The Lockeian Foundations of the Declaration of Independence and the United States Constitution

Perhaps inevitably, leading individuals in the American colonies focused on the freedom versus oppression spectrum in justifying revolution against their British rulers in 1776. For they were confronting an allegedly external oppressor that, nevertheless, had established a civil society characterized, for the most part, by its support of life, liberty and property. The colonies, in 1776, certainly were not characterized by the anarchistic conditions of a Hobbesian jungle.

The colonists were not revolting because their lives and liberties were threatened externally or internally. Nor were they revolting, except in the most trivial sense, because their properties were threatened by a plundering government. The taxes involved in the 'no taxation without representation' battle-cry were minimal, indeed were far below the levels that subsequent governments of the United States would impose. The colonists were revolting because their liberties potentially were threatened by an autocratic government.

4.1. *The declaration of independence*

The American Declaration of Independence states that government is an artifice instituted among men to secure rights. The Declaration views these rights as preceding government and as being derived from the Creator. In this sense, they are natural rights. They are more important than government. Indeed, they are the end or purpose of government (Zuckert, 1994, p. 3). The Declaration also states, as a self-evident truth, that all men are created equal, implying that, by nature, human beings are not subject to the rule or authority of any other human beings. These notions have clear roots in the writings of John Locke in *The Second Treatise* (1690).

The Declaration justifies the emergence of government through the consent of the governed, implying that government derives its authority through a social contract. It unequivocally affirms a universal right in all peoples to alter or abolish governments that fail to secure the rights of individuals, thus justifying the American Revolution. These notions also fully accord with Locke's writings in the *Second Treatise* (1690). There can be no question but that the Founding Father signatories to the Declaration embraced the philosophy of John Locke, and placed themselves unequivocally in favor of freedom over oppression (Zuckert, 1994, pp. 3–25).

4.2. *The constitution*

The Constitution of the United States was a compromise document forged by the several confederate states at the Philadelphia convention. As such, it is a blend of differing philosophies mixed with a good dose of political pragmatism. The three most important texts that influenced the Founding Fathers with respect to the popular basis of political authority were John Locke's *Second Treatise of Government* (1690), Charles Secondat Montesquieu's *On the Spirit of Laws* (1748) and David Hume's *Of the Original Contract* (1752). Each of these texts focused attention, albeit in differing ways, on the spectrum of liberty versus oppression. Thomas Hobbes's *Leviathan* (1651) is singularly absent from the parchment of the Constitution (Kurland & Lerner, 1987).

Although the Constitution begins by declaring that, 'We the People of the United States. . .do ordain and establish this Constitution for the United States of America', it is misleading to infer that the Constitution is based on the consent of the governed. For this to be true, the consent necessarily must be real, not fictional, and unanimous, not majoritarian (Barnett, 2004, p. 11).

In reality, the Constitution was approved by a majority of the delegates to conventions in each state. These delegates themselves were elected by a majority of those who voted for delegates. The greater part of Americans was not permitted to vote for any candidate. Though voting requirements varied across local jurisdictions, nowhere could women, children, indentured servants, or slaves vote. Property requirements further limited the voting rights of white males and free black males. Furthermore, those voting in 1787 surely could not bind, by their consent, their mostly unborn posterity.

If a duty of obedience to the commands of lawmakers exists in the absence of consent, one must ask, from what source does it arise? The answer to this question is of critical importance to understanding the nature of the United States Constitution. Fundamentally, the commands of lawmakers carry with them a duty of obedience, even without consent, 'if there is a procedural assurance that they do not violate the rights of the persons on whom they are imposed and that their requirements are necessary to protect the rights of others' (Barnett, 2004, p. 53).

The Founding Fathers knew this well and crafted the Constitution, together (most especially) with the first ten amendments, on the basis of the natural rights that individuals enjoy in the state of nature. As James Madison stated in his speech to the House of Representatives, 'the pre-existent rights of nature "are" essential to secure the liberty of the people' (quoted in Barnett, 2004, p. 81). According to this account, natural rights constitute 'the set of concepts that define the moral space within which persons must be free to make their own choices and live their own lives if they are to pursue happiness while living in society with others' (*ibid.*, p. 80).

It is important to note that natural rights provide for the bounded freedom of the individual, by establishing the rights to several property, freedom of contract, first possession, self-defense and restitution. A Constitution that preserves and protects these rights in civil society provides for the properly bounded freedom of all citizens, a condition that we call liberty. Liberty is not license and is not to be confused with modern variants of unrestrained libertarian philosophy.

So it was that the Founding Fathers justified the United States Constitution in terms of the 'transcendent and precious right of the people to abolish or alter their governments' (*Federalist* No. 40). It should be noted, however, that Madison also recognized that, in so doing, popular government should seek to express 'the cool and deliberate sense of the community, and should not be driven by the pique of those who merely cannot have things their way (*Federalist* No. 63).

Article 4, Section 4 of the Constitution guarantees a republican form of government to every state in the Union. At the core of the notion of republican government was the principle that the many should rule and not the elitist few, and most especially, no king. Hamilton and Madison refined this notion by distinguishing a republic from a democracy in terms of its basis of representation. A properly constructed republic entailed rejecting the right of equal suffrage in the national legislature accorded to the small states under the Articles of Confederation, but allowing for some deviation from the one-man, one-vote principle, in order to protect small states from total domination by the large (*Federalist* Nos. 22, 39 and 57).

The Founding Fathers also had to overcome Montesquieu's warning (invoked by the anti-federalists) that republics could thrive only in small and fairly compact territories (Kurland & Lerner, 1987, p. 97). Madison, in particular, successfully counter-argued that the enlargement of the sphere is found to lessen the insecurity of private rights (*ibid.*). Of course, the success of this argument depended to no small extent on the 'great compromise' that offered the small states equal representation with large states in the U.S. Senate.

Central to the constitutional debate was the proposed shift from a confederacy to a federalist form of government. The insular and diverse communities that had developed in British North America over some 170 years of imperial rule jealously guarded their independence from any dominant central government. Madison recognized the tension, but argued forcefully for making significant inroads into the authority of the states (*ibid.*, p. 148). In the event, however, Madison and his federalist colleagues had to settle for a combination of restraints and restrictions that did not provide the federal government with a complete national veto over all state actions (US Constitution, Art. 1, §§9–10; Art. 6).

Crucially, the Constitution, unlike the Articles of Confederation that preceded it, is silent on the question whether individual states are free to secede from the Union, and whether individual states are free to nullify federal laws that impacted adversely upon their peoples. The Tenth Amendment clearly provides that '[t]he powers not delegated to the United States by the Constitution, nor prohibited to it by the States, are reserved to the States respectively, or to the people.' Therefore, in principle, at least, it would seem that the rights to secede and to nullify remain with the individual States.

The Constitution also is silent concerning the doctrine of the separation of the powers of the legislative, executive and judicial branches of government. Yet the framework of the political system, as established by the Constitution, clearly relies upon that doctrine. In this respect, the Constitution is consistent with the philosophy of John Locke in the *Second Treatise* as refined and made relevant to the American situation by James Madison.

Locke had argued that legislative supremacy was a foregone conclusion and that 'all other Powers in any Members or parts of the Society [are] derived from and subordinate to it' (*Second Treatise*, ¶150). Madison counter-argued that good government requires that the legislature must be prevented from 'drawing all power into its impetuous vortex' (*Federalist* No. 48). Following Hamilton's suggestion that '[e]nergy in the executive is a leading character in the definition of good government' (*Federalist* No. 70), Madison further argued that not only liberty, but also governmental energy, is dependent on an effective separation of powers.

In *Federalist* No. 51, Madison developed a much more potent doctrine of the separation of powers than that advanced by Locke. He did so by advocating a separation of powers between distinct levels of government as well as within each level of government. This argument for protecting states' rights against any potential encroachment by an unconstrained federal government was essential for the ratification of the Constitution.

Left unresolved by the Constitution was the issue of who would resolve disputes concerning the relevant jurisdictions of the separated powers. That issue would be resolved by the Supreme Court of the United States in *Marbury v. Madison* (1803). The damaging consequences for the Constitution itself inherent in the nature of that resolution would not become apparent until 1937 in the Supreme Court's majority decision in *West Coast Hotel v. Parrish.*

The Constitution placed a further check on populism within the legislature by establishing a bicameral legislature. The popular lower chamber within the legislature, the House of Representatives, would reflect the magnitude of the electorate in each State with all representatives elected for simultaneous two-year terms. The upper house within the legislature, the Senate, despite Madison's objections, was composed of two senators from each State, appointed for non-simultaneous six year terms by their respective state legislatures. The Senate was viewed as the aristocratic brake, designed to constrain the populist engine of the House of Representatives, and to serve as a guarantor of property rights against redistributive pressures.

The original Constitution, ratified in 1787, did not contain a bill of rights, despite the pressures placed in favor of such a bill by such leading anti-federalists as George Mason and Patrick Henry. James Madison was a foremost critic of including such a listing of individual rights in a parchment that strictly limited the powers of the federal government, as was Alexander Hamilton (see Federalist No. 84). Yet, within two years, the U.S. Congress, by a two-thirds majority in each House, proposed twelve amendments to the several states, ten of which were ratified to form the basis of a bill of rights.

James Madison, in a dramatic change of political perspective, was primarily responsible for master-minding the passage of these amendments through the House of Representatives. Madison's approach to the bill of rights, however, differed radically from that of the anti-federalists. In consequence, the bill of rights focused specifically on protecting negative and not positive freedoms, thereby consolidating the Lockeian nature of the United States Constitution.

5. The Winds of War

Although the United States owed its founding to a revolutionary war, and its Constitution to the continuing threat of harassment by the all-powerful British Navy, nevertheless its fundamental documents are drawn heavily from the philosophy of John Locke. As such, they are designed primarily to protect individual liberty by limiting the power of the state rather than to secure order through the provision of unlimited governmental power. Unfortunately, a sequence of five major wars – the Civil War, the First World War, the

Second World War, the Cold War, and the War on Terror – has wrought havoc on this design, fragmenting the parchment of the Constitution as politicians and judges, in response to Hobbesian pressures, systematically breached their oaths of office to preserve, protect and defend the Constitution.

5.1. *The civil war: 1860–1865*

When Abraham Lincoln took the oath of office in March 1861, seven southern states already had seceded from the Union in order to maintain the 'peculiar institution' of slavery and to promote free trade favorable to their agricultural interests. Lincoln delivered his inaugural address shielded behind a military cordon, with streets lined with soldiers and with riflemen watching from the rooftops and from the windows in the wings of the Capitol.

Lincoln's inaugural address clearly delineated a Hobbesian philosophy that would remain with him until his assassination in April 1865: 'Plainly the central idea of secession is the essence of anarchy', he argued. Furthermore, 'A majority held in restraint by constitutional checks and limitations, and always changing easily with deliberate changes of popular opinions and sentiments, is the only true sovereign of a free people. Whoever rejects it does, of necessity, fly to anarchy or to despotism' (quoted in Hummel, 1996, pp. 138–139).

From the outset, Lincoln demonstrated his ignorance of or his disdain for the Constitution. The Constitution is silent on the issue of secession. The tenth amendment clearly states that '[t]he powers not delegated to the United States by the Constitution, nor prohibited by it to the States, are reserved to the States respectively, or to the people'. In his inaugural address, Lincoln instead argued, 'I hold that ... the Union of these States is perpetual' and '[t]he Union is unbroken, and to the extent of my ability I shall take care, as the Constitution itself expressly enjoins upon me, that the laws of the Union be faithfully executed in all the States' (*ibid.*, pp. 137–138).

The Confederate attack on Fort Sumter encouraged Lincoln to issue a proclamation calling up the militia, an act that catapulted four additional states and several territories into the Confederacy. Maryland, as a divided border state that separated Washington, DC, from the Northern Union States, became a political tinderbox. In fear for his life, in April 1861, Lincoln chose to breach the Constitution by suspending the *writ of habeas corpus* along the line between Philadelphia and the District of Columbia and by placing Maryland under military rule, even though that state had not voted to secede. Essentially this was an impeachable act.

The Supreme Court and the Congress, both badly crippled by changes in their memberships at the start of the Civil War, were in poor shape to play their judicial and legislative roles in protecting the Constitution. Nevertheless, Chief Justice Roger Taney, a consistent supporter of states' rights, as guaranteed by the Constitution, attempted to control the behavior of the executive branch by invalidating Lincoln's suspension of *habeas corpus*. Taney questioned the action of the president in *Ex parte Merriman* in May 1861.

Merriman was a pro-Confederate Maryland political leader who was arrested without trial, under the authority of Lincoln's suspension of *habeas corpus*, for allegedly participating in the destruction of railroad bridges. Merriman petitioned Taney, as the presiding judge of the circuit court of Baltimore, for a *writ of habeas corpus*. Taney issued the writ, but the military commander to whom it was addressed refused to produce Merriman. The Chief Justice then issued a writ of attachment ordering the military commander to be apprehended. Again, the Chief Justice was rebuffed. Holding a session at chambers, on May 28, 1861, now as Chief Justice and not as presiding circuit court judge, Taney declared Merriman entitled to his freedom and filed an opinion condemning Merriman's arrest as an arbitrary and illegal denial of civil liberty (Belz, 1992, p. 153).

In his opinion, Taney stated that military detention of civilians like Merriman was unconstitutional because only Congress had authority to suspend the *writ of habeas corpus*. He based this conclusion on the fact that the provision authorizing its suspension appears in Article 1 of the Constitution, dealing with the powers of the legislative branch. In a broader analysis, Taney described the president as a mere administrative officer, charged with the faithful enforcement of the law. As such, the president had a duty not to execute laws on his own authority, but rather to executive the laws 'as they are expounded and adjudged by the co-ordinate branch of the government, to which that duty is assigned by the Constitution' (*ibid.*). Taney noted that if Lincoln's action was allowed to stand then 'the people of the United States are no longer living under a Government of laws, but every citizen holds life, liberty and property at the will and pleasure of the army officer in whose military district he may happen to be found' (quoted in Hummel, 1996, p. 142). This, of course, is precisely what Thomas Hobbes advocated in *Leviathan*.

Lincoln responded by ignoring Taney's opinion. In order to intimidate the Chief Justice, Lincoln wrote out standing orders for the Chief Justice's arrest, although these were never in fact served. The President did not ignore, however, the outspoken Maryland legislature, when it lodged a protest with Congress. Rather, Secretary of State Seward ordered a military raid that jailed 31 legislators, the mayor of Baltimore, one of the state's Congressmen and key anti-administration publishers and editors: 'At the state's next election in the fall of 1861, federal provost marshals stood guard at the polls and arrested any disunionists who attempted to vote' (*ibid.*, p. 143).

Lincoln further arranged for special furloughs to Marylanders who had joined the Union army, so that they could return home to vote. Under such circumstances, it is not surprising that the new legislature strongly endorsed the war. Note, however, what all this implies. It implies that a despotic king, albeit one with a limited term in office, once again reigns over the 'colonies'. In the telling words of James Ryder Randle's song, 'Maryland, My Maryland':

The despot's heel is on thy shore, Maryland!
His torch is at thy temple door, Maryland!

Throughout the Civil War, the Supreme Court deferred to the internal security policy of the president, even when executive action exceeded *habeas corpus* suspension, as in *Ex parte Vallandigham* (1864). In April 1863, Union General Ambrose Burnside issued an order prohibiting in the area of his command any declarations of sympathy for the enemy, and declared that persons who assisted the enemy would be tried under military authority. Former Democratic representative Clement Vallandigham condemned the order and urged resistance to it. He was arrested, tried and convicted by a military commission. His imprisonment was commuted by Lincoln into banishment beyond Confederate lines. From Canada, Vallandigham petitioned the Supreme Court for a writ of *certiorari* to review directly the decision of the military commission. With Chief Justice Taney not participating, the Court denied *certiorari*, asserting that the Court lacked jurisdiction over a military commission (Belz, 1992, p. 153).

More generally, the Supreme Court refrained from decisions that might impact on war-related policies of the executive branch, offering the president wide discretion, a discretion that he systematically abused by violating the various provisions of the bill of rights.

5.2. *The first world war: April 1917–November 1918*

The First World War represented a historical landmark for the United States in the sense that, for the first time, American armies fought on European soil. Arguing – without any obvious justification, since America's actual contribution to the war would be relatively small – that the nation faced a crisis of unprecedented proportion, President Woodrow Wilson and the U.S. Congress moved swiftly to extend the authority of the federal government, once war was declared in April 1917.

Leviathan quickly replaced constitutional democracy. The Supreme Court, under the jingoistic leadership of Chief Justice Edward D. White, stood complaisantly by while virtually every right guaranteed to Americans under the Constitution was nullified or abridged (Vaughn, 1992, p. 941). Both during and after the war, the Supreme Court upheld almost all of the federal government's wartime violations of the Constitution.

In May 1917, the Selective Service Act instituted a wartime military draft. This legislation was upheld unanimously by the Supreme Court in January 1918 in *Arver v. United States*, arguing unrealistically that the draft was not involuntary servitude, as defined by the Thirteenth Amendment. Also in 1918, in *Cox v. Wood*, the Court refused relief to a man who sought discharge from the armed forces on grounds that the draft could not be used to enforce military service overseas. In *Ruthenberg v. United States* (1918), the Court rejected claims by socialists that their constitutional rights had been violated because both the grand jury and the trial jury at their trial for not registering for the draft had been made up entirely by individuals from other political parties.

In August 1917, the Lever Food Control Act subjected fuel and food to federal regulation and empowered the president in an 'extreme' emergency to dictate price schedules for any industry. In *United States v. L. Cohen Grocery Co.* (1921), the Supreme Court (unusually) invalidated a section of the Lever Act dealing with food, on the ground that the legislation had not set clear standards for what constituted unreasonable prices. However, the Court did not deny the authority of the government to fix prices during times of war.

In November 1918, the War Prohibition Act banned the making and sale of alcoholic beverages during the war. Even though this act was passed after the Armistice, the Court sustained its validity in the *War Prohibition Cases* of late 1919, holding that federal regulatory authority continued even after the wartime emergency had passed. The Court again upheld prohibition in *Rupert v. Caffey* (1920), rejecting the argument that the Act encroached on the police powers of the states.

A similar pattern of approving the augmented discretionary power of the state is apparent in other cases. In *Northern Pacific Railway Co. v. North Dakota* (1921), a unanimous Supreme Court endorsed a section of the Army Appropriation Act of 1916 that empowered the president to take over and run railroads during wartime. The Court also rejected challenges to the Trading with the Enemy Act in a sequence of cases decided between 1919 and 1921, *Rumely v. McCarthy* (1919), *Central Union Trust Co. v. Carvin* (1921), and *Stoehr v. Wallace* (1921). The Court further rejected challenges, in *Dakota Central Telephone v. South Dakota* (1919), to the federal government's takeover of telegraph and telephone lines and, in *Commercial Cable v. Burleson* (1919), to the federal government's use of private cable property during the war.

Perhaps even more serious, from the perspective of individual liberty, were the restrictions on freedom of speech imposed by President Wilson's government. Not since the Alien and Sedition Act of 1798, had the federal government so severely invaded the First Amendment rights of American citizens (Vaughn, 1992, p. 942).

In June 1917, the Espionage Act made it a felony to cause insubordination, to interfere with enlistments, or to transmit false statements that obstructed military operations. It also established postal censorship, giving the postmaster general the power (used capriciously) to ban from the mails any material deemed to be seditious or treasonable. In October 1917, the Trading with the Enemy Act created a Censorship Board to coordinate and to make recommendations about censorship. The Sedition Act of May 1918 was enacted to repress anarchists, socialists, pacifists and certain labor leaders. The Act made it a felony to disrupt recruiting or enlistments, to support Germany or its allies, or to disrespect the American cause.

The government prosecuted some 2,200 Americans under the Espionage and Sedition acts, convicting more than 1,000 of them. No cases concerning the constitutionality of these statutes came before the Supreme Court during the war, though several cases concerning civil liberties were adjudicated by the Court after the Armistice.

In *Schenck v. United States* (1919), the Court validated government security legislation, relying on the 'bad tendency' test which held that the government did not have to establish a cause-and-effect relationship between a statement and an illegal act. Intent alone was sufficient to establish guilt. The case involved a prosecution under the Espionage Act for distributing anti-draft leaflets to American military personnel. Appellant Schenck argued unsuccessfully that the Act violated the First Amendment. The Court unanimously concluded (with Justice Holmes writing the opinion) that free speech was not an absolute right.

In *Abrams v. United States* (1919), the Court upheld the Sedition Act. Abrams and others were charged with publishing leaflets condemning the American expeditionary force in Russia and calling for a general strike. Justice Clarke, writing for the majority, contended that the pamphlets sought to 'excite, at the supreme crisis of the war, disaffection, sedition, riots and. . .revolution'. As such, they were not protected by the First Amendment. On this occasion, Justice Holmes, writing for the minority, argued that the prosecution had failed to prove that the leaflets exercised any impact on the war effort.

The First World War enhanced the discretionary authority of the federal government, at the expense of the states. It strengthened the power of the president relative to Congress. The Supreme Court, by its unjustifiable deference to the other offending branches of the federal government, also violated the Constitution and opened doors that would later allow unscrupulous governments to exploit so-called crises by riding rough-shod over the precious individual liberties supposedly protected by the Founding Fathers.

5.3. *The second world war: December 1941–August 1945*

The Supreme Court presiding during the Second World War was significantly more liberal than its First World War counterpart, albeit with a weak Chief Justice, Harlan Stone, who was utterly unable to control his fractious colleagues (Belknap, 1992b, p. 943). In consequence, the Court was more protective of the First Amendment rights of American citizens. Predictably, however, a Court forged to protect the interventionist policies of the New Deal rejected all challenges to the wartime economic regulations imposed by the federal government. The Court also repeatedly subordinated other constitutional rights to the alleged demands of military necessity.

In 1941, President Roosevelt, exercising his claimed emergency war powers, created the Office of Price Administration (OPA). OPA received congressional approval in the Emergency Price Control Act of 1942, which empowered the agency to set prices and ration commodities. The Court protected OPA from every legal challenge leveled against it.

In *Yakus v. United States* (1944), the Court rejected the challenge that the statute delegated too much authority to an administrative agency. In an *obiter dicta* opinion, Chief Justice Stone suggested that federal war powers gave Congress itself the authority to fix prices. If the six majority justices truly believed that they could read such an invasion of the separation of powers into the Constitution, they must have been smoking weed long before the 1960s made it a national pastime.

In *Bowles v. Willingham* (1944), the Court rejected a due process challenge to a requirement that OPA rent controls had to go into effect before their validity might be challenged. In *Steuart and Bros. v. Bowles* (1944), the Court upheld the right of the OPA to suspend, without any benefit of judicial process, fuel-oil deliveries to a retail dealer who sold oil in violation of the agency's coupon-rationing system. The Court defied the lessons of elementary price theory by determining that judicial process was not required because OPA's suspension order did not constitute punishment, but rather served to promote the efficient distribution of fuel oil.

So careless were the Supreme Court justices of the unconstitutionality of federal government regulations that they upheld, as a valid exercise of the war power, the Housing and Rent Act of 1947, which was not even enacted until after President Truman had proclaimed that the war was at an end. Evidently, the constitutional laxity of the Court, and its deference to the legislative and executive branches on issues of wartime regulatory interventions, spilled over into the postwar era, and, by degrading the Fifth Amendment rights of American citizens, further opened doors for the unconstitutional economic expansion of the federal government throughout the second half of the twentieth century.

Although the Supreme Court consistently upheld First Amendment, freedom of expression rights throughout the war, the same cannot be said concerning its role with respect to civil liberties. The following judgments epitomize the wartime deference of the Court to unconstitutional behavior by President Roosevelt and the executive branch in this latter field.

In *Duncan v. Kahanamoku* (1946), the Court confronted issues relating to the imposition of martial law in the Territory of Hawaii, ruling that establishing military tribunals to try civilians there had been illegal. However, the Court based its judgment on the fact that the armed forces failed to comply with the Hawaiian Organic Act, ignoring the constitutional provision governing suspension of the *writ of habeas corpus*. Moreover, the Court delayed its decision until two years after the termination of military government in Hawaii.

A much more serious transgression of constitutional rights by the executive branch concerned its treatment of Japanese-Americans living on the West Coast. The government trampled on the constitutional rights of some 70,000 US citizens (together with an additional 42,000 non-citizens), imposing upon them punishments without indictment or trial, curfews, bans from coastal areas, and ultimately, detention in concentration camps. The Supreme Court deferred to these war crimes on the part of President Roosevelt.

In *Hirabayashi v. United States* (1943), the Court ruled unanimously that the curfew order was constitutional. In *Korematsu v. United States* (1944), the Court upheld the validity of the exclusion order. Justice Hugo Black, speaking for the Court, acknowledged that, in the absence of a war, this kind of curtailment of the civil rights of a specific racial group would be unconstitutional. He argued, however, that hardships are part of war and that Japanese-Americans must be required to bear this one because national security required it. Justice Frank Murphy, who dissented, and who thus honored his oath of office, characterized the judgment in *Korematsu* as a plunge into the ugly abyss of racism.

Of course, the idea that the enemy has no rights has enormous appeal to the ignorant, to the malign, and to those who feel themselves to be inadequate, and who therefore seek out reasons why certain groups are inherently inferior to themselves. As such, the Supreme Court decisions damning Japanese-Americans to federal-government-imposed serfdom would contribute greatly to a similar hysteria that swelled up and destroyed the lives of law-abiding American citizens during the early years of the Cold War between the United States and the Soviet Union.

Once again, a major war had allowed an ambitiously aggressive president (Roosevelt) the opportunity to punch holes in the Constitution, to consolidate the relative power of the presidency over the other branches of the federal government and to enhance the authority of the federal government relative to that of the states and the people. Because economic regulation was so general in this war, the shift away from capitalism and towards socialism was of great moment, some indeed, would argue, irreversible (Higgs, 1987, 2004).

5.4. *Communism and the cold war: 1947–1990*

By 1947, the US government clearly was aware that the naïve trust placed by President Roosevelt in Marshal Josef Stalin ('Uncle Joe' as FDR used to call him) had been entirely misplaced, especially so at the Yalta Conference in 1944. As the Soviet Empire made its way across Eastern and Central Europe and into Asia and Africa, the United States committed itself to a policy of containment. In a thermo-nuclear age, the Cold War assumed novel and frightening dimensions.

Because the Soviet Union justified its imperial expansion through the rhetoric of communism, President Truman utilized a virulent anticommunist rhetoric as a justification for the American containment policy. This rhetoric activated concern about the presence of communism within the United States, concern heightened by allegations that Soviet spies had passed nuclear information on to the Soviet Union. Although American communists were very few, and posed only a minimal threat to national security, political opportunists, like Senator Joseph R. McCarthy, ruthlessly exploited the issue for electoral gain (Belknap, 1992a, p. 171).

The anti-communist hysteria in the United States resulted in a number of federal government interventions designed to prevent espionage and subversion. The Internal Security Act of 1950 and the Communist Control Act of 1954 were two examples, each leading to criminal prosecutions and deportations of radicals, the official designation of certain organizations as subversive, and the introduction of loyalty oath requirements.

Many of these, of course, constituted flagrant breaches of the bill of rights. The most notorious of these interventions were those instigated by Senator Joseph R. McCarthy, Chairman of the House Committee on Un-American Activities (HUAC). HUAC investigations resulted in the incarceration of many prominent Americans who refused to name communist acquaintances, and destroyed the careers of many others, in a process correctly compared by Arthur Miller to the Salem witch-trials in his famous play, *The Crucible*.

These patterns of unconstitutional behavior occurred under Republican (Eisenhower) as well as Democratic (Truman) administrations, and were condoned by Republican as well as by Democratic legislatures. Inevitably, challenges to this anti-communism crusade made their way to the Supreme Court. The Court oscillated in its reaction to the legality of these egregious invasions of constitutional rights.

During the early postwar years, when hysteria was at its peak, the Vinson Court generally rejected challenges to anti-communist legislation. Thus, in *American Communications Association v. Douds* (1950), the Court affirmed the constitutionality of a provision in the Taft-Hartley Act that required labor union officials to file affidavits disavowing membership in the Communist Party. In *Dennis v. United States* (1951), the Court rejected a First Amendment challenge to the Smith Act by communist leaders convicted of violating that law. Although Chief Justice Vinson had been a staunch supporter of President Roosevelt's New Deal throughout the 1930s, as a Democratic Party member of the House Ways and Means Committee, he became an unquestioning cold warrior, with no sympathy for the civil rights of communists in the post-Second World War era.

By 1953, when Chief Justice Vinson died and the leadership of the Court passed to Chief Justice Warren, anti-communist hysteria was beginning to wane, as indicated by the Senate's censure of McCarthy in December 1954.

By 1955, the Warren Court's decisions began, at least for a time, to reflect this shift in majority public opinion.

In *Peters v. Hobby* (1955) and in *Cole v. Young* (1956), the Court reinstated federal employees who had been discharged under the loyalty-security programs. In *Watkins v. United States* (1957), a decision handed down on June 17th, a day its critics would call 'Red Monday', the Court overturned the contempt conviction of a man who had refused to answer questions asked by HUAC. In *Service v. Dulles* (1957), the Court ordered the federal government to reinstate an alleged security risk and, in *Yates v. United States* (1957), it reversed the Smith Act convictions of a number of California Communist leaders.

Republicans in Congress reacted adversely to this change of direction by the Court. Senator William Jenner introduced a bill designed to take away the appellate jurisdiction of the Supreme Court in five types of loyalty and subversion cases, yet another example of a failure to observe an oath of office. The bill failed, in large part, because the Warren Court oscillated back towards its earlier unconstitutional stance in favor of anti-communist interventions, as a result of strategic 'switches in time' by the pivotal justices Felix Frankfurter and John M. Harlan (Belknap, 1992a, p. 172).

In *Barenblatt v. United States* (1959) the Court entered a judgment supportive of HUAC, in direct conflict with its Red Monday (*Watkins*) ruling. In *Scales v. United States* (1961), the Court upheld a Smith Act conviction for membership in the Communist Party, in direct conflict with *Yates*. Once again, this change of direction proved to be temporary. With the retirement of Frankfurter in 1963, the Court reverted once again to constitutionality (*ibid.*).

The Cold War was not of such a nature as to encourage the federal government to mobilize production and distribution under the terms of a command economy. So the unconstitutional thrust towards regulation evident in the hot wars is less evident (at least for war–related purposes). In the only significant war-related regulatory venture, the Court upheld the Constitution against an over-reaching executive branch. In *Youngstown Sheet & Tube Co. v. Sawyer* (1952), the Court rejected the argument that President Truman had inherent constitutional authority to issue an executive order seizing private steel mills to prevent strike disruption during the Korean War. This well-grounded judgment undoubtedly constrained subsequent presidents from attempting similar over-reaches of authority throughout the remainder of the Cold War.

5.5. *The war on terror: September 2001*

The successful terrorist attacks on the World Trade Center and the Pentagon on September 11, 2001, quickly followed by an anthrax attack launched through the US Post Office, brought with them a profound Hobbesian shock that pulsated through American society and permeated the American political marketplace. President George W. Bush responded by placing the United States at the forefront of the War on Terror. Within months, the United States and its allies launched a successful war against the Taliban regime in Afghanistan and, in March 2003, went on a war footing again to topple the regime of Saddam Hussein in Iraq. As water runs downhill, so both the president and the Congress violated the bill of rights as they allowed order to dominate liberty as the primary objective of their policies.

On October 26, 2001, the US Congress passed and President Bush signed into law the USA PATRIOT Act, an acronym for 'Uniting and Strengthening America by Providing Appropriate Tools Required to Intercept and Obstruct Terrorism'. The legislation was rushed through Congress, with little time for debate and discussion. The Senate voted 98–1 in its favor, and the House 357–66. Perhaps the only saving grace in this largely unconstitutional legislation is its sunset provision. The Act will die on December 31, 2005, unless it is reenacted. There is little chance that it will die.

The Act violates the US Constitution in several ways. It provides sweeping new powers of detention and surveillance to the executive branch of the federal government and to law enforcement agencies, while depriving the courts of meaningful judicial oversight to ensure that the new law enforcement powers are not abused. It authorizes the Secretary of State to designate any group, foreign or domestic, as a terrorist organization, an authority that is not subject to judicial review. It permits investigations based on lawful First Amendment rights, if that activity, somehow, can be tied to intelligence purposes.

The Act undermines the privacy protections of the Fourth Amendment, by weakening the line that divides intelligence gathering and gathering evidence for criminal investigations, and so expands the ability of the federal government to spy through wiretaps, computer surveillance, accessing medical, financial, business and educational records, and initiating secret searches of homes and offices. It undermines the due process procedures guaranteed by the Fifth, Sixth, and Fourteenth Amendments, which for over a century have extended to non-citizens, by permitting the federal government to detain foreigners indefinitely, even if they have never been convicted of a crime.

Yet more problematically, the Act eliminates much of the judicial oversight established during the 1970s following revelations that the CIA and the FBI had spied on over a half-million American citizens during and after the McCarthy era. In conjunction with the consolidation of the intelligence agencies under the centralized leadership of an Intelligence Tsar, the Patriot Act opens the door wide to major new possibilities of executive branch abuse of the individual rights of US citizens. Unless challenges to the Act are sustained by the Supreme Court, executive branch abuse will be unconstrained from any prospect of redress, and the police state predictably will tighten its grip, especially once terrorists again successfully attack the American homeland.

As a central part of the War on Terror the executive branch currently pursues a policy of detaining, indefinitely and incommunicado, US citizens and non-citizens designated as enemies of the war (Silverglate, 2005, p. 22). Many non- US citizens are detained in Guantanamo Bay, Cuba, on a naval base governed by a perpetual lease between the United States and Cuba, in an attempt to place the prisoners far beyond the reach of due process and judicial review. Yet, in three landmark decisions, a divided Rehnquist Supreme Court, reached out to bring at least a few of these wretched souls back under some semblance of the rule of law.

In *Rasul v. Bush* (2004), the Supreme Court reversed a judgment favorable to the federal government handed down by the US Court of Appeals for the District of Columbia. Four British and Australian citizens had been captured by the American military in Pakistan and Afghanistan during the War on Terror, and had been transported to the American military base at Guantanamo Bay. Their families filed suit seeking a *writ of habeas corpus* that would declare the detention unconstitutional in that it violated the Fifth Amendment's due process clause.

The government countered that the federal courts had no jurisdiction to hear the case because the prisoners were not American citizens and were being held in territory over which the United States did not have sovereignty. The District Court agreed with the government, and the Court of Appeals affirmed the district court's judgment.

The Supreme Court, in a 6-to-3 decision, written by Justice John Paul Stevens, determined that the degree of control exercised by the United States over the Guantanamo Bay base was sufficient to trigger the application of habeas corpus rights. The fact that ultimate sovereignty remained with Cuba was irrelevant. Justice Stevens also confirmed that the right to habeas corpus is not dependent on citizenship status. The detainees were therefore free to bring suit challenging their detention as unconstitutional.

In *Hamdi v. Rumsfeld* (2004), the Supreme Court passed judgment on the detention of an American citizen, Yaser Hamdi, who had been arrested by the United States military in Afghanistan. Hamdi was accused of fighting for the Taliban, an enemy combatant of the United States. He was transferred to a military prison in Virginia.

A defense attorney filed a petition for a writ of certiorari in the Virginia federal district court, arguing that Hamdi's detention violated his Fifth Amendment right to due process by holding him indefinitely without access to an attorney or to a trial. The government countered that the executive branch had the right, during wartime, to declare individuals who fight against the United States to be enemy combatants, and thus to restrict their access to the court system.

The district court ruled for Hamdi, ordering the government to release him. On appeal, the Fourth Circuit Court reversed, finding that the separation of powers required federal courts to practice restraint during wartime. The Supreme Court partly reversed this latter decision in a four-justice plurality partly joined by two additional justices. Justice Sandra Day O'Connor, writing for the majority, concluded that, although Congress had authorized Hamdi's detention, Fifth Amendment due process guarantees a citizen held in the United States as an enemy combatant the right to contest that detention before a neutral decision-maker.

However, Justice O'Connor applied a flexible due process standard in which the Court 'would not be offended by a presumption in favor of the Government's evidence, so long as that presumption remained rebuttable, and so long as a fair opportunity for rebuttal were provided'. This is a remarkable concession to the government, effectively reversing the onus of proof in a criminal case. Moreover, the majority judgment left open the possibility that the neutral decision-maker might be a military tribunal, and not a civilian court of law.

In *Rumsfeld v. Padilla* (2004), the Supreme Court passed judgment on a habeas corpus petition filed on behalf of Jose Padilla, an American citizen who had been arrested in Chicago's O'Hare International Airport after returning from Pakistan in 2002. Initially, Padilla was detained as a material witness in the government's investigation of the *al Qaeda* terrorist network. Later, he was declared to be an enemy combatant, who could be held in prison indefinitely without an access to either an attorney or to the courts.

Donna Newman, who had represented Padilla while he was being held as a material witness, filed a petition for habeas corpus on his behalf. The US District Court for the Southern District of New York ruled that Newman had standing to file the petition even though Padilla had been moved to a military brig in South Carolina. However, the Court also ruled that the government had the power to detain him as an enemy combatant notwithstanding the federal Non-Detention Act which states that 'no citizen shall be imprisoned or otherwise detained by the United States except pursuant to an Act of Congress'.

A divided Second Circuit Court of Appeals reversed judgment on the enemy combatant ruling, finding that the Authorization for Use of Military Force did not meet the requirement of the Non-Detention Act and that the president could not declare American citizens captured outside a combat zone to be enemy combatants.

The Supreme Court did not pass judgment on the merits of the case. In a 5-to-4 opinion, written by Chief Justice Rehnquist, the Court found that the case had been filed improperly, incorrectly naming Donald Rumsfeld as the defendant. The Court determined that the case must be re-filed in South Carolina, naming the brig commander as defendant. The government now has the advantage of pleading its case before a much more sympathetic Fourth Circuit federal district court. Once again, the Supreme Court has exposed itself to the view that it leans over backward to accommodate the executive branch in the latter's pursuit of the so-called War on Terror.

6. Conclusions

Evidence outlined in this paper demonstrates that the US Constitution, drafted by Founding Fathers who shared a Lockeian vision of society, simply cannot contain the pressures that mount during Hobbesian episodes, when the country places itself in a state of war. Although, to some degree, the Supreme Court attempts to re-establish the credibility of the Constitution during intervening periods of peace, fault-lines remain that are easily exploited by ambitious presidents.

The situation is especially ominous at the present time, in that President Bush has declared a War on Terror that can never be successfully concluded. Such a war is a paradise for any ambitious president and for his *coterie* of self-serving sycophants; but it is a Hobbesian nightmare for ordinary citizens who surrender their precious rights to *Leviathan*, in return for a vague promise to protect their lives. The Hobbesian social contract that characterizes the United States of American at the turn of the twenty-first century is a ragged remnant of that rich parchment forged in Philadelphia by Founding Fathers who truly understood and cherished a constitution of liberty.

References

Barker, E. (1960). *Social Contract: Essays on Locke, Hume and Rousseau.* Oxford University Press: Oxford.

Barnett, R. E. (2004). *Restoring the Lost Constitution: The Presumption of Liberty.* Princeton University Press: Princeton, NJ.

Belknap, M. (1992a). Communism and the Cold War. In K. L. Hall (Ed.), *The Oxford Companion to the Supreme Court of the United States*, 171–172. Oxford University Press: New York and Oxford.

Belknap, M. (1992b). World War II. In K. L. Hall (Ed.), *The Oxford Companion to the Supreme Court of the United States* (pp. 943–945). Oxford University Press: New York and Oxford.

Belz, H. (1992). Civil War. In K. L. Hall (Ed.), *The Oxford Companion to the Supreme Court of the United States* (pp. 152–154). Oxford University Press: New York and Oxford.

Bobbio, N. (1993). *Thomas Hobbes and the Natural Law Tradition.* University of Chicago Press: Chicago.

Higgs, R. (1987). *Crisis and Leviathan: Critical Episodes in the Growth of American Government.* Oxford University Press: New York and Oxford.

Higgs, R. (2004). *Against Leviathan.* The Independent Institute: Oakland, CA.

Hobbes, T. ([1642] 1839–1845). *De Cive.* In W. Molesworth (Ed.), *The English Works of Thomas Hobbes*, vol. 2. J. Bohn: London.

Hobbes, T. ([1650] 1839–1845). *Elements of Law.* In W. Molesworth (Ed.), *The English Works of Thomas Hobbes*, vol. 4. J. Bohn: London.

Hobbes, T. ([1651] 1839–1845). *Leviathan.* In W. Molesworth (Ed.), *The English Works of Thomas Hobbes*, vol. 3. J. Bohn: London.

Hume, D. ([1752] 1987). Of the Original Contract. In E. F. Millere (Ed.), *Essays, Moral, Political and Literary*. Liberty Classics: Indianapolis, IN.
Hummel, J. R. (1996). *Emancipating Slaves, Enslaving Free Men: A History of the American Civil War*. Open Court: Chicago and La Salle, IL.
Kurland, P. B., & Lerner, R. (Eds.). (1987). *The Founders' Constitution*, vol. 1. University of Chicago Press: Chicago.
Locke, J. ([1690] 1967). Two Treatises of Government. In P. Laslett (Ed.), Cambridge University Press: Cambridge.
Montesquieu, C.S. ([1748] 1989). *The Spirit of Laws*. In A. M. Cohler, B. C. Miller, & H. S. Stone (Ed. and trans.). Cambridge University Press: Cambridge.
Rowley, C. K. (1996). What is Living and What is Dead in Classical Liberalism? *The Independent Review, 1*(1), 9–28.
Rowley, C. K. (1998a). Locke, John (1632–1704). In P. Newman (Ed.), *The New Palgrave Dictionary of Economics and the Law* vol. 2, (pp. 594–601). Macmillan: London and New York.
Rowley, C. K. (1998b). State of Nature and Civil Society. In P. Newman (Ed.), *The New Palgrave Dictionary of Economics and the Law* vol. 3, (pp. 514–523). Macmillan: London and New York.
Silverglate, H. (2005). Why the Supreme Court's Widely Praised Rulings are bad for America. *Reason, 36*(8), 22–29.
Vaughn, S. (1992). World War I. In K. L. Hall (Ed.), *The Oxford Companion to the Supreme Court of the United States*, 941–943. Oxford University Press: New York and Oxford.
Warrender, H. (1957). *The Political Philosophy of Hobbes: His Theory of Obligation*. Clarendon Press: Oxford.
Zuckert, M. J. (1994). *Natural Rights and the New Republicanism*. Princeton University Press: Princeton, NJ.

Cases cited

Abrams v. United States, 250 U.S. 616 (1919)
American Communications Association v. Douds, 339 U.S. 382 (1950)
Arver et al. v. United States, 245 U.S. 366 (1918)
Barenblatt v. United States, 360 U.S. 109 (1959)
Bowles v. Willingham, 321 U.S. 504 (1944)
Central Union Trust v. Carvin, 254 U.S. 554 (1921)
Cole v. Young, 351 U.S. 536 (1956)
Commercial Cable v. Burleson, 250 U.S. 360 (1919)
Cox v. Wood, 247 U.S. 3 (1918)
Dakota Central Telephone v. South Dakota, 250 U.S. 163 (1919)
Dennis v. United States, 341 U.S. 494 (1951)
Duncan v. Kahanamoku, 327 U.S. 304 (1946)
Hamdi v. Rumsfeld, U.S. 6696 (2004)
Hirabashi v. United States, 320 U.S. 81 (1943)
Korematsu v. United States, 323 U.S. 214 (1944)
L. Cohen Grocery Co. v. United States, 255 U.S. 81 (1921)
Marbury v. Madison, 5 U.S. 137 (1803)
Merriman, Ex parte, F. Cas. 9487 (1861)
Northern Pacific Railway Co. v. North Dakota, 236 U.S. 585 (1919)
Peters v. Hobby, 349 U.S. 331 (1955)
Rasul v. Bush, 03 U.S. 334 (2004)

Rumely v. McCarthy, 250, U.S. 283 (1919)
Rumsfeld v. Padilla, U.S. 1027 (2004)
Rupert v. Caffey, 251 U.S. 264 (1920)
Ruthenberg v. United States, 245 U.S. 480 (1918)
Scales v. United States, 367 U.S. 203 (1961)
Schenck v. United States, 249 U.S. 47 (1919)
Service v. Dulles, 354 U.S. 363 (1957)
Steuart & Bros. v. Bowles, 322 U.S. 398 (1944)
Stoehr v. Wallace, 255 U.S. 239 (1921)
Vallandigham, Ex parte, 68 U.S. 243 (1864)
War Prohibition Cases, 251 U.S. 146 (1919)
Watkins v. United States, 354 U.S. 178 (1957)
West Coast Hotel v. Parrish, 300 U.S. 379 (1937)
Yakus v. United States, 321 U.S. 414 (1944)
Yates v. United States, 354 U.S. 298 (1957)
Youngstown Sheet & Tube Co. v. Sawyer, 343 U.S. 579 (1952)

Public Choice (2005) **124:** 57–73
DOI: 10.1007/s11127-005-4746-z

Constitutional political economy in the European Union

DENNIS C. MUELLER
Department of Economics, University of Vienna, BWZ – Bruenner Str. 72, A-1210 Vienna
(E-mail: dennis.mueller@univie.ac.at)

Accepted March 2005

Abstract. This article surveys recent research in constitutional political economy in Europe. Although not all of the works discussed necessarily focus only on European constitutional issues or are written by Europeans, European constitutional issues figure importantly in each area surveyed. The article examines the literatures linking constitutional institutions to economic growth, government size, government deficits and corruption, bicameralism, direct democracy and federalism. Three exclusively European topics also are covered: constitutional issues in the transition countries, the structure of the European Union and the draft constitution for the European Union.

1. Introduction

The distinguishing feature of constitutional political economy is to view democracy as a two-stage process – in the first stage the rules of the political game to be played in stage two are drawn up; in stage two the game is played. Although participants in the process are assumed to be rational egoists, the different characteristics of the choices made at each stage, the fact that constitutional choices are assumed to be long-lived in comparison to everyday political choices, and in particular the different levels of uncertainty assumed at each stage lead to quite different sorts of outcomes.

Constitutional political economy, or as it is also often called, *constitutional economics*, can be said to have been born with the publication of *The Calculus of Consent* in 1962. Much of the work of James Buchanan, coauthor of this classic in public choice with Gordon Tullock, since the publication of *The Calculus* has fallen within the domain of constitutional economics. Appropriately enough, when the journal *Constitutional Political Economy* was launched in 1990, its two managing editors were at Buchanan's home university, George Mason, and Buchanan was listed as an advisory editor.

Buchanan (1986, p. 366) has remarked that he and Tullock "more or less explicitly considered our exercise to be an implicit defense of the Madisonian structure embodied in the United States Constitution." A second major contribution to the constitutional political economy literature by Buchanan, *The Limits of Liberty* (1975), clearly was stimulated by and was in a sense a reaction to the tumultuous events in the United States during the late 1960s and early '70s. Thus, it can fairly be said that constitutional political economy was a very American contribution to social science, both in terms of the origin of the pioneering contributors to the field and the perspectives that they brought to it.

In recent years, however, it is possible to discern a shift in the center of gravity of the field toward Europe. This shift was signaled symbolically by the move of one of the founding editors of *Constitutional Political Economy*, Viktor Vanberg, from the United States to Europe. Today, two of the journal's three editors are located in Europe. The shift in center of gravity can be most visibly seen, however, in the recent literature in the field. Many of the leading scholars studying constitutional questions from a public choice perspective today are Europeans, and many of the questions they examine concern European institutions.

This development is not particularly surprising, perhaps, once one considers the importance of constitutional issues in popular politics on both sides of the Atlantic. The US Constitution is viewed with reverence by most American citizens and by many academicians working in political science and public choice. Proposals to make substantial changes in it seldom appear and are viewed with considerable skepticism if not fear when they do surface. Although the recent proposal for a constitutional amendment to ban same-sex marriages sparked the interest of some citizens and politicians in the United States – including the president – I do not anticipate that it will generate a great deal of research in the constitutional political economy field.

In contrast, constitutional issues of substantive importance have sprung to the fore in great number and variety in recent years in Europe. Most salient of these is the recently drafted constitution for the European Union (hereafter EU). But even before it appeared, the various treaties that were signed by EU countries presented a host of constitutional issues to explore. Each new expansion of the EU has raised important constitutional issues, and the collapse of communism in Eastern Europe in 1989 and the Soviet Union in 1991 forced the affected countries into a constitution writing or rewriting process of major proportions. Some western European countries, like Great Britain, also have introduced substantial constitutional reforms recently, and others, like Sweden, have been actively considering them.[1]

In this essay I discuss *some* of the recent research in constitutional political economy in Europe. In selecting topics to discuss, I have chosen not to limit myself to studies that explicitly employ the two-stage framework pioneered by Buchanan and Tullock, but rather to employ a broader definition of constitutional political economy. Namely, I shall discuss eight areas of research, which are directly concerned with constitutional questions that either exclusively pertain to Europe or do so to a large degree. In the final section of the article I then speculate a bit about the future development of constitutional political economy in Europe.

2. The Consequences of Constitutional Institutions for Economic Growth

In a by now classic article, North and Weingast (1989) demonstrated the importance in 17th century England of the strengthening of constitutional institutions that committed the state to protect property rights, enforce contracts and maintain other economic institutions that foster growth.[2] More generally, North has stressed the link between the development of strong property rights and economic institutions in England and the Netherlands and their early economic success compared to that of France and Spain (North & Thomas, 1973; North, 1990, 1995).

What has been true for Europe historically also has been found to be true in cross-country panel data sets covering the post-World War II era. Strong *economic* institutions (enforcement of property rights, respect for the sanctity of private contracts, and so on) are positively related to economic growth. Interestingly enough, the relationship between political liberties and economic growth is less consistent than that between economic liberties and growth.[3]

In recent work, La Porta, Lopez-De-Silanes, Shleifer and Vishny (1997, 1998) examined the content and historical development of legal institutions in different countries to determine which ones best align the interests of the owners (shareholders) and managers of corporations. They concluded that the *common* law systems found in the Anglo-Saxon countries and former British colonies offer outside and minority shareholders greater protection against managerial abuse of their positions than do *civil* law systems. Greater shareholder protection in turn has been found to be positively associated with the size of a country's external capital markets, which in turn are positively related to country growth rates and the investment performance of firms.[4] Although the laws and rules that define a country's corporate governance institutions are not usually included in its constitution, like its constitution the basic legal framework of a country – whether it has a common law or civil law system – tends to change slowly over time. Thus, this more recent research that is not confined to Europe reconfirms the basic conclusions of North and his coauthors for Europe. The constitutional and legal institutions that define the economic liberties of a country have a profound impact on its economic performance.

3. Electoral Laws, form of Government and Economic Performance

A constitution defines the rules of the political game a country plays, and no constitutional rules are more important than those governing elections and the selection of the chief executive.[5] A large literature going back at least to Maurice Duverger (1954), has established a close relationship between the number of representatives elected from a political district and the number of parties winning seats in the legislature.[6]

In an impressive body of research over the past decade, Persson and Tabellini (1999, 2000, 2003, 2004a,b) and Persson, Roland, and Tabellini (2000) have explored the relationships between electoral rules, numbers of active political parties, whether a country has a presidential system or not, and various measures of economic performance. In the empirical part of their research program, they have of course used samples of countries from around the world. Since multiparty systems are heavily concentrated in Continental Europe, their findings for these systems can be interpreted as findings for Continental Europe. Persson and Tabellini's theoretical models predict more rent seeking and corruption in multiparty systems, because individual members of parliament are less accountable to the voters when they run as members of party lists than when they have to defend their own seats in single-member districts. They also predict larger government sectors, more redistribution and larger budget deficits in multiparty systems, because of inefficiencies of bargaining among parties in coalition governments, and because single-party governments, which are found more often in single-member district systems, are more accountable to the voters. Presidential systems are expected to lead to smaller governmental sectors, because they generally contain stronger checks and balances than parliamentary systems. By and large, Persson and Tabellini's empirical findings corroborate their models.[7]

4. Bicameralism

Bicameralism is another institution that is not peculiar to Europe, but interest in the properties of bicameral systems has been high on the continent in recent years, and again much of the empirical evidence regarding the effects of bicameralism includes European countries. Thus, we include it in our survey.

Buchanan and Tullock (1962, Ch. 16) were the first scholars to look at bicameralism from a constitutional perspective. They argued that bicameral systems effectively increase the size of the majority needed to pass legislation. Bicameralism has this effect, *if* representatives in the second chamber are drawn from different constituencies than representatives in the first chamber, *and* the second chamber has veto power over the first. When these conditions are met, then a group which obtained a bare majority of seats in the first chamber could not also possess a bare majority in the second, and thus would effectively need a super-majority across the entire country to pass legislation in both chambers.

Tsebelis and Money (1997, p. 215) claim that the conditions needed to sustain this argument apply to only one country – the United States, and I claim that they are not even necessarily satisfied there. It would be easy to identify

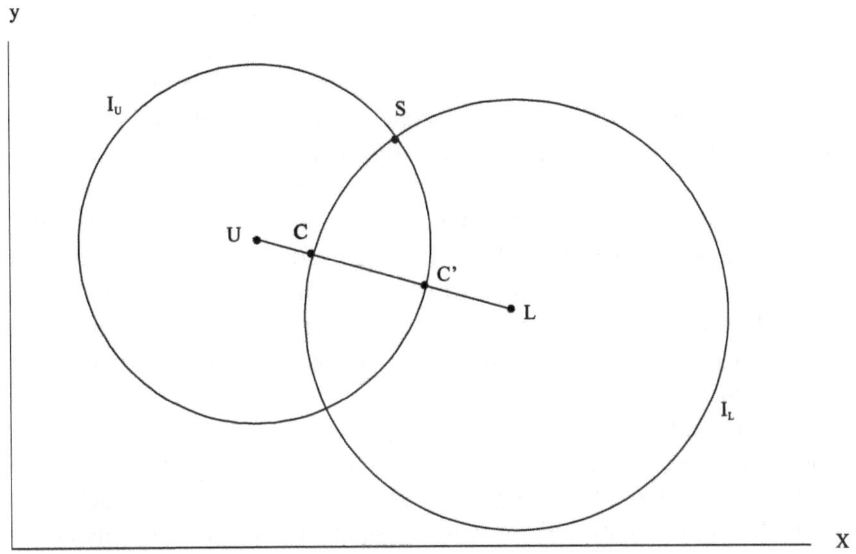

Figure 1. Outcomes with Bicameralism.

26 states with populations that summed to more than half of the US population. An ideological group that elected the representatives to both houses from these 26 states would then be able to determine legislative outcomes, just as it could if only one chamber had decision-making power.

Nevertheless, bicameralism often will *effectively* increase the required majority in the US legislative branch, and more generally shares the salient property of all supra-qualified majority rules of increasing the likelihood of the status quo's victory. To see this consider Figure 1, which depicts a two-dimensional issue space.[8] The upper house favors the combination *U* and the lower house *L*. If legislative authority rested solely with the lower house, point *L* would defeat the status quo, *S*. But under a bicameral system, the two houses must agree on some compromise, if *S* is to be overturned. If we treat the bargainers from each chamber as unitary actors with circular indifference curves centered on their ideal points, then any compromise reached must fall in the lens formed by the two indifference curves passing through *S*, I_U and I_L. The line connecting the ideal points, *U* and *L*, is the Pareto set for the two actors, and thus an agreement on the segment CC' falling in the lens formed by the two indifference curves is expected. Where the final compromise lies will depend on the relative bargaining strengths of the representatives of each chamber. The closer *S* lies to the *UL*-line, the shorter is CC', and the less room there is for bargaining. Should *S* fall on the *UL*-line, it could not lose to any point in the figure.

In Figure 1 a core exists. With more than two dimensions a core often does not exist. Tsebelis and Money (1997, Ch. 3) argue that even when a core does not exist, agreements between the two chambers that defeat the status quo are likely to be found in some central space like the uncovered set.[9] They also hypothesize that the speed at which compromises are reached and the division of the gains from collective action depend on both the institutional structure for reaching compromises and the degrees of impatience in the two chambers. They test their predictions with data from France for the period 1959–85, where they argued that the composition of the National Assembly varied dramatically over time, thus changing the degree of impatience in this chamber. Their results seem to confirm their hypotheses. The more uncertainty there is about the degree of impatience of the other chamber, the longer it takes to reach a decision. The more patient chamber also gains at the expense of the other chamber.

Bradbury and Crain (2002) also have presented evidence that the composition of the two chambers affects outcomes using data from state legislatures in the United States. The further apart are the median voters in each chamber, the less redistribution there is in the state and the smaller is its budget. Congleton (2003a,b) likewise presents time-series evidence for Sweden and Denmark that seems to show that the shift from bicameral to unicameral systems increased the size of the state sector.

Both the theoretical and empirical literatures on bicameralism confirm the fundamental proposition of public choice – institutions matter. Different outcomes can be expected from a bicameral than from a unicameral legislature. What they do not demonstrate, however, is that the outcomes from two chambers are *superior* to those from one chamber, if this chamber employs a supra-majority rule. As the required majority rises the probability of cycles falls,[10] just as this probability falls as one goes from one to two chambers. Less redistribution and a smaller government sector can be expected when a unicameral legislature uses a supra-qualified majority rule. Requiring large majorities to pass legislation should benefit the patient legislators who hold out for bigger shares of the gains from collective action. Tsebelis and Money (1997) show that the results from a bicameral system should be different from a unicameral system, even when the latter uses a supra-majority rule. Neither they nor any one else has yet demonstrated that the results from a bicameral system would be *better* than those from a unicameral system coupled with a supra-majority rule.[11]

5. Direct Democracy

Direct democracy is yet another political institution that is not unique to Europe, but an institution to which European public choice scholars have devoted considerable attention. Switzerland makes the most use of direct democracy of any country in the world, and it has been the focal point of research by European public choice scholars.

Direct democracy might, of course, either improve the outcomes of the political process or make them worse. An argument why they might be made worse would be that citizens are poorly informed about the issues and their decisions will therefore be inferior to than those of legislative representatives and bureaucrats, who are well-educated and informed about the issues. A second charge leveled against direct democracy, when it takes the form of referenda, is that it is overly influenced by interest groups.

Proponents of direct democracy see it as a potential check on budget-maximizing politicians and bureaucrats. The weight of the empirical evidence supports this position. The following conclusions emerge from this literature.

1. The outcomes in communities that make use of direct democracy (hereafter DD) come closer to the preferences of the median voter than do the outcomes in communities lacking these institutions (Pommerehne, 1978; Matsusaka, 2004).
2. In general, expenditures are lower in DD communities (Pommerehne, 1976, 1978; Pommerehne & Schneider, 1978). This finding seems to confirm the hypothesis that representatives and bureaucrats seek larger budgets. Interesting in this regard, however, are the findings of John Matsusaka (2004) for the United States. His data for the post-World War II period confirmed the findings from Switzerland – expenditures were lower in cities and states that used DD. However, before the war DD led to *higher* expenditures. Matsusaka's explanation for this finding is that the great migration of people from the countryside to the cities during the late 19th and early 20th centuries left urban voters in state legislatures under-represented as redistricting lagged population movements. Urban voters demand more public services than rural voters and thus the median voter favored larger budgets than the median representative. As such, the main feature of DD is to shift outcomes toward the preferences of the median voter. This shift reduces the size of the public sector when representatives favor larger budgets than the median voter, which today is probably the usual case.
3. Budget deficits are lower in the presence of DD (Feld & Kirchgässner, 1999).
4. There is less manipulation of the political business cycle in the presence of DD (Pommerehne, 1978).
5. There is less under-reporting of taxable income with DD (Weck-Hannemann & Pommerehne, 1989).
6. The economy of a direct democracy is more productive (Feld & Savioz, 1997).
7. Citizens are happier in a DD (Frey & Stutzer, 2000, 2002).

This is an impressive list of advantages. Indeed, Kirchgässner, Feld, and Savioz (1999) are so impressed with DD's performance in Switzerland that they claim that the institution is ripe for exporting. Feld and Kirchgässner (2004) advocate building institutions of DD into the new European Union Constitution. There has been much talk in the EU in recent years of the need to close "the democratic deficit". The draft constitution certainly fails to do this. Making greater use of the institutions of direct democracy could be an important step toward closing the deficit.

6. Federalism

Both the United States and Canada have strong federalist systems, and thus not surprisingly federalism (or, as it is more often discussed in public finance, fiscal federalism) has received a great deal of attention by public economics scholars in these countries. In recent years, federalism also has been a topic of much interest, both in popular discourse and academia in Europe. There are several explanations for this interest. First, the pax Americana that now rules Europe following the collapse of communism has produced pressures in several countries like England and Spain for more decentralized political institutions with local and regional communities having more control over their taxes and expenditures. An additional factor facilitating smaller sized governments is the expansion of liberalized trade since World War II, which has made countries less dependent on their internal markets (Alesina & Spolare, 1997; Alesina, Spolare, & Wacziarg, 2000). In some countries, like Sweden, there has been discussion of a complete constitutional overhaul with the introduction of strong federalist institutions as one possible outcome.[12] Finally, the issue of whether the European Union itself should be organized more along federalist lines has been raised and hotly debated outside of academia and to some extent inside it as well.

Much of this debate has been around the question of how centralized should collective decision-making in the EU be. Both proponents and opponents of greater federalism seem to equate more federalism with more centralism, and thus opponents of centralism are opponents of a federal EU.[13] But instead of seeing the issue as a choice between centralization and decentralization, one can see it as a choice between different institutions for representing individual preferences – a choice between a federation and a confederation. The key difference here is that in a confederation an individual's preferences are *indirectly* represented at the central level by representatives chosen by the elected government in his country. In a federal state the citizen chooses representatives for the legislature of the central government directly. Which institutional structure is best suited for representing individual preferences depends on how these preferences are distributed within the larger community (Mueller, 1997, 2002). Both a federation and a confederation can in principle be highly decentralized, *if the constitution is designed in such a way as to protect the lower states from the central state.*[14]

As it functions today, the EU is a cross between a confederation and a federation. If one examines the evolution of the EU, it is easy to see how this hybrid arose. The occasion of drafting a new constitution for the EU was a golden opportunity to rationalize this part of the EU's political institutions, an opportunity that the EU's drafters unfortunately failed to seize. Debate over federalism in the EU can be expected to continue well into the future.

7. The Transition Countries

The collapse of communism in Eastern Europe in 1989 and in the Soviet Union in 1991 also presented golden opportunities for putting some of the knowledge of political institutions developed by public choice scholars over the preceding 40 years into practice. One country – Russia – did in fact invite two leading public choice scholars, Peter Ordeshook and Thomas Schwartz, to help it draft a new constitution. The final product did not, however, incorporate their ideas so much as the wishes of Boris Yeltsin, who wanted the constitution to create a strong president, a post that he would occupy after the constitution went into effect. The Russian experience confirms the first law of constitution writing – those who are likely to hold office under the new constitution should not be involved in its writing lest they draft a constitution to serve *their* interests and not those of the citizens.[15]

One might have expected the shift from communist dictatorships to democracies to have precipitated great debates in each country as to what kind of democratic institutions best suited a given country – two party or multiparty, federalist or unitary, to name two of the choices. Such debates did not take place. Perhaps there was not time for them or the urgency of the transformation of economic institutions and the efforts that they took left no energy for a serious look at the possible political options. The Eastern European countries all modeled their democratic institutions along the lines of their West European neighbors on the continent – multiparty parliamentary systems. Former members of the Soviet Union followed Russia and introduced presidential systems (Roland, 2002, pp. 37–38).

Shortly after the fall of communism, the *East European Constitutional Review* was launched jointly by the University of Chicago Law School and the Central European University. (The University of Chicago was later on replaced by the New York University School of Law.) As its name implies, this journal has been devoted to reporting constitutional developments in the transition countries, and to articles analyzing these developments. Although these articles generally do not employ the rational actor methodology of public choice, the journal contains a wealth of information that would be of value to any public choice scholar who decided to apply this methodology to the analysis of the many issues raised by political transitions.

Somewhat surprisingly, not many such scholars have chosen to follow this path. One exception has been Stefan Voigt (1999). He develops a *positive* theory of constitutions, in which constitutional contracts are the result of bargaining among the major interest groups in a society. Constitutional change comes about when the bargaining positions of one group change significantly, thus requiring a rewriting of the constitution. Such a change in bargaining power occurred in Poland during the 1980s with the rise of the labor union Solidarity, and eventually produced the constitutional shift from communism to a democratic constitution.[16]

8. The European Union

The literature reviewed in Section 3 focuses primarily on electoral rules and their impact on various measures of performance. The empirical testing of hypotheses relies on cross-national comparisons. The advent of the European Union and its unique and evolving institutional structure has provided scholars working in the public choice-rational choice traditions with an additional set of institutions to analyze. An already fairly large literature has tried to understand and explain how collective decisions are made in the European Union.

One strand of this literature focuses on power indexes. A *power index* assigns a score of s to each voter i for every coalition in which i is pivotal, that is to say the coalition is a winning coalition with i and a losing coalition without i. The two most popular power indexes are the Shapley-Shubik and Banzhaf indexes.[17] Although these indexes have been around for some 50 years, they had limited impact on the analysis of political institutions and political outcomes – until at least they were applied to the European Union. This can easily be explained for the United States by the fact that there is weak party discipline in the Congress, and thus each Member of Congress has essentially the same, low score. In contrast, both the Council and the Parliament of the European Union yield different scores for the various actors, and thus have provided a fertile ground for the use of power indexes. Because countries are assigned different numbers of votes in the Council, they receive different power index scores. Still more variety is added by assuming that different groups of countries are more likely to form coalitions – the rich versus the poor, big versus small, old members versus new.

In the European parliamentary systems, the executive and legislative branches are combined, and the calculation of power indexes is meaningless, once a government has been formed. Those not in the government coalition are essentially without power, while each party in the government has the power to bring it down, whenever the coalition forming the government is minimal-winning, which is generally the case.[18] In the European Union, on the other hand, the executive and legislative branches are effectively separated, and the calculation of power indexes for the Parliament can be a meaningful exercise. As in the Council, countries are allocated different numbers of seats in the Parliament based on their populations, so that power indexes can be calculated for each country under the assumption that all representatives from a country vote the same way. Alternatively, separate power indexes might be calculated for each party in a country, or for each party coalition in the Parliament recognizing that social democratic parties in the Parliament tend to form one coalition, Christian democratic parties a second coalition, liberal parties a third, and so on. The continual expansion of the EU has provided renewed opportunities for calculating power indexes and tracking the changes in individual countries' and parties' voting power.[19]

Where the above-described literature looks inside of the Council and Parliament and tries to calculate the power of the different members, the second line of research on EU institutions treats the Council and Parliament as well as the Commission as unitary actors. Each body is assumed to have a set of preferences defined over an issue space. Each body acts in sequence following the procedures laid down in the various treaties that until now have served as the EU's constitution, and the analysis predicts when and where equilibria will exist. Here again the changes in procedures that accompany each new treaty have helped keep analysts using these spatial models busy.[20]

9. The European Union's Draft Constitution

The Treaty of Nice, agreed to in 2001 by the heads of the 15 countries that made up the EU at the time, introduced additional changes in the allocations of votes and seats in the Council and Parliament, and provided for the expansion of the EU by ten additional countries. The public reception of the Treaty was at best lukewarm and set in motion the creation of a convention to draft a genuine constitution for the European Union that would close "the democratic deficit" that appeared to exist between the Union's political elite, who favored an "ever closer union" of the EU's ever-expanding number of member states, and the Union's apparently skeptical or uninterested citizenry.

The occasion of drafting a constitution for the EU was, of course, a great opportunity to apply some of the knowledge of political institutions accumulated over the last 50 years by public choice-rational choice scholars. Several of these scholars stepped forward and offered suggestions for the content of the new constitution.[21] There is scant evidence that these offerings were even considered in the drafting of the new constitution.

Given that the goal in writing a new constitution was to close the "democratic deficit," one might have expected – or hoped – that citizens would have been involved in constituting the membership of the convention, as say by electing them. Such was not the case, however. The Union's political elite selected from amongst themselves the participants in the convention, and they went off and drafted a document of great length and complexity, which in the summer of 2003 was offered up for adoption as the new EU constitution. Thus, the European Union also chose to violate the first law of constitution writing. Although the political elite professed a desire to close the democratic deficit, when it came time to actually write the constitution they felt it was too important a task to entrust in any way to the citizens. A majority of countries will not even trust the citizens to decide in a referendum whether the document that the elite drafted should be adopted.

10. Conclusions

In an important sense, virtually *all* of public choice falls in the domain of constitutional political economy, since it deals with the consequences of democratic institutions that are typically imbedded in constitutions. A demonstration that the simple majority rule is prone to cycling has implications for the design of constitutions, because it informs us of a cost of using this voting rule to aggregate preferences. The literature reviewed in this essay has been more directly concerned with constitutional issues, however.

Every country has a constitution of some sort – written or unwritten. Thus, it is artificial to concentrate on constitutional political economy in Europe alone, and so I have cited some works that do not deal with Europe. On the other hand, it is fair to say that there has been greater interest in constitutional issues by public choice scholars in Europe in recent years, and certainly that more has been happening on the constitutional front in Europe than in the United States. Interest in constitutional issues is likely to remain strong in Europe for the foreseeable future. Regardless of the outcome of the various national referenda being held on the draft European Union Constitution, the EU's constitutional structure undoubtedly will continue to evolve as new challenges arise and new entrants appear. Some of the former communist countries in Europe are likely to get around to redrafting their constitutions to improve the performance of their democratic institutions and, looking further to the East, one might hope that some of the former members of the Soviet Union eventually will decide to become true democracies, and will draft constitutions which allow them to achieve this goal. This activity on the constitutional front in Europe should further ensure that a large number of European public choice scholars continue to develop and extend the field of constitutional political economy.

Notes

1. For a brief overview in English of some of the proposals under discussion in Sweden, see Petersson, Karvonen, Smith, and Swedenborg (2004).
2. See also Weingast (1997).

3. For evidence linking the strength of economic institutions to growth, see Abrams and Lewis (1995), Keefer and Knack (1995) and Knack (1996). For further discussion and references to the literature, see Mueller (2003a, pp. 548–554).
4. La Porta, Lopez-De-Silanes, Shleifer, and Vishny (1997, 1998) establish the link between legal institutions and the size of a country's external capital markets, while Levine and Zervos (1998) present evidence of a positive link between the size of a country's equity market and its rate of economic growth. Gugler, Mueller, and Yurtoglu (2003, 2004) present evidence of better investment performance by corporations in countries with strong corporate governance institutions.
5. A reading of the public choice literature of the last 50 years would lead one to expect that the *voting rule* used by a country's legislature should be of great importance. Since nearly all legislatures use the simple majority rule for most of their decisions, there is little scope for testing this proposition empirically. If one regards it as a legislature, then a major exception to this practice has been the Council of the European Union in which the governments of the member countries are represented.
6. For a review of this literature, see Mueller (2003a, pp. 264–278).
7. For a review of their own work and references to other contributions to this literature, see Persson and Tabellini (2004a).
8. This figure and discussion follows Tsebelis and Money (1997, pp. 73–76).
9. For descriptions of the uncovered set, see Miller (1980), McKelvey (1986) and Mueller (2003a, pp. 236–241).
10. See Caplin and Nalebuff (1988).
11. For further discussion, see Mueller (1996, Ch. 13; 2003b).
12. For a discussion of various issues regarding the potential for federalism in Sweden, see Molander (2004).
13. Vaubel (1994) has been a strong opponent of EU centralization. See also Aroney (2000).
14. Alas, this is no easy task. For discussions of how decentralization can be preserved in federalist systems, see (Mueller, 1996, Ch. 6; Schneider, 1996; and Filippov, Ordeshook, & Shvetsova, 2004).
15. For further discussion and examples, see Mueller (1996, Ch. 21).
16. Voigt (1999, pp. 131–137). Also see the essays in Voigt and Wagener (2002).
17. See Shapley and Shubik (1954) and Banzhaf (1965).
18. A coalition is minimal-winning if the removal of any member party makes it a losing coalition. For further discussion and evidence, see Mueller (2003a, pp. 280–284).
19. Some of the more important contributions to this literature are Herne and Nurmi (1993), Widgrén (1994, 2004), Lane, Mæland, and Berg (1995), Hosli (1996, 1997), Laruelle and Widgrén (1998), Lane and Mæland (2002) and Steunenberg (2002b). For a short but informative review of the literature, see Dowding (2002).
20. See, for example, Steunenberg (1994), Tsebelis (1994, 1995, 1997), Crombez (1996, 1997) and Tsebelis and Garrett (2000).
21. See, Berglöf, Eichengreen, Roland, Tabellini, and Wyplosz (2003), Blankart and Mueller (2004), and the proposed constitution of the European Constitutional Group, http://www.european-constitutional-group.org/.

References

Abrams, B. A., & Lewis, K. A. (1995). Cultural and institutional determinants of economic growth: A cross-sectional analysis. *Public Choice*, *83*(3–4), 273–289.

Alesina, A., & Spolare, E. (1997). On the number and size of nations. *Quarterly Journal of Economics*, *112*(4), 1027–1056.

Alesina, A., Spolare, E., & Wacziarg, R. (2000). Economic integration and political disintegration. *American Economic Review*, *90*(5), 1276–1296.
Aroney, N. (2000). Mueller on European federation: A reply from the perspective of australian federalism. *Public Choice*, *105*(3–4), 255–272.
Banzhaf, J. F., III (1965). Weighted voting doesn't work: A mathematical analysis. *Rutgers Law Review*, *19*(2), 317–343.
Berglöf, E., Eichengreen, B., Roland, G., Tabellini, G., & Wyplosz, C. (2003). *Built to Last: A Political Architecture for Europe*. CEPR: London.
Blankart, C. B., & Mueller, D. C. (Eds.) (2004). *A Constitution for the European Union*. MIT Press: Cambridge, MA.
Bradbury, J. C., & Crain, W. M. (2002). Bicameral legislatures and fiscal policy. *Southern Economic Journal*, *68*(3), 646–659.
Buchanan, J. M. (1975). *The Limits of Liberty: Between Anarchy and Leviathan*. University of Chicago Press: Chicago.
Buchanan, J. M. (1986). Better than plowing. *Banca Nazionale del Lavoro Quarterly Review*, *39*(159): 359–375.
Buchanan, J. M., & Tullock, G. (1962). *The Calculus of Consent: Logical Foundations of Constitutional Democracy*. University of Michigan Press: Ann Arbor.
Caplin, A., & Nalebuff, B. (1988). On 64%-majority rule. *Econometrica*, *56*(4), 787–814.
Congleton, R. D. (2003a). *Improving Democracy through Constitutional Reform: Some Swedish Lessons*. Kluwer: Dordrecht.
Congleton, R. D. (2003b). On the merits of bicameral legislatures: Policy stability within partisan polities. In M. J. Holler, H. Kliemt, D. Schmidtchen, & M. E. Streit (Eds.), *European Governance*, (pp. 29–49). Mohr Siebeck: Tübingen.
Crombez, C. (1996). Legislative procedures in the european community. *British Journal of Political Science*, *26*(2), 199–228.
Crombez, C. (1997). Policy making and commission appointment in the EU. *Aussenwirtschaft*, *52*(1–2), 63–82.
Dowding, K. (2002). Rational choice and institutional change. An overview of current theories. In B. Steunenberg (Ed.), *Widening the European Union*, (pp. 21–38). Routledge: London.
Duverger, M. (1954). *Political Parties: Their Organization and Activity in the Modern State*. Wiley: New York.
Feld, L. P., & Kirchgässner, G. (1999). Public debt and budgetary procedures: Top down or bottom up. In J. M. Poterba & J. von Hagen (Eds.), *Fiscal Institutions and Fiscal Performance* (pp. 151–179). NBER Conference Report Series. University of Chicago Press: Chicago.
Feld, L. P., & Kirchgässner, G. (2004). The role of direct democracy in the European Union. In C. B. Blankart & D. C. Mueller (Eds.), *A Constitution for the European Union* (pp. 203–235). MIT Press: Cambridge, MA.
Feld, L. P., & Savioz, M. R. (1997). Direct democracy matters for economic performance: An empirical investigation. *Kyklos*, *50*(4), 507–538.
Frey, B. S., & Stutzer, A. (2000). Happiness, economy and institutions. *Economic Journal*, *110*(466), 918–938.
Frey, B. S., & Stutzer, A. (2002). *Happiness and Economics: How the Economy and Institutions affect Well-Being*. Princeton University Press: Princeton.
Filippov, M., Ordeshook, P. C., & Shvetsova, O. (2004). *Desiging Federalism*. Cambridge University Press: Cambridge.
Gugler, K., Mueller, D. C., & Yurtoglu, B. B. (2003). The impact of corporate governance on investment returns in developed and developing countries. *Economic Journal*, *113*(491), F511–F539.

Gugler, K., Mueller, D. C., & Yurtoglu, B. B. (2004). Corporate governance and the returns on investment. *Journal of Law and Economics*, *47*(2), 598–633.

Herne, K., & Nurmi, H. (1993). The distribution of a priori voting power in the EC council of ministers and the European parliament. *Scandinavian Political Studies*, *16*(3), 269–284.

Hosli, M. O. (1996). Coalitions and power: Effects of qualified majority voting in the council of the european union. *Journal of Common Market Studies*, *34*(2), 255–273.

Hosli, M. O. (1997). Voting strength in the european parliament: The influence of national and partisan actors. *European Journal of Political Research*, *31*(3), 351–366.

Keefer, P., & Knack, S. (1995). Institutions and economic performance: Cross-country tests using alternative institutional measures. *Economics and Politics*, *7*(3), 207–227.

Kirchgässner, G., Feld, L. P., & Savioz, M. R. (1999). *Die direkte Demokratie*. Helbing & Lichtenhahn: Basel.

Knack, S. (1996). Institutions and the convergence hypothesis: The cross-national evidence. *Public Choice*, *87*(3–4), 207–228.

Lane, J.-E., & Mæland, R. (2002). Enlargement and the council of ministers. In B. Steunenberg (Ed.), *Widening the European Union* (pp. 121–143). Routledge: London.

Lane, J.-E., Mæland, R., & Berg, S. (1995). The EU parliament, seats, states and political parties. *Journal of Theoretical Politics*, *7*(3), 395–400.

La Porta, R., Lopez-de-Silanes, F., Shleifer, A., & Vishny, R. (1997). Legal determinants of external finance. *Journal of Finance*, *52*(3), 1131–1150.

La Porta, R., Lopez-de-Silanes, F., Shleifer, A., & Vishny, R. (1998). Law and finance. *Journal of Political Economy*, *106*(6), 1113–1155.

Laruelle, A., & Widgren, M. (1998). Is the allocation of voting power among EU states fair? *Public Choice*, *94*(3–4), 317–339.

Levine, R., & Zervos, S. (1998). Stock markets, banks and economic growth. *American Economic Review*, *88*(3), 537–558.

Matsusaka, J. G. (2004). *For the Many or the Few: The Initiative, Public Policy, and American Democracy*. Chicago University Press: Chicago.

McKelvey, R. D. (1986). Covering, dominance, and institution-free properties of social choice. *American Journal of Political Science*, *30*(2), 283–314.

Miller, N. R. (1980). A new solution set for tournaments and majority voting: Further graph-theoretical approaches to the theory of voting. *American Journal of Political Science*, *24*(1), 68–96.

Molander, P. (Ed.). (2004). *Fiscal Federalism in Unitary States*. Kluwer: Dordrecht.

Mueller, D. C. (1996). *Constitutional Democracy*. Oxford University Press: Oxford.

Mueller, D. C. (1997). Federalism and the European Union: A constitutional perspective. *Public Choice*, *90*(1–4), 255–280.

Mueller, D. C. (2002). Constitutional issues regarding European Union expansion. In B. Steunenberg (Ed.), *Widening the European Union* (pp. 41–57). Routledge: London.

Mueller, D. C. (2003a). *Public Choice III*. Cambridge University Press: Cambridge.

Mueller, D. C. (2003b). Comment on congleton. In M. J. Holler, H. Kliemt, D. Schmidtchen, & M. E. Streit (Eds.), *European Governance* (pp. 50–54). Mohr Siebeck: Tübingen.

North, D. C. (1990). *Institutions, Institutional Change, and Economic Performance*. Cambridge University Press: Cambridge.

North, D. C. (1995). The paradox of the west. In R. Davis (Ed.), *Origins of Modern Freedom in the West* (pp. 7–34). Stanford University Press: Stanford.

North, D. C., & Thomas, R. P. (1973). *The Rise of the Western World: A New Economic History*. Cambridge University Press: Cambridge.

North, D. C., & Weingast, B. R. (1989). Constitutions and commitment: The evolution of institutions governing public choice in seventeenth-century england. *Journal of Economic History*, *49*(4), 803–832.

Persson, T., & Tabellini, G. (1999). The size and scope of government: Comparative politics with rational politicians. *European Economic Review*, *43*(4–6), 699–735.

Persson, T., & Tabellini, G. (2000). *Political Economics – Explaining Economic Policy*. MIT Press: Cambridge, MA.

Persson, T., & Tabellini, G. (2003). *Economic Effects of Constitutions*. MIT Press: Cambridge, MA.

Persson, T., & Tabellini, G. (2004a). Constitutions and economic policy. *Journal of Economic Perspectives*, *18*(1), 75–98.

Persson, T., & Tabellini, G. (2004b). Constitutional rules and fiscal policy outcomes. *American Economic Review*, *94*(1), 25–45.

Persson, T., Roland, G., & Tabellini, G. (2000). Comparative politics and public finance. *Journal of Political Economy*, *108*(6), 1121–1161.

Petersson, O., Karvonen, L., Smith, E., & Swedenborg, B. (2004). *A New Constitution for Sweden*. SNS Förlag: Stockholm.

Pommerehne, W. W. (1976). Private versus öffentliche müllabfuhr; ein theoretischer und empirischer vergleich. *Finanzarchiv*, *35*(2), 272–294.

Pommerehne, W. W. (1978). Institutional approaches to public expenditures: Empirical evidence from swiss municipalities. *Journal of Public Economics*, *9*(2), 163–201.

Pommerehne, W. W., & Schneider, F. (1978). Fiscal illusion, political institutions, and local public spending. *Kyklos*, *31*(3), 381–408.

Roland, G. (2002). The political economy of transition. *Journal of Economic Perspectives*, *16*(1), 29–50.

Schneider, F. (1996). The design of a minimal european federal union: Some ideas using the public choice approach. In J. Casas Pardo & F. Schneider (Eds.), *Current Issues in Public Choice* (pp. 203–220). Edward Elgar: Cheltenham.

Shapley, L. S., & Shubik, M. (1954). A method for evaluating the distribution of power in a committee system. *American Political Science Review*, *48*(3), 787–792.

Steunenberg, B. (1994). Decision making under different institutional arrangements: Legislation by the european community. *Journal of Institutional and Theoretical Economics*, *150*(4), 642–669.

Steunenberg, B. (Ed.). (2002a). *Widening the European Union*. Routledge: London.

Steunenberg, B. (2002b). An even wider union. In B. Steunenberg (Ed.), *Widening the European Union* (pp. 97–118). Routledge: London.

Tsebelis, G. (1994). The power of the european parliament as a conditional agenda-setter. *American Political Science Review*, *88*(1), 128–142.

Tsebelis, G. (1995). Conditional agenda-setting and decision-making *inside* the European parliament. *Journal of Legislative Studies*, *1*(1), 65–93.

Tsebelis, G. (1997). Maastricht and the democratic deficit. *Außenwirtschaft*, *52*(1–2), 29–56.

Tsebelis, G., & Garrett, G. (2000). Legislative politics in the European Union. *European Union Politics*, *1*(1), 9–36.

Tsebelis, G., & Money, J. (1997). *Bicameralism*. Cambridge University Press: Cambridge.

Vaubel, R. (1994). The political economy of centralization and the european community. *Public Choice*, *81*(1–2), 151–190.

Voigt, S. (1999). *Explaining Constitutional Change*. Edward Elgar: Cheltenham.

Voigt, S., & Wagener, H.-J. (Eds.) (2002). *Constitutions, Markets and Law – Recent Experiences in Transition Economies*. Edward Elgar: Cheltenham.

Weck-Hannemann, H., & Pommerehne, W. W. (1989). Einkommensteuerhinterziehung in der Schweiz: Eine empirische analyse. *Schweizerische Zeitschrift für Volkswirtschaft und Statistik*, *125*(4), 515–556.

Weingast, B. R. (1997). The political foundations of democracy and the rule of law. *American Political Science Review*, *91*(2), 245–263.

Widgrén, M. (1994). Voting power in the ec decision making and the consequences of two different enlargements. *European Economic Review*, *38*(5), 1153–1170.

Public Choice (2005) **124:** 75–93
DOI: 10.1007/s11127-005-4747-y

Collective versus unilateral responses to terrorism

TODD SANDLER
School of International Relations, University of Southern California, Von Kleinsmid Center 330, Los Angeles, CA 90089-0043, USA (E-mail: tsandler@usc.edu)

Accepted March 2005

Abstract. Global terrorism presents collective action issues for targeted nations. Proactive measures (e.g., preemptive strikes) against terrorists create external benefits for all at-risk nations. In contrast, defensive actions deflect attacks to softer targets, thereby giving rise to external benefits to protected foreign residents and external costs to venues abroad. Coordinated antiterrorism measures are particularly difficult to achieve when many nations must participate and nonparticipants can undo the efforts of others. Thus, freezing terrorists' assets or abiding by a no-negotiation pledge pose difficult collective action problems. These same concerns do not plague decisive action against domestic terrorism.

1. Introduction

Terrorism is the premeditated use or threat of use of violence by individuals or subnational groups to obtain a political or social objective through intimidation of a large audience beyond that of the immediate victims. Terrorists try to circumvent the normal political process through violence perpetrated on a public who may then pressure the government to concede to the terrorists' demands. On 11 September 2001 (henceforth, 9/11), the four hijacked planes graphically illustrated the havoc and destruction that terrorists can wreak on society. If a targeted government views its future (discounted) costs from a sustained terrorist campaign as greater than that of conceding to terrorists' demands (including reputation costs), then a government may grant concessions (Lapan & Sandler, 1993). In the absence of caving in, governments must institute antiterrorist measures.

The modern era of transnational terrorism began in 1968 with terrorists traveling between countries and maintaining a presence in multiple countries to achieve their greatest impact. A watershed transnational terrorist event was the 22 July 1968 hijacking of an El A1 Boeing 707 en route from Rome to Tel Aviv with 10 crew members and 38 passengers, including three hijackers identified with the Popular Front for the Liberation of Palestine (PFLP) (Mickolus, 1980, pp. 93–94). This event is noteworthy for a number of reasons. First, there was clear evidence of state-sponsorship after the plane landed in Algiers, because Algeria took advantage of the situation and held some of the hostages until 1 September 1968 when a deal was finally struck.[1] Second, the incident forced the Israelis to negotiate directly with the Palestinian terrorists

(Hoffman, 1998, p. 68). Third, massive media coverage demonstrated to other terrorists that such events could capture worldwide attention. Fourth, one of the terrorists helped land the plane in Algiers; hence, 9/11 was not the first instance where a terrorist flew a hijacked airplane (Mickolus, 1980, p. 94). Fifth, a ransom of $7.5 million was paid by the French to the hijackers and 16 Arab prisoners from the 1967 Arab-Israeli war were released by Israel. The hijackers were flown to a safe location with their ransom; two of the hijackers subsequently were involved in hijackings in 1972 (Mickolus, 1980). This incident clearly depicts the *transnational externality* (i.e., uncompensated interdependency involving multiple countries) that modern terrorism can imply where, e.g., a grievance in the Middle East affects a flight leaving a European airport. To protect against such events, airports must institute adequate security measures against the spillover of terrorism from abroad. The news coverage resulted in an externality in the form of additional hijackings. Moreover, paid ransoms encouraged further incidents worldwide owing to the promise of high rewards.

More recently, the skyjackings of 9/11 created transnational externalities because the deaths and property losses at the World Trade Center (WTC) involved upwards of 80 countries. Subsequent efforts to bolster security in the United States and Europe appear to be shifting attacks to developing countries – e.g., Indonesia, Morocco, Saudi Arabia, Kenya, Turkey and Malaysia (Sandler, 2005). The devastation of 9/11 raised the bar in terms of the kind of carnage that a future terrorist act must produce to capture similar news coverage. That, in turn, induces the terrorists to innovate in order to find new means to cause even greater destruction. This innovation process is an *intertemporal* externality that today's terrorists impose on tomorrow's victims.

Modern-day transnational terrorism raises some essential dilemmas. Terrorists appear able to address their collective action concerns through cooperation among themselves, while governments are less adept at collective responses and primarily resort to unilateral (suboptimal) responses. For transnational terrorism, there is a propensity for nations to focus on defensive rather than proactive countermeasures. Defensive actions may merely deflect attacks to less-protected venues, leading nations to work at cross-purposes (Arce & Sandler, 2005; Sandler & Lapan, 1988; Sandler & Siqueira, 2003). Moreover, there is a clear tendency for at-risk nations to rely on a prime-target nation to carry the burden for direct action against the terrorists. In contrast, governments appear properly motivated to strike the right balance between defensive and proactive responses against domestic terrorism.

The primary purpose of this paper is to explain the collective action failures that plague targeted countries in their efforts to respond to global terrorism. To accomplish this task, I employ some simple game theory to examine alternative antiterrorism responses to a common transnational terrorism threat. Three game forms are prevalent: prisoners' dilemma, asymmetric dominance and stag hunt. The last is particularly germane for analyzing cases where a degree of coordination is required to accomplish some gain. For example, countries that do not freeze terrorists' assets can greatly undo the actions of those that do. I address the asymmetries between governments and terrorists that underlie many collective action concerns, driven by opposing externalities relevant to today's networked terrorists who harbor common grievances. Terrorists' own actions may foster efforts for nations to address collective action concerns. As the severity of attacks escalates, nations become more willing to follow the lead of prime-target nations to take actions such as freezing terrorists' assets. I also underscore some of the public choice dilemmas where political freedoms provide a favorable environment that some terrorists may exploit.

2. Preliminaries

At the outset, domestic terrorism must be distinguished from transnational terrorism. The former is solely a host country affair where its citizens resort to terrorist attacks on other citizens or their property with the intention of furthering a domestic political or social agenda through violence and intimidation. The bombing of the Alfred P. Murrah Federal Building in Oklahoma City on 19 April 1995 was a domestic terrorist event, because Timothy McVeigh and his accomplices were American citizens, as were the victims of the blast. Moreover, this bombing did not have ramifications for other countries.

By virtue of its victims, targets, institutions, supporters, terrorists' demands, or perpetrators, transnational terrorism involves more than a single country. The train bombings in Madrid on 11 March 2004 were transnational terrorist incidents because many of the terrorists were foreign nationals who came to Madrid to stage their attack. Moreover, the bombing victims included some non-Spanish citizens. In addition, the bombing had far-reaching implications for other European countries that then had to take precautions against similar attacks. The four hijackings on 9/11 also were transnational terrorist acts with global consequences as to their victims, security concerns, and financial impact. Although domestic terrorism is far more prevalent than transnational terrorism (National Memorial Institute for the Prevention of Terrorism, 2004), the latter generates cross-border externalities that are difficult to address, and leads to collective action failures when unilateral responses by governments work against global welfare. For example, US efforts to secure its borders have transferred most terrorist incidents against US interests to foreign venues. Although 40% of all transnational terrorist attacks are against US people or property, few have occurred on US soil in recent years (Sandler, 2003). Transnational terrorism, as practiced by Al-Qaida and its loose network of affiliates, poses a greater threat than domestic terrorism to world security as fundamentalist groups seek maximum carnage and financial repercussions (Hoffman, 1998).

Counterterrorism consists of government actions to inhibit terrorist attacks or curtail their consequences. There are two main categories of antiterrorism policies – proactive and defensive. Proactive or offensive measures target the terrorists, their resources, or their supporters directly. By weakening the ability of terrorists to operate, proactive policies reduce the frequency and prevalence of attacks against all at-risk targets. Such actions include attacking terrorist camps, assassinating terrorist leaders, freezing terrorist assets, retaliating against a state-sponsor, gathering intelligence, and infiltrating a terrorist group.

Defensive or passive policies try to protect a potential target against an attack or to ameliorate the damage in case of an attack. Defensive measures may involve the installation of technological barriers (e.g., bomb-sniffing devices, metal detectors, or biometric identification), the hardening of targets (e.g., barriers in front of federal buildings), the deployment of security personnel (e.g., sky marshals on commercial flights), and the institution of terrorist alerts. While some proactive policies may provoke a terrorist backlash, defensive measures usually do not have this potential downside (Rosendorff & Sandler, 2004). By reducing the terrorists' probability of success and increasing their operations' costs, defensive actions attempt to dissuade terrorists by reducing their expected net benefits from attacks. If, however, the authorities make one type of attack harder without affecting the costliness of other types of attacks, then such partial measures can merely induce terrorists to *substitute* one mode of attack for another relatively cheaper one – e.g., the installation of metal detectors at airports reduced skyjackings but increased other types of hostage-taking missions (Enders & Sandler, 1993, 1995, 2004; Enders et al., 1990). Similarly, defensive actions that make one country more secure may merely transfer attacks to less-secure venues abroad.

3. Asymmetries Between Nations and Terrorists

To appreciate the collective action problems posed by transnational terrorism, one must recognize the asymmetries that distinguish the behavior of targeted nations and their terrorist adversaries. These asymmetries provide tactical advantages to terrorists who target assets from powerful nations.

Nations must guard everywhere, while terrorists can identify and attack the softest targets. Efforts by nations to harden targets induce terrorists to redirect their attacks to less-protected venues. As rich countries mobilized their defensive measures following 9/11, the developing world stayed the venue of choice from which to attack Western interests. In 2003, there were 190 transnational terrorist attacks, with none in North America and 24 incidents in Europe.[2] There were, however, 70 attacks in Asia, 53 in Latin America, and 37 in the Middle East. Although there were no transnational attacks in the United States in 2003, there were 82 anti-US attacks on foreign soil: 46,

Latin America; one, Eurasia; two, Africa; six, Asia; 11, Middle East; and 16, Western Europe. During 2002, there were 198 transnational terrorist incidents, with none in North America and only nine in Western Europe. Asia was the preferred venue with 101 attacks.

Nations are target-rich; terrorists are target-poor. Terrorists may hide in the general population in urban centers, thereby maximizing collateral damage during government raids to capture them. Nations have to be fortunate on a daily basis, while terrorists only have to be fortunate occasionally.[3] As such, terrorists can sit back and pick the most opportune time to strike, as they did on 9/11. Unlike liberal democracies that are constrained in their reaction to terrorist threats, terrorists can be unrestrained in their brutality, as demonstrated by attacks perpetrated by fundamentalist terrorists in recent years. Nations are not well-informed about terrorists' strength, whereas terrorists can easily discover how many governmental resources are being allocated to antiterrorist activities. In the United States, this information is a matter of public record. This asymmetric information is amply illustrated by US estimates of al-Qaida strength as "several hundred to several thousand members", reported by the US Department of State (2001, p. 68) just five months before 9/11. The 7 October 2001 invasion of Afghanistan indicated that Al-Qaida had far more members than the State Department's upper-bound estimate. Such misleading figures not only hamper the military in terms of planning antiterrorist operations, but they also make it more difficult to convince other countries to contribute troops to preemptive raids on training camps and terrorist infrastructure.

Another asymmetry concerns the organizational structure adopted by governments and terrorists. Governments are hierarchical, whereas terrorist organizations are nonhierarchical with loosely tied networks of cells and affiliated terrorist groups (Arquilla & Ronfeldt, 2001). Terrorist cells and groups can operate independently of one another. Moreover, captured terrorist leaders can provide only limited intelligence owing to the looseness of the network and the virtual autonomy of many of its components. Recent espionage scandals indicate that government informants can do much damage to the integrity of an intelligence organization.

Beyond some point, government size can limit its effectiveness in waging an antiterrorist campaign. Also, a larger government has more targets to protect and can create greater grievances from taxes used to finance the bureaucracy. In contrast, a larger terrorist group can engage in a more effective campaign that may signal to the government that an accommodation is less costly. Hirshleifer (1991) introduced the notion of the "paradox of power" in conflict situations, where smaller forces may have a strategic advantage over larger, militarily superior forces. In particular, small insurgencies, including terrorists, can cause more damage per operative insofar as some technologies of conflict favor the small force that can hide and strike large targets.

A final asymmetry is the most essential for understanding why nations have greater difficulty in addressing their collective action problem than the terrorists. National strength provides a false sense of security, thereby inhibiting governments from appreciating the need for coordinated action. Nations also do not agree on which groups are terrorists – e.g., until fairly recently, the European Union (EU) did not view Hamas as a terrorist organization despite its suicide bombing campaign. In democracies, leaders' interests in the future are limited by the length of the election cycle and their likelihood of reelection. Agreements made with leaders of other countries to combat terrorism may be rather short-lived if a government changes. For example, the new Spanish Prime Minister Zapatero pulled the country's troops out of Iraq following his surprise win in the national elections stemming from the alleged link between the 11 March 2004 train bombing and Spanish support for the US-led war on terror. This short-term viewpoint limits intergovernmental cooperative arrangements that could follow from a repeated-game analysis, based on a tit-for-tat strategy. Because many counterterrorism actions among governments abide by a prisoners' dilemma game structure (see Section 4), a myopic viewpoint works against solving the problem through repeated interactions, unless agreements can have a permanency that transcends a change in governments. The high value that governments place on their autonomy over security matters also inhibits their addressing collective action issues successfully.

A much different situation characterizes the terrorists who have cooperated in networks since the onset of modern-day terrorism. From the late 1960s, terrorist groups have shared personnel, intelligence, logistics, training camps and resources (Alexander & Pluchinsky, 1992; Hoffman, 1998). More recently, Al-Qaida forged a loosely linked network when Osama bin Laden began franchising other Islamic groups (Raufer, 2003; Hoffman, 2003). Despite different political agendas, terrorist groups share similar opponents – e.g., the United States and Israel – that provide some unity of purpose. For example, the left-wing terrorists groups in Europe during the 1970s and 1980s were united in their political orientation and their goal to overthrow a capitalistic system (Alexander & Pluchinsky, 1992). Terrorist groups cooperate because of their relative weakness compared with the well-armed governments that they confront. Given their limited resources and grave risks, terrorists have little choice but to cooperate to stretch resources. Terrorist leaders tend to be tenured for life so that they view intergroup interactions as continual. This long-term orientation means that terrorist groups can successfully address prisoners' dilemma interactions through punishment-based tit-for-tat strategies. The temptation to renege on an agreement with another terrorist group for a short-term gain is tempered by the long-run losses from the lack of future cooperative gains. Terrorists appear to place less weight than governments on their autonomy, provided that shared actions further their goals. Unlike their government adversaries, terrorists are motivated to address their collective action concerns.

4. Proactive Versus Defensive Policies

As a generic proactive policy, I examine efforts to preempt a terrorist group by, say, attacking the terrorists' bases and training camps. I then compare and contrast preemption with a generic defensive policy – i.e., actions to deter an attack by fortifying vulnerable targets.

4.1. *Preemption*

In panel a of Figure 1, a symmetric preemption game is displayed for two targeted countries (i.e., nations 1 and 2), each of which must decide whether or not to launch a preemptive strike against a common terrorist or state-sponsor threat. The attack is meant to weaken the terrorists and limit their future actions. Given the common threat posed by the terrorists, each preempting country provides a pure public benefit of B for itself and the other at-risk nation. More benefits are achieved when both countries attack the terrorists, as combined action does more harm to the terrorists.

In each cell of the 2×2 game matrix, the left-hand payoff is that of nation 1 and the right-hand payoff is that of nation 2. The cost of preemption is c for each preemptor, where $c > B$. I assume that isolated action results in less benefits than costs so that a collective action problem occurs.[4] If nation

		nation 2 Preempt	Status quo
nation 1	Preempt	$2B - c, 2B - c$	$B - c, B$
	Status quo	$B, B - c$	Nash 0, 0

a. Symmetric prisoners' dilemma ($2B > c > B$)

		nation 2 Preempt	Status quo
nation 1	Preempt	$2B_1 - c_1, 2B_2 - c_2$	Nash $B_1 - c_1, B_2$
	Status quo	$B_1, B_2 - c_2$	0, 0

b. Asymmetric dominance ($B_1 > c_1$ and $2B_2 > c_2 > B_2$)

Figure 1. Alternative preemption scenarios.

1 preempts alone and nation 2 maintains the status quo, then nation 1 nets $B - c < 0$, while nation 2 receives the free-rider benefit of B. These payoffs are interchanged when the nations' roles are reversed in the bottom left-hand cell. When both nations join forces, each nets $2B - c$ from the two preemption actions, where $2B$ is assumed to be greater than c. All-around inaction gives payoffs of 0 to both nations. Given these assumptions, each nation's dominant strategy is to do nothing, because $B > 2B - c$ and $0 > B - c$. The underlying game is a prisoners' dilemma with a Nash equilibrium of mutual inaction. If the symmetric case is extended to n nations with each preemptor providing B in benefits for all at-risk nations at a provision cost of $c > B$ to the preemptor, then the outcome is for no nation to act. A repeated-game version is not promising owing to the short-run view that nations take of such interactions with other governments.

A more optimistic case arises in the asymmetric version in panel b of Figure 1, where benefits and costs are tailored by subscripts to the two nations. Nation 1 is a prime target of the terrorists with more to gain from any action that weakens the terrorists. Suppose that nation 1 receives a benefit of B_1 from its own preemptive action or that of nation 2. Moreover, B_1 exceeds its preemption costs of c_1. Since $B_1 > c_1$, nation 1's dominant strategy now is to preempt, which is analogous to the United States after 9/11. Nation 2 is in an analogous situation to that in panel a; thus, $2B_2 > c_2 > B_2$ and nation 2's dominant strategy is still to do nothing. As each nation exercises its dominant strategy, the Nash equilibrium results in nation 1 preempting unilaterally. The underlying game is one of "*asymmetric dominance*". With the United States sustaining 40% of transnational terrorist attacks worldwide, its willingness to preempt alone or to lead a coalition is easy to understand. By focusing so many attacks on US interests, the terrorists motivate US proactive responses. If terrorists had not concentrated their campaign on a couple of nations, there would be even fewer proactive measures against terrorism. The Nash equilibrium in panel b is not necessarily the social optimum (based on the compensation principle) insofar as the sum of benefits from mutual preemption may exceed that of the Nash equilibrium. Matrix b can be extended to n nations with m prime targets and $n - m$ nonprime targets. As such, the subset of prime targets is motivated to take aggressive actions against the terrorists.

Next suppose that some at-risk nation adopts proactive measures (even symbolic ones) to support a prime-target nation's actions, as Spain and Japan did in the US war on terror. Their supportive efforts put their people in greater jeopardy. In this scenario, nation 2's assumed inequality changes to $c_2 > 2B_2$ in panel b of Figure 1. Nation 2's dominant strategy is to do nothing – as illustrated by Spain's withdrawal from Iraq following the 11 March 2004 train bombing where this inequality became apparent. Terrorists have a clear motive to attack countries that bolster the proactive measures of prime-target countries.

		nation 2 Deter	Status quo
nation 1	Deter	Nash $b - C - C_1, b - C - C_2$	$b - C, -C_2$
	Status quo	$-C_1, b - C$	0, 0

$(C + C_i > b > C), i = 1, 2$

Figure 2. Deterrence: Symmetric prisoners' dilemma

4.2. *Defensive measures*

Next, I consider deterrence as a means to limit terrorists' success by hardening a target at an expense of C to the deterrer. In Figure 2, such action provides a benefit of b greater than C for the deterrer. Unlike preemption with its public benefits, defensive measures have a public cost of C_i because the attack may be deflected to country i as country j takes precautionary actions. If nation 1 deters alone, then it gains $b - C$, while nation 2 suffers a cost of $-C_2$ as it becomes a more desirable target. When nation 2 deters alone, the payoffs are reversed with nation 1 sustaining a deflection cost of $-C_1$. No action gives 0 payoffs, while mutual deterrence provides payoffs of $b - C - C_i$ for nation i, $i = 1, 2$. Since $b > C$, the dominant strategy in the game matrix is for both countries to deter. As each nation plays its dominant strategy, the Nash equilibrium of this prisoners' dilemma is for everyone to deter, which gives both nations a negative payoff based on the parameters assumed. The payoffs for mutual deterrence include $-C_i$ because I implicitly assume only two countries and that the terrorists are bent on attacking some target no matter how well protected. Thus, matching deterrence upgrades leads to net costs, so that $C + C_i > b$, as assumed. The deterrence game is analogous to the problem of the commons, with all players trying to achieve a gain while ignoring the external-cost consequences of their actions.

If this game is extended to n nations with analogous parameters, then the suboptimality of the Nash equilibrium worsens as more nations take defensive measures to shift the attack elsewhere. In today's world of globalized terrorism, the game's outcome is that the terrorists will stage their attacks in those nations with the least defensive measures – the so-called soft targets. In these venues, the terrorists will hit the interests of those nations against which they have the greatest grievances. Thus, the paucity of attacks in North America and Europe in 2002–2003 is consistent with this prediction, as is the large percentage of attacks against US people and property abroad.

Shoring up the softest target implies its own collective action problem. Bolstering the defense of soft targets provides purely public benefits to all nations whose people or property are in jeopardy. In a globalized world, this may involve improving many nations' defensive capabilities. The underlying symmetric game for shoring up the softest target is surely a prisoners' dilemma with no action at the equilibrium. With nonsymmetric players, the prime-target nations have the most to gain from increasing the capabilities of soft targets. Thus, one of the four pillars of US counterterrorism policy is to improve the antiterrorism abilities of those countries that seek assistance (US Department of State, 2004). No country – not even the United States – has the requisite resources to enhance all countries' counterterrorism activities. Since 9/11, the United States has been spending large amounts on its own proactive and defensive responses, which limits its capacity to help others. There is also a moral-hazard problem associated with strengthening another country's capabilities, since the latter may purposely use this money for domestic concerns and not protect the providing country's interests. Thus, US aid to country *X* might either be used to protect non-US targets in *X* or else replace *X*'s usual security expenditures.

4.3. *Choice between preemption and deterrence*

Even though preemption implies public benefits and private costs, while deterrence implies public costs and private benefits, the prisoners' dilemma applies to both situations in their symmetric presentation. What would happen if a nation has three strategic options: deter, status quo, and preempt? Arce and Sandler (2005) examined this question and found that the deter strategy dominates in two-nation symmetric scenarios. Ironically, the mutual-deter Nash equilibrium provides the smallest summed payoff in the associated 3×3 game matrix. These authors vary the game form for the embedded preemption game (e.g., chicken is allowed) but uncover a robustness of their results. Even when a fourth policy choice – deterring *and* preempting – is included, the deter choice dominates.

For domestic terrorism, nations are able to balance proactive and defensive measures. Israel clearly applies both in its domestic struggle against Hamas and Hezbollah. In their fight against leftist terrorists in the 1970s and 1980s, countries in Europe used proactive and defensive campaigns. The former resulted in the capture of Direct Action in France, the Red Brigades in Italy, and the Combatant Communist Cells in Belgium in the 1980s (Alexander & Pluchinsky, 1992). Why do tactics to combat domestic terrorism generally differ from those used by non-prime-target nations to fight transnational terrorism? First, the host nation is the only target of domestic terrorism. Defensive actions are not applied to transfer the attack abroad as in the case of transnational terrorism. Any transference of domestic attacks takes place among targets within the nation. A centralized government can internalize any transference externality when deciding defensive allocations for the country.

There is no centralized supranational government to serve the same purpose for transnational terrorism. Second, the benefits of a proactive campaign against domestic terrorism are *private* to the venue nation. As such, the nation cannot free ride on any other nation's efforts, since other nations are not in jeopardy. For domestic terrorism, the central government removes much of the strategic maneuvering that characterizes policy decisions for transnational terrorism.[5] Third, defensive measures require protecting *all* potential targets, while proactive responses only necessitate intelligence-based raids against the terrorists or their resources. There is a cost-effectiveness in instituting a focused proactive campaign; defensive action may lead to virtually limitless spending.

5. Coordination Dilemma: Freezing of Terrorists' Assets

Obviously, other game forms can apply to countermeasures in the war on terror. A common game form for some policy choices is a "stag-hunt" assurance game, where both parties are best off if they take identical measures. When a player takes the measure alone, this player receives the smallest payoff and the player who does nothing earns the second-greatest payoff. This kind of scenario is descriptive of a host of counterterrorism policies where two or more nations must act in unison for the best payoffs to result. Examples include freezing terrorist assets, denying safe haven to terrorists, applying sanctions to state-sponsors, or holding to a no-negotiation policy. Even one nation that breaks ranks can ruin the policy's effectiveness for all others. To illustrate such scenarios, I use freezing terrorist assets as a generic example and begin with a two-nation symmetric case.

Matrix a in the top of Figure 3 displays this scenario where the highest payoff of F results from mutual action, followed by a payoff of A from doing nothing either alone or together. The smallest payoff, B, comes from freezing assets alone since the terrorists can merely transfer their assets elsewhere, leaving the acting country with some banking losses but few safety gains. Since $F > A > B$, there is no dominant strategy. There are, however, two pure-strategy Nash equilibriums: both countries freeze assets or neither freezes assets.

A third Nash equilibrium involves mixed strategies in which each pure strategy is played in a probabilistic fashion. To identify this mixed-strategy equilibrium, I determine the probability q of nation 2 freezing terrorist assets *that make nation 1 indifferent* between freezing terrorist assets and doing nothing. Similarly, I derive the probability p of action on the part of nation 1 that makes nation 2 indifferent between the two strategies. Once p and q are identified, equilibrium probabilities for maintaining the status quo simply equal $1 - q$ and $1 - p$ for nations 2 and 1, respectively. The relevant probabilities are indicated for matrix a besides the respective column and row. The

		nation 2		
		Freeze	Status quo	
nation 1	Freeze	*F*, *F*	*B*, *A*	p
	Status quo	*A*, *B*	*A*, *A*	$1-p$
		q	$1-q$	

a. Freezing assets: Scenario 1

		nation 2		
		Freeze	Status quo	
nation 1	Freeze	*F*, *F*	*B*, *E*	p
	Status quo	*E*, *B*	*A*, *A*	$1-p$
		q	$1-q$	

b. Freezing assets: Scenario 2

Figure 3. Alternative freezing assets scenarios.

calculations for q (or p not shown) go as follows:

$$qF + (1-q)B = qA + (1-q)A, \tag{1}$$

from which we have

$$q = (A-B)/(F-B). \tag{2}$$

when q exceeds this value, cooperation in the form of both countries freezing terrorist assets is the best strategic choice. An identical expression holds for p owing to symmetry. The ratio in (2) represents the *adherence probability* that each nation requires of the other to want to coordinate its freeze policy.[6] A smaller equilibrium probability favors successful coordination, because a nation requires less certainty of its counterpart's intention to freeze assets in order to reciprocate.

From Equation (2), either a larger gain (F) from a mutual freeze or a smaller status-quo payoff (A) promotes the coordination equilibrium by reducing the required adherence probability. An event like 9/11 not only raises F but lowers A as nations realize the benefits from limiting terrorists' resources and the catastrophic consequences that inaction may have for all. As terrorists escalate the carnage to capture the media's attention, nations are increasingly drawn to coordinate counterterrorism activities when unified action is required. Following 9/11's unprecedented casualties, many more nations participated in freezing assets,[7] but participation is by no means universal. Differentiating the right-hand side of (2) with respect to B shows that a decrease in the payoff associated with unilaterally freezing assets inhibits cooperation by raising p or q.[8]

This game scenario can be readily generalized to n homogeneous nations, where at least n nations must freeze assets if each participant is to receive a payoff of F. For less than n freeze participants, each adherent receives B for cooperating and the nonadherents get A. If nations are uncertain about the intentions of other nations, then freezing assets is a desired policy provided that a nation believes that the $n-1$ required additional participants will follow through with a collective probability greater than q. This then implies that each nation must be expected to cooperate by at least the $n-1$st root of q, which for even modest groups may require near certainty. This is not an encouraging finding. If, however, the required number of adherents for coordination gains can be limited, then this decreases the assurance probabilities. For an agreement to freeze assets, this is best accomplished by first unifying some of the major financial-center nations – i.e., the United States, the United Kingdom, Switzerland, Japan and Germany. A concern with this strategy is that some near-catastrophic terrorist acts are not very costly – e.g., the 1993 WTC bomb cost just $400 and caused $500 million in damages (Hoffman, 1998) – so that near-universal freezes may be required.

In matrix b in Figure 3, an alternative scenario is displayed where not freezing assets, when the other nation freezes, gives the second highest payoff to the noncooperator, so that $F > E > A > B$. This scenario implies that the nation that does not join the freeze can profit by providing a safe haven for terrorists' funds. The nation may be motivated to do so if it does not view its own people or property as likely targets of the terrorists. The two pure-strategy Nash equilibriums are for a mutual freeze or no action along the diagonal of the matrix. For the mixed-strategy Nash equilibrium, the adherence probabilities are now:

$$p = q = (A - B)/[F - B + (A - E)], \tag{3}$$

which are greater than those in (2), because $(A - E) < 0$. Hence, coordinating a freeze becomes more difficult owing to profitable opportunities available to less scrupulous nations that can greatly limit gains from action to freeze assets, eliminate safe havens, or abide by no-negotiation pledges (see, e.g., Lee, 1988).

Policies that penalize noncompliance can reverse the ranking of A and E, so that $A > E$. As a consequence, adherence becomes easier to achieve. There are two practical problems: (i) to identify nations that accept terrorists' funds and (ii) to convince nations to punish nonadherents. Since nations hide their bad behavior, singling out nations for punishment is not so easy. Imposing sanctions is itself a prisoners' dilemma game that presents its own collective action concern.

In Figure 4, a final freeze scenario allows for asymmetry where nation 2 has more potential nonadherence profits but fewer gains from acting alone than its counterpart. That is, I assume that $F > E_i > A > B_i$, $i = 1, 2$, where $E_2 > E_1$ and $B_1 > B_2$. The pure-strategy Nash equilibriums are still the matching-behavior outcomes along the diagonal of the matrix in Figure 4. For the mixed-strategy equilibrium, the adherence probabilities are:

$$p = \frac{A - B_2}{F - B_2 + (A - E_2)} > \frac{A - B_1}{F - B_1 + (A - E_1)} = q. \tag{4}$$

To act, nation 2 needs greater assurance than nation 1 that the other nation will freeze assets. Such asymmetry is likely to work against consummating a freeze.

When coordination is required for a counterterrorism measure, many factors work against getting sufficient action. A crucial consideration is the minimum number of nations required for coordinating antiterrorism activities. As this minimum increases, nations must have greater assurance that others will cooperate for them to follow suit. Any policy action that limits this minimum bolsters cooperation. As the threat of terrorism escalates, coordination of counterterrorism is encouraged because cooperative outcomes have greater payoffs and unilateral action has smaller payoffs. The application of technology to track money flows can identify duplicitous nations that hamper other nations' actions by providing safe havens to terrorists' assets. Retribution against these "spoiler" nations can foster more fruitful coordination by sending a clear signal that profiting from terrorism has consequences. Efforts by the International Monetary Fund and World Bank to assist countries in tracking asset transfers can lower the costs of unilateral action, thereby boosting efforts to freeze terrorists' assets.

		nation 2: Freeze	Status quo	
nation 1	Freeze	F, F	B_1, E_2	p
	Status quo	E_1, B_2	A, A	$1 - p$
		q	$1 - q$	

$F > E_i > A > B_i$, $i = 1, 2$; $E_2 > E_1$ and $B_1 > B_2$

Figure 4. Asymmetric freezing assets scenario.

6. Public Choice Dilemma

The recent terrorism literature has shown that there appears to be a positive association between terrorism and democracy (Eubank & Weinberg, 1994, 2001; Li & Schuab, 2004; Schmid, 1992). This association is traced to factors in a liberal democracy that can provide a favorable environment for transnational terrorist activities. For example, freedom of the press allows terrorists to publicize their cause through news coverage of terrorist attacks. Media coverage of ghastly events also serves terrorists' needs to create an atmosphere of fear where everyone feels at risk. File footage is reshown periodically on anniversaries of events and when related incidents occur, so that these events remain in the public consciousness. Restraints on governments' powers limit the ability of authorities to hold terrorist suspects or to gather intelligence. Obviously, 9/11 has eroded some of these restraints as civil society became more willing to trade away some civil liberties for greater security. Freedom of association also provides an environment conducive to terrorism. Modern democratic states are not only target-rich, but also present opportunities for funding and military training. Information is also readily available on building bombs and guerrilla tactics in an open society. In contrast, an autocracy is a less supportive environment for terrorism. If a terrorist group in an autocracy wants to publicize its cause, then it may stage incidents in democracies where news coverage is more complete and the environment is more supportive. Crossing borders is generally easier in a liberal democracy than in an autocracy which, in turn, encourages the export of terrorism and the prevalence of transnational externalities.

This association between democracy and transnational terrorism presents a real public choice dilemma. Usually, democratic ideals work in a country's favor – e.g., democratic countries do not tend to go to war with one another. There are a number of research issues that require further empirical analysis to understand the public choice implications of transnational terrorism. First, the staging of terrorist events in liberal democracies requires study. To date, there has been no careful and convincing study on whether transnational terrorism is originating in or spilling over to democratic countries. The level of this alleged externality needs to be investigated in order to determine the appropriate policy response. For example, enhanced border security can address some spillover terrorism. Second, the influence of the type of democracy on the level of terrorism requires analysis. Which kind of democratic system – proportional representation or majoritarian system – is more conducive to terrorism? Since proportional representation gives more views, even extreme ones, a presence in government, terrorism may be less prevalent under proportional representation than under a majoritarian system. The impact of the type of democratic system on the level of terrorism has not been investigated.[9] Third, the role of rent seeking as a motive for terrorism requires further analysis. A paper by Kirk (1983) argued that government size encourages more terrorism because of greater potential rents to capture. His analysis probably does not apply in today's world where fundamentalist-based terrorism is the driving force, since these terrorists' goals do *not* appear to be distribution driven. Many fundamentalist groups – e.g., Al-Qaida – view all nonbelievers as enemies and want an Islamic state (White, 2003). In those countries where there are *rival* terrorist groups, a rent-seeking explanation of terrorism may be appropriate. Each terrorist group is in a contest with other groups for the provision of a public good in the form of a political change that favors the group's constituency. Rent-seeking costs are the expense of the terrorist campaign that promotes the terrorists' demands. Such costs represent a lower bound on the expense that the campaign imposes on society, because damage to the latter must also be included.

7. Concluding Remarks

The paper applies elementary noncooperative game theory to explore the collective action dilemmas that confront nations as they address a global terrorist threat. Although incentives are conducive for terrorists to form networks and cooperate, incentives are less supportive for targeted nations to coordinate their counterterrorism policies. Both proactive and defensive measures often imply an underlying prisoners' dilemma game in which insufficient action characterizes offensive efforts and too much action characterizes defensive responses. For proactive measures, a prime-target country is anticipated to act. By concentrating their attacks on a couple of target countries, terrorists motivate these countries to strike back and privilege all at-risk countries with their actions to weaken the terrorists. If countries realize that defensive measures may merely divert attacks abroad where their people and property are still targeted, then there will be a smaller tendency to overspend on defensive measures. For domestic terrorism, there is a better balance struck between proactive and defensive responses because a central government can internalize the externalities among targets that plague responses at the transnational level.

Collective action concerns may be particularly troublesome for counterterrorist actions requiring sufficient transnational coordination, where nonparticipating countries can severely undermine the efforts of the cooperators. Such coordination concerns apply to efforts to freeze terrorists' assets, eliminate terrorists' safe havens, deny terrorists' weapons, and maintain a no-negotiation policy. As the number of participants required for cooperative gains to be realized increases, the associated assurance probabilities also increase. Thus, in the case of freezing terrorists' assets, a few nations that safeguard these assets can provide terrorists with the means to engage in some large-scale attacks. This is especially true because deadly events may be relatively cheap to finance. Sanctions for nonparticipants can improve coordination possibilities but raise a collective action problem of their own, since sanctions provide purely public benefits. By targeting countries and their interests at home and abroad, today's terrorists worsen the coordination problem for at-risk countries. As terrorists escalate the damage from their acts, they, however, increase the likelihood of coordination success on the part of targeted countries. Following 9/11, many more countries started to freeze terrorists' assets.

Acknowledgments

The author is the Robert R. and Katheryn A. Dockson Professor of International Relations and Economics. The author's research was financed in part from the Dockson endowment. While assuming full responsibility for any shortcomings, the author has benefited from comments by Hirofumi Shimizu and Kevin Siqueira on an earlier draft.

Notes

1. The Algerians immediately freed the 23 non-Israeli passengers. On 27 July 1968, they released the Israeli women and children hostages (Mickolus, 1980, p. 94). The remaining hostages were held at an Algiers military base under the "protection" of the Algerian government.
2. The figures in this paragraph come from US Department of State (2004, pp. 176–181).
3. This asymmetry paraphrases what Irish Republican Army (IRA) terrorists said in a letter after they learned that their 12 October 1984 bombing of the Grand Hotel in Brighton had narrowly missed killing Prime Minister Margaret Thatcher. Their letter said, "Today, we were unlucky. But remember we have only to be lucky once. You will have to be lucky always." See Mickolus et al. (1989, vol. 2, p. 115).
4. If $B > c$, then the dominant strategy is for both nations to preempt – a scenario that we virtually never see for multiple countries.
5. Before 9/11, airlines tried to save money in their employment of security personnel. The deployment of federally trained screeners removes this strategic option.
6. Another interpretation for mixing is that p and q denote the uncertain beliefs that the nations have for the likelihood that the other country will act.
7. Since 9/11, $200 million of alleged terrorist assets have been frozen (White House, 2003).
8. $dq/dB = dp/dB = (A - F)/(F - B)^2 < 0$, so that a smaller B is associated with greater adherence probabilities.
9. Recently Reynal-Querol (2002) showed that the incidence of civil wars is lower with proportional representation than with majoritarian systems. Her analysis can be applied to the incidence of transnational terrorism.

References

Alexander, Y., & Pluchinsky, D. (1992). *Europe's Red Terrorists: The Fighting Communist Organizations*. Frank Cass: London.

Arquilla, J., & Ronfeldt, D. (2001). The advent of Netwar (Revisited). In J. Arquilla & D. Ronfeldt (Eds.), *Networks and Netwars*, 1–25. RAND: Santa Monica, CA.

Arce, D. G., & Sandler, T. (2005). Counterterrorism: A game-theoretic analysis. *Journal of Conflict Resolution, 49*(2), 183–200.

Enders, W., & Sandler, T. (1993). The effectiveness of anti-terrorism policies: A vector-autoregression-intervention analysis. *American Political Science Review, 87*(4), 829–844.

Enders, W., & Sandler, T. (1995). Terrorism: Theory and applications. In K. Hartley & T. Sandler (Eds.), *Handbook of Defense Economics*, Vol. 1, 213–249. North-Holland: Amsterdam.

Enders, W., & Sandler, T. (2004). What do we know about the substitution effect in transnational terrorism? In A. Silke (Ed.), *Researching Terrorism: Trends, Achievements, Failures*, 119–137. Frank Cass: Ilford.

Enders, W., Sandler, T., & Cauley, J. (1990). UN conventions, technology, and retaliation in the fight against terrorism: An economic evaluation. *Terrorism and Political Violence, 2*(1), 83–105.

Eubank, W. L., & Weinberg, L. (1994). Does democracy encourage terrorism? *Terrorism and Political Violence, 6*(4), 417–435.

Eubank, W. K., & Weinberg, L. (2001). Terrorism and democracy: Perpetrators and victims. *Terrorism and Political Violence, 13*(1), 155–164.

Hirshleifer, J. (1991). The paradox of power. *Economics and Politics, 3*(3), 177–200.

Hoffman, B. (1998). *Inside Terrorism*. Columbia University Press: New York.

Hoffman, B. (2003). Al Qaeda, trends in terrorism, and future potentialities: An assessment. *Studies in Conflict & Terrorism, 26*(6), 429–442.

Kirk, R. M. (1983). Political terrorism and the size of government: A positive institutional analysis of violent political activity. *Public Choice, 40*(1), 41–52.

Lapan, H. E., & Sandler, T. (1993). Terrorism and signaling. *European Journal of Political Economy, 9*(3), 383–397.

Lee, D. R. (1988). Free riding and paid riding in the fight against terrorism. *American Economic Association Papers and Proceedings, 78*(2), 22–26.

Li, Q., & Schuab, D. (2004). Economic globalization and transnational terrorism: A pooled time-series analysis. *Journal of Conflict Resolution, 48*(2), 230–258.

Mickolus, E. F. (1980). *Transnational Terrorism: A Chronology of Events 1968–1979*. Greenwood Press: Westport, CT.

Mickolus, E. F., Sandler, T., & Murdock, J. M. (1989). *International Terrorism in the 1980s: A Chronology of Events*, 2 vols. Iowa State University: Ames.

National Memorial Institute for the Prevention of Terrorism. (2004). Preventing Terrorism or Mitigating its Effect. Available at http://www.mipt.org.

Raufer, X. (2003). Al Qaeda: A Different Diagnosis. *Studies in Conflict & Terrorism, 26*(6), 391–398.

Reynal-Querol, M. (2002). Political systems, stability and civil wars. *Defence and Peace Economics, 13*(6), 463–483.

Rosendorff, P., & Sandler, T. (2004). Too much of a good thing? The proactive response dilemma. *Journal of Conflict Resolution, 48*(5), 657–671.

Sandler, T. (2003). Collective action and transnational terrorism. *World Economy, 26*(6), 779–802.

Sandler, T. (2005). Recognizing the limits to cooperation behind national borders: Financing the control of transnational terrorism. In I. Kaul & P. Conceição (Eds.), *Public Finance in a Globalizing World: Innovations in Theory and Practice*. Oxford University Press: New York, forthcoming.

Sandler, T., & Lapan, H. E. (1988). The calculus of dissent: An analysis of terrorists' choice of targets. *Synthèse, 76*(2), 245–261.

Sandler, T., & Siqueria, K. (2003). Global terrorism: Deterrence versus preemption. Unpublished manuscript, School of International Relations, University of Southern California, Los Angeles, CA, USA.

Schmid, A. P. (1992). Terrorism and democracy. *Terrorism and Political Violence*, *4*(4), 14–25.

United States Department of State. (2001). *Patterns of Global Terrorism*, 2001. US Department of State: Washington, DC.

United States Department of State. (2004). *Patterns of Global Terrorism*, 2003. US Department of State: Washington, DC.

White, J. R. (2003). *Terrorism: 2002 Update*. Wadsworth/Thomason Learning: Belmont, CA.

White House. (2003). Progress Report on the Global War on Terrorism. Available at http://www.state.gov/s/ct/rls/rpt/24087.htm.

Public Choice (2005) **124:** 95–114
DOI: 10.1007/s11127-005-4748-x

Government growth in the twenty-first century

RANDALL G. HOLCOMBE
Department of Economics, Florida State University, Tallahassee, FL 32306-2045 USA
(E-mail: holcombe@garnet.acns.fsu.edu)

Accepted March 2005

Abstract. Public choice explanations of government growth fall into three main categories: budget-maximization theories, rational-choice models, and path-dependent models like the "ratchet hypothesis". The strengths and weaknesses of these theories as explanations for government growth are considered along with some facts about the actual growth of government to conjecture about its trajectory in the twenty-first century. Government size seems to have been constrained in the past primarily by its ability to raise revenue. Growth rates in the new century thus appear to depend on factors constraining government's ability to continue to expand the tax base.

1. Introduction

The massive worldwide growth of government in the twentieth century was a truly remarkable phenomenon, and one that has interested the community of public choice scholars since the discipline was in its infancy. Looking ahead to the twenty-first century, will this growth continue, or is the era of big government over, as Bill Clinton said in 1995?[1] This paper examines this issue by looking at the theories that public choice analysis has offered to explain government growth, along with some facts about the past growth of government, to try to gain some insight on what lies ahead.

The task would be more straightforward if there were one well-established theory of government growth, but public choice scholars have offered many hypotheses. After reviewing the existing theories along with the facts of government growth, this paper suggests that there is a single factor underlying government growth: growth in the availability of revenues. Government will spend as much as it can collect from its citizens so, as Brennan and Buchanan (1980) suggest, the key to understanding the future course of government growth is to develop an understanding of the constraints that governments face in raising revenue. That the course of twenty-first century government growth will depend primarily on the ability of governments to extract revenues from their citizens may be a controversial conclusion, so the paper will proceed by examining the existing public choice literature on government size and government growth along with some historical facts to indicate why this conclusion appears consistent with both the facts and the literature.

2. The Two Dimensions of the Literature

Explanations for the growth, or size, of government in the public choice literature differ on two different dimensions. First, some of the literature focuses on the size of government, while some looks at the growth in government. Second, there are, broadly, three different categories of explanations for government's growth or size: budget-maximization models, rational-choice models, and path-dependent models. Looking at the first dimension, in one sense it may appear that theories about the growth of government and theories about the size of government amount to the same thing, because government growth is the first derivative of government size. An explanation for one is therefore an explanation for the other. However, if there is a path dependency in government growth, models designed to explain government size may not capture the elements that lead to government growth. Thus, it becomes important to separate the sometimes subtle differences between theories of government size and theories of government growth.

Looking at the second dimension, many public choice explanations of government growth rest on a model that depicts the size of government as a collective choice of its citizens. While there is an element of truth to this – in that collective choice mechanisms can act as a constraint on government action – the depiction of government size as an outcome of collective choice stands at odds with the literature on revenue-maximizing or budget-maximizing government, where government spends as much as it can, subject to certain constraints. These two explanations become more consistent with each other if collective choice mechanisms are viewed as constraints on the activities of government rather than as mechanisms that cause outcomes to reflect constituents' preferences. The third major category of explanation is that there is a path dependency in government spending, which would make any static model of collective choice misleading in the analysis of government growth. Because there is no one established public choice theory of government growth, any single explanation is likely to be controversial, including the explanation offered here. It is offered not with any hope that it is the last word on the subject, but rather with the hope that it will stimulate interest in further research on the topic.

3. Budget Maximization

Before Niskanen's (1971) book, *Bureaucracy and Representative Government*, public choice almost exclusively examined the demand side of the public sector, neglecting the supply side. Demand-side models were dominated by the median voter model, which as Holcombe (1989) explains, was almost always taken to imply that the public sector is a reflection of the median voter's preference.[2] Niskanen created a minor revolution within public choice with his assumption of budget-maximizing government bureaucracy that led directly to a number of studies on government growth (Borcherding, 1977). In the context of government growth, Niskanen's model of budget-maximizing bureaucracy explains why government is excessively large, but not why it has grown. Perhaps its greatest impact on the literature on government growth is the assumption – persuasively justified, but an assumption nevertheless – of budget maximization.

While Niskanen's model was seen by some as a critique or refutation of the median voter model, it is in fact built on the median voter model, and Niskanen (1971, pp. 139 & 143) refers to the demander in his model as the median voter in a number of places. The median voter's demand still determines the budget size, even though the outcome is higher government spending than the median voter prefers. Similarly, Romer and Rosenthal (1978) clearly depict the median voter's preference as determining the level of government spending, even though government spends more than the median voter prefers. In both cases, the institutional structure depicted by the models acts merely as a constraint on the actions of expenditure-maximizing politicians.

This budget-maximizing assumption manifests itself in a slightly different form in Brennan and Buchanan (1980), who depict government as a revenue-maximizing Leviathan that may be limited by constitutional constraints on its behavior. As with Niskanen's bureaucracy model, this is a model of big government but not growing government, and again the driving force behind the model is an assumption of revenue maximization. In this literature, constitutions and democratic institutions serve only the function of imposing constraints on the size of a budget- or revenue-maximizing government, and without these constraints the models give no indication as to how large government could actually grow. Of course, government size will always be constrained by the maximum amount of revenue that government could possibly collect – the Laffer curve[3] – but the point is that in these models, government tries to spend as much as it possibly can, and constitutions, democratic institutions, and so forth do not determine the optimal amount of government spending, they only constrain excessively large government from spending even more. If the constraint is loosened, government grows; if the constraint is tightened, government shrinks, but unlike the median voter model, collective decision-making does not produce what citizens most prefer – it only constrains excessively large government to some degree.

Along these same lines, Becker and Mulligan (2003) note the constraining effect of the deadweight loss associated with taxes. If taxes are collected more efficiently, deadweight losses go down, which reduces the political pressure against taxes and causes taxes to rise and government to get larger. Similarly, Holcombe and Mills (1995) argue that deficit finance is constrained by the political opposition it generates, and Buchanan and Wagner (1977) argue that the acceptance of Keynesian economic policy measures relaxed a political constraint on deficit finance, allowing government to spend more than had that constraint remained in place. What these works have in common is that the size of government is constrained by political opposition. If factors change to lessen the political opposition to government revenue generation, government grows.

Kau and Rubin (1981) find that virtually all of the increase in the size of the United States government from 1929 to 1970 can be explained by reductions in the cost to government of collecting taxes. Similarly, David Friedman (1977) argues that the size and shape of nations is designed to maximize government revenue. Budget maximization or revenue maximization has been well-established as a working hypothesis in a number of public choice models for decades, although not everyone accepts the assumption's validity. The main alternative, at least as presented in the public choice literature, is to view actual outcomes in the public sector as a reflection of citizen preferences as expressed through the political process.[4]

4. Rational-Choice Models of Government Size

The median voter model has already been noted as an example of a model that suggests that the size of government reflects the preferences of citizens as expressed through a collective decision-making procedure, but there are a number of other models pointing to the same conclusion. For example, Becker (1983) and Wittman (1989, 1995) describe collective decision-making institutions as creating a kind of political marketplace in which competing demands of various interests are weighed against each other and the result is an optimal allocation of resources in the public sector, analogous to the way that a competitive market would allocate resources in the private sector. These models were not intended to explain government growth, but if government spending optimally reflects the preferences of its citizens, the implication is that government grows because people have a preference for larger government.

Meltzer and Richard (1981) develop a model explicitly built on the median voter model, and argue that government has grown because of extensions of the franchise that have changed the position of the median voter. Similarly, Lott and Kenny (1999) argue that government grew in the twentieth century because women were extended the vote and women prefer larger government than men. Peltzman (1980) argues that government grows because people vote themselves more redistributive benefits, and suggests that a more equal distribution of income has produced more of this rent-seeking behavior, leading to larger government. Models of government growth such as these do not argue that government size is optimal, but rather that it is the outcome of a collective choice process that reflects the preferences of those who choose.

In these cases, the set of people who could choose was expanded to include people who wanted bigger government, or in Peltzman's case, the distribution of income changed to make the existing electorate favor more government redistribution, and government grew. These models are similar to the median voter model in that the size of government is a result of a democratic choice, but they take into account changes in the group of people who are able to express their preferences through voting.

Baumol (1967) offers another explanation for government growth: because of the labor-intensive nature of government services, productivity will grow more in the private sector than in the public sector, so utility-maximizing individuals will want to shift their consumption away from private sector consumption toward public sector consumption. Baumol was arguing that this shift has not happened to the extent that would be optimal, so government is too small; nonetheless, if differences in relative productivity growth between the public sector and private sector pointed toward a shift in production toward the public sector, this would result in individuals collectively choosing a larger public sector. Downs (1960) likewise argues within his median voter framework that voters tend to choose inefficiently low levels of government expenditures.

Institutional differences may lead some types of political decision-making to result in higher governmental expenditures than others. Persson and Tabellini (1999, 2003) and Mueller (2002) explain that interest groups tend to be more successful in lobbying European parliamentary governments than the more decentralized government in the United States, resulting in larger transfer expenditures in European governments. Institutions may vary, resulting in different-sized governments, but the underlying size of government is a result of a collective choice mechanism that makes government activities a product of group preferences.

The various explanations for government growth, or government size, offered in this section differ in a number of ways, but they have the common element that they consider the size of government to be a reflection of the preferences of its citizens aggregated through a collective choice mechanism. As in much of the public choice literature, the collective decision-making process in these models is depicted as a method of transforming the preferences of a group of people into an outcome that reflects the group's preferences. In many of the models the outcome is not necessarily efficient because institutions do not necessarily aggregate preferences to produce the optimal level of output, but in models like those of Becker (1983) and Wittman (1995), the political system also weighs the intensities of preferences in order to generate an optimal allocation of resources. In either case, government growth is a result of a collective preference for larger government, as citizen preferences are aggregated through a rational choice mechanism.

5. Path Dependency and the "Ratchet Hypothesis"

One of the earlier theories of government growth is the ratchet hypothesis, first put forward by Peacock and Wiseman (1961) and supported by Rassler and Thompson (1985), Higgs (1987) and others. The theory is that government responds to crises like wars and depressions by ratcheting up expenditures, and then after the crises pass, expenditures fall somewhat but remain above their pre-crisis level. Thus, government growth is a series of ratchets upward in government spending in response to crisis. While it does appear that spending ratchets up after crises and remains above its pre-crisis level, Holcombe (1993) notes that in an empirical examination of expenditure levels, the trend growth of government expenditures in the twentieth century has been so substantial that any ratchets are completely swamped by the trend, and do not show up as statistically significant increases. Yet as Higgs (1991) notes, the ratchets may still be there, because government can grow in dimensions other than expenditures.

The ratchet hypothesis appears at odds with the rational choice models of government growth (or government size), unless a past crisis causes people to believe that continued higher government expenditures can help avert a future crisis. As Holcombe (1996, 2002, ch. 9) shows, after the ratchet upward following World War I there was a substantial increase in the growth of non-military federal government spending and regulation in the 1920s, and after World War II non-military federal government expenditures rose from 7.8% of GDP to 10%, following military spending decreases in each case. Clearly, the non-military expenditure increases after these major wars were not a rational-choice response to the crisis that had passed. Rather, as military expenditures receded after the wars, the increased revenue used to finance the wars left money available for an increase in non-military expenditures. Both World War I and World War II were financed in part by major income tax increases, and while after the wars rates fell some from their wartime highs, they never fell to their pre-war levels.

Prior to World War I the highest marginal income tax rate was 7%, and it went to 77% in 1918. The top marginal rate fell back to 25% in the 1920s, which was below the wartime high but more than three times higher than the pre-war rate. Similarly, from 1936 to 1939 the top marginal income tax rate was 79%, levied on incomes above $5 million.[5] It was raised to 94% of incomes above $200,000 during World War II, and the rate came down only to 91% of incomes above $200,000 in the 1950s.[6] Rates that would not have been tolerated prior to the war were accepted as a part of the war effort and, once in place, the federal government was able to maintain much of the tax increase after the crisis had passed. Government grew because revenue was available after the wars that could not have been collected prior to them. Citizens would not have accepted these tax increases during normal times, but were willing to accept them as a response to crises.

Another factor that aided government revenue collection during World War II was the implementation of income tax withholding on wage income. Again, it is unlikely that citizens would have accepted withholding without the crisis, but once implemented citizens did not rebel against the status quo. Note, however, that in the 1980s there were several attempts made to institute withholding on dividend and interest income, but without a crisis to justify it, they were rejected because of public opposition. One would think that because interest and dividend withholding would have its largest impact on the rich, whereas wage withholding affects the average (median?) citizen much more, interest and dividend withholding would meet with less political opposition than wage withholding.[7] Two observations are relevant here: first, because wage withholding was implemented in response to a crisis, it was more acceptable politically, bolstering the ratchet hypothesis; second, once a change has been implemented and becomes part of the status quo, it becomes difficult to reverse.

Both the ratchet hypothesis and the evidence just reviewed suggest that there is a path dependency in the level of government expenditures that cannot fully be captured in a comparative-statics framework. Institutions and citizen preferences act as constraints on the level of government expenditures, but if a constraint is temporarily relaxed, resulting in an increase in government expenditures, that constraint will not fully be reimposed to cause government expenditures to fall back to their former level. Olson (1982) presents a similar theory of path dependency, arguing that as political systems mature, interest groups become more firmly entrenched and are able to divert ever larger shares of national income away from expenditures in the public interest to support their own private interests, leading to the decline of nations.

If these theories of path-dependent government growth are descriptive, they call into question models suggesting that the level of government expenditures is optimal by some measure. These theories suggest that the level of government expenditures is not the result of some process that responds only to current conditions, but rather is dependent upon historical circumstances that have allowed government expenditures to rise. While a crisis may have some impact on what citizens believe to be the optimal level of government expenditures, it is implausible to think, for example, that because of World Wars I and II citizens believed that non-military expenditures should be higher after the war than before. More likely, a constraint on government revenues that could not have been relaxed during peacetime was relaxed because of the war, and was not able to be reimposed after the war. This suggests a revenue-maximizing government coupled with institutional rigidities and path-dependent institutional developments along the lines described by Olson (1982), and not a process that somehow reflects the static preferences of citizens at that particular point in time.

Path-dependency theories of government growth do not have as solid a behavioral foundation as the rational choice models discussed in the previous section. Yet this may reflect as much on the way that models of individual rational choice are applied to collective choice mechanisms than on the ratchet hypothesis itself. Brennan and Lomasky (1993) suggest that rational choice models do not apply all that closely to political choice, and Caplan (2001, 2003) has argued that voters not only are rationally ignorant but also rationally irrational. Rational choice models may not apply very well to collective choice mechanisms where any one individual has a negligible impact on the overall collective choice. There is a substantial literature that incorporates psychological findings into economics, discussed by Kahneman (2003), which suggests that the axioms of neoclassical utility maximization do not hold so strongly in real-world choices. Kahneman, Knetsch, and Thaler (1991) discuss the endowment effect, loss aversion, and the status quo bias, all of which are relevant to the ratchet hypothesis. People may be reluctant to trade their freedoms or their incomes for governmental growth, but once those things have been ceded and become a part of the status quo, they are equally reluctant to sacrifice the benefits of the government programs that have resulted from government growth.

The status-quo bias may be especially powerful with regard to government expenditure programs. Interest groups lobby government for expenditure programs that benefit them, and along the lines of Becker (1983), the legislature weighs the interests for and against programs to decide whether to implement them, or how much should be spent on them. Once the programs are established, a new interest group is created in the form of the government bureaucracy that will administer the programs, adding to the strength of interests that favor the expenditure. Furthermore, as Niskanen (1971) argues, that bureaucracy becomes the legislature's experts on the program, adding to the bias in favor of keeping the program. As Tullock (1982) observed, many new government programs are started, but few existing programs are terminated. This status-quo bias, well-established in the economics literature both inside and outside of public choice, provides at least a partial foundation to support the ratchet hypothesis and path dependency in government expenditures.

Path-dependency theories underscore the differences between theories of government growth and theories of government size. Theories of government size suggest that certain factors determine the size of government, and that if those factors change, the size of government will change in response. As it happens, the theories of government size cited above all hypothesize that changes occurred to make government larger, but presumably if those changes were reversed, government would shrink. Theories of government size treat government growth as the first derivative of government size. If there is a path dependency, however, the theories discussed in this section suggest that once government has grown that growth is difficult to reverse. In this path-dependent environment, the size of government is not simply a function of current conditions, but is a result of events that may be well past. It is plausible to argue, for example, that had World War II not occurred, political forces would have prevented income tax withholding, and as a result the federal government in the United States would be substantially smaller than it is now. Events that occurred sixty years ago have left their mark on the level of current government expenditures completely independently of current conditions.

6. Non-Expenditure Growth

Most of the literature on government growth has focused on expenditure growth, perhaps because expenditure growth is relatively easy to quantify, and this paper follows the literature in that regard. However, government can grow in other dimensions too, and these other dimensions may be at least as significant as expenditure growth. Higgs (1987, 1991) emphasizes regulatory growth, the power to confiscate property, and the ability of government officials to act unilaterally, without any checks on their behavior, as other dimensions in which government has grown. Holcombe (2002) discusses the erosion of individual rights which have been replaced by the power of the majority, and Posner (1971) describes regulation as a type of taxation. Gwartney and Lawson (2003) have quantified economic freedom across countries, and Gastil (1978) has quantified political rights and civil liberties, which are other dimensions along which government can grow beyond simply the level of expenditures.

Growth in these non-expenditure dimensions of government is relevant for two reasons. First, it may have impacts as significant, or more significant, than expenditure growth. For example, if we accept Posner's (1971) description of regulation as a form of taxation, researchers who focus only on the budgetary actions of government are leaving out an important dimension of government growth. Second, these non-expenditure dimensions may be related to the underlying causes of government expenditure growth, in which case one could not fully understand expenditure growth without an understanding of these other dimensions of government growth. Expenditure growth may have been facilitated by the increasing scope of government in other areas. This argument should resonate with public choice scholars who may look for the roots of government growth in political institutions. While recognizing the potential importance of government growth in non-budgetary dimensions, this paper primarily follows the literature by focusing on expenditure growth.

7. Public Choice – or Compulsion?

Public choice, as an area of inquiry, has tended to describe public sector outcomes as a reflection of group preferences. The public sector is a result of a collective decision-making process that produces what the group prefers. The analogy of a political marketplace holds up to a degree, but fails to be a complete analogy because transactions in the private marketplace are undertaken voluntarily whereas compulsion underlies all government activity. As Yeager (2001, p. 234) puts it,

> not even a democratic state is a mechanism voluntarily operated by its citizens to attend to their common concerns. Even under political democracy the essence of the state is compulsion. Any call for a particular government activity is a call for supporting it, if ultimately necessary, by force.

As applied to the topic of government growth, government has been able to grow because it has been able to force citizens, through taxation, to pay for its ever-increasing size.

Whereas public choice has often viewed government as the product of collectively expressed preferences, the literature on government growth has deviated from this approach to a degree. Both the budget maximization literature and the path dependency-ratchet hypothesis literature depicts a government that has interests at odds with its citizens. This literature suggests that the suppliers of government programs – politicians and bureaucrats – want to enlarge their domains, and the electoral process – the demand side of the market – has acted only as an ineffective constraint. Government does not try to reflect the preferences of its citizens, following this line of reasoning, but tries to override them to command more resources for itself.

In this context, the public choice literature offers two starkly contrasting views of the public sector. In one view, the public sector is a result of a collective decision-making process in which various interests interact in a political marketplace through voting, lobbying, and other political activities, and the political marketplace allocates resources in a manner analogous to more ordinary competitive markets. In the other view, public officials try to maximize governmental revenues and expenditures, and the political process and constitutional rules act as constraints on the government's size. Even this second view, however, rests on an ultimate foundation of agreement, albeit with one side having an advantageous bargaining position. Niskanen's budget-maximizing bureaus can only produce as much as their sponsors will agree to; Romer and Rosenthal's budget-maximizing agenda setters can only get as much as the voters will agree to; Brennan and Buchanan's revenue-maximizing Leviathan can only tax as much as the constitution allows. Even here the analogy seems to allude more to a reluctant customer dealing with a monopoly supplier than to a citizenry that is forced to comply whether they consent or not.

Ironically, this element of compulsion is more a part of neoclassical public finance than it is a part of public choice. For example, optimal tax theory, based on Diamond and Mirrlees (1971) and Mirrlees (1971), depicts a welfare (not budget) maximizing government that redistributes income by forcibly taking it from some people and giving it to others. While one might make the excuse that this is unobjectionable because the government has the welfare of its citizens in mind, what the model of optimal taxation argues is that it is optimal for the government to take income from some people forcibly in order to further its objectives. In contrast, public choice analysis has often depicted such a government action as the result of a collective agreement. In a democracy, giving people the right to vote gives the appearance of legitimacy to government action, as Edelman (1964) notes, obscuring the coercion that underlies everything government does. If coercion were not necessary, then there would be no reason for government to get involved.

It may be comforting to think that in optimal tax models government is forcibly taking money from some to give to others to increase the utility of the recipients, but normally economists assume that people act to maximize their own utility, not the utility of others. Thus, Niskanen's (1971) argument as to why those in government maximize their utility by maximizing their budgets supports the Leviathan model of government and suggests that money forcibly taken from taxpayers is done not to maximize social welfare, but to maximize the utility of those who are taking it. Taxation is, as Usher (1992) explains, a form of predation.

The implications of this line of reasoning for public choice theory in general are substantial, but for present purposes two ideas will be carried forward. First, the model of revenue and expenditure maximizing government makes sense as a description of governmental behavior, and is in many ways more descriptive than a model of a political marketplace in which resources are allocated through bargaining among various interests. Yes, the demands of various interests must be accounted for if political leaders want to survive in office, but, as Bueno de Mequita et al. (2003) argue, this is different from a marketplace where people enter into agreements for mutually advantageous trades. Second, one might question the effectiveness of electoral and constitutional constraints on government, because government can implement its policies by force and in general does not need the agreement of the electorate. The first idea – of budget-maximizing government – is well-established in public choice. The second idea – about the ineffectiveness of electoral and constitutional constraints in the face of government coercion – is not as well-established. If anything, public choice has served to reinforce the idea of the effectiveness of electoral constraints on government. Democracy does constrain government action to a degree, undoubtedly, but to the degree that political competition is limited by barriers to entry, which is an old idea in public choice (Tullock, 1965), incumbents do not face a true competitive market, and are in a position to use the force of government to further their own ends.

One gets a different picture of the causes of government growth if one looks at the size of government as a result of the rational choice of its citizens as opposed to viewing it as the result of a revenue-maximizing government that is able to extract revenues from its citizens by force. Bringing in this element of compulsion may lend more insight both to the causes of government growth and to public choice analysis in general.[8]

8. Government Growth in the Nineteenth Century

Any complete theory of government growth must be able to explain not only why government has grown rapidly in the twentieth century, but also why at other times there was relatively little government growth. Governments around the world grew substantially in the twentieth century, but grew much more slowly in the nineteenth, and even retrenched by some measures. Real per capita federal government expenditures in the United States (in 1990 dollars) were $79.76 in 1870, and were $79.56 in 1895, twenty-five years later (Holcombe, 2002, p. 140). Real per capita federal expenditures were unchanged for a quarter of a century, and when one considers the substantial real income growth during the period, government expenditures actually fell as a percentage of income.

When looking at national governments, one explanation for the relatively slow growth of government in the nineteenth century was the increasing openness of the expanding world economy, allowing capital to shift beyond national borders more easily and thereby limiting the ability of national governments to tax it. In the United States, the ease of westward movement accelerated with the growth of the railroads, allowing people to move to the frontier to escape the reach of government. By the end of the nineteenth century the continent was populated from coast to coast, closing the frontier,[9] and the twentieth century was dominated by two world wars and a cold war that divided the world and made international capital movements much more risky. This offers a tentative explanation for why the growth of national governments slowed considerably or even stopped in the nineteenth century, but accelerated in the twentieth, which is consistent with the budget-maximizing assumption. Taxable resources became more mobile in the nineteenth century, but became less mobile in the twentieth.

While national government growth was limited in the nineteenth century, local government growth in the United States was substantial. Holcombe and Lacombe (2004) show that while there was minimal state and federal government growth in the nineteenth century, per capita local government revenues

Table 1. Federal, state, and local government expenditures as a share of total government expenditures

Year	Federal (%)	State (%)	Local (%)
1870	43.4	13.7	42.9
1913	23.3	12.7	64.0
1922	35.5	15.1	49.4

Source: Holcombe and Lacombe (2001, p. 188).

and expenditures grew substantially throughout the century, especially so after 1870. Local governments spent about $28 per resident in 1820, which increased to $122 per resident in 1850 and $253 per resident in 1870 (all in 1990 dollars).[10] In 1870, local government expenditures were slightly less than federal government expenditures in the United States, with local expenditures making up 42.9% of total government expenditures and federal expenditures making up 43.4%. By 1913 local government expenditures were 64% of the total while federal expenditures had fallen to 23.3% of total government expenditures, as shown in Table 1. So while the nineteenth century was a century of minimal federal government growth, it was also a century of substantial local government growth.

This growth in 19th century local governments might be explained in part by rising infrastructure demands as cities were expanding and the economy was being transformed from a rural one based on agriculture to an urban one based on manufacturing, but this explanation does not fit many of the facts of local government growth. As Holcombe and Lacombe (2004) note, expenditure growth was not concentrated on infrastructure, but on all types of public and non-public goods. In comparisons of two cities that were similar in many ways – Boston and Baltimore – growth rates were found to be more highly correlated with increases in tax bases than with the demand for public services. The evidence suggests that nineteenth-century city governments grew because agglomeration economies attracted economic activity to cities, and cities could use property taxes to raise revenue from a relatively immobile tax base. Thus, city government growth resulted from access to a larger tax base that could not escape city taxes, rather than to demand-side factors.

Furthermore, when analyzing the factors underlying 19th century local government growth, such as an increasingly urbanized population and infrastructure demands, it is worth noting that these factors continued through the 20th century, suggesting that local government expenditures should have continued growing faster than federal expenditures. Yet the opposite is true: by 1922 federal government expenditures had risen to 35.5% of total government expenditures, while local expenditures had fallen to less than half of total government expenditures, as Table 1 shows. What happened in that decade from 1913 to 1922? The two biggest factors affecting this change were World War I and the creation of the federal income tax in 1913. As explanations of federal government growth, World War I fits the ratchet hypothesis while the creation of the federal income tax fits the explanation that it is the supply of funds available to a budget-maximizing government – rather than the demand for government expenditures – that drives government growth.

In the nineteenth century, increased competition at the national level and increased international mobility reduced the ability of national governments to raise tax revenues, whereas reduced factor mobility at the local level due to agglomeration economies in cities increased the ability of local governments to raise revenues.[11] In the twentieth century, greater mobility due to advances in transportation technology reduced some of the locational advantages that cities had, while the income tax increased the federal government's tax base and international hostilities inhibited international capital movements, which increased the revenue-generating ability of national governments. These stylized facts regarding federal versus local government growth in the nineteenth and twentieth centuries are more consistent with the hypothesis that government is a budget-maximizing institution that spends as much revenue as it can raise than with the hypothesis that government spending reflects the demands of its citizens.

9. An Explanation for Nineteenth and Twentieth Century Government Growth

The facts of the preceding two centuries are consistent with the hypothesis that government growth has occurred because revenue- and expenditure-maximizing governments have been able to appropriate ever-increasing shares of private sector production. This explanation implies that collective choice mechanisms and constitutional constraints do not determine the size or growth rate of government, but, along the lines of Brennan and Buchanan (1980), they act as constraints that keep the government from getting larger. Those in government find ways to erode the constraints on spending that they face, causing government to grow, but there is only the loosest connection between group preferences for government growth and the actual path of government growth. Existing constraints on government's power to tax are easier to maintain than new constraints are to implement, or than old constraints are to reimpose once they have been removed. This status quo bias creates a path dependency in government growth and suggests that given the nature of the constraints on government's size, it is easier to remove them to allow government to grow than it is to impose them to force government to shrink.

This theory of government growth has as its foundation the assumption of expenditure and revenue maximization on the part of those in government, and while this budget-maximization hypothesis is well-established and frequently employed in public choice, it is far from proven.[12] Even if it is accepted, the budget-maximization proposition as applied to government growth is ambiguous. As Buchanan and Lee (1982), Levi (1988) and Holcombe (1994) note, different policies are implied depending upon the time horizon of those who have government power, and a budget maximizer with a long time horizon might prefer government to take a smaller share of income in order to encourage income growth. Nevertheless, the budget-maximization hypothesis stands in stark contrast to theories which suggest that government growth is a reflection of citizen preferences, and the facts behind two centuries of government growth align more closely with the hypothesis of budget-maximizing Leviathan government than with the hypothesis that the size of government is a reflection of citizen preferences. Citizen preferences act to constrain government, but there is a path dependency in government growth so that any static theory of government size based on current conditions leaves out an important part of the story.

Both economic and political constraints can limit the size of government. Economic constraints represent an absolute limit to the amount of revenue the government can extract. Revenue-maximizing tax rates depicted by the Laffer curve represent an economic constraint. Political constraints can keep government smaller than this through constitutional limits and through political mechanisms, but as Peacock and Wiseman (1961), Buchanan and Wagner (1977), Olson (1982), Higgs (1987), Holcombe (2002), and others have suggested, once these political constraints are relaxed, it is difficult to reimplement them.

10. The Role of Ideas

The closest the public choice literature comes to discussing the role of ideas on the size and growth of government is in models that depict government size as a function of citizen preferences. But those preferences tend to be modeled as static in nature (e.g., Republicans versus Democrats) rather than being analyzed as a dynamic interaction of ideas and the scope of government. Keynes (1936, p. 383) famously said that "the ideas of economists and political philosophers, both when they are right and when they are wrong, are more powerful than is commonly understood. Indeed the world is ruled by little else." Perhaps the growth of government in the twentieth century was due partly to the ideas of Marx (1906), and others. But in the early twenty-first century the ideas of Friedman (1962) and Hayek (1944) appear to have more popular support than those of Marx, and their ideas have been popularized by politicians like Ronald Reagan and Margaret Thatcher.

Higgs (1987) attributes the growth of twentieth century government to a change in ideology around the beginning of that century. If ideas have as much influence as Keynes and Higgs suggest, the resurgence of interest in classical liberal ideas may point toward a retrenchment in the size of government in the twenty-first century. But according to most of the theories reviewed here, the appetite of Leviathan is not swayed by ideas, and narrow special interests appear to dominate the general public interest in the political process.

11. Government Growth and Public Choice Theory

Not surprisingly, the public choice literature on government growth has much in common with public choice scholarship more generally. Yet there are at least two facets of the literature on government growth that deviate somewhat from the median of the literature, and those two facets might shed additional light on other public choice issues. First, a significant part of the literature on government growth has focused on the coercive nature of government action, depicting government as a revenue-maximizing Leviathan restrained by various constitutional and electoral constraints. Following this line of reasoning, government's actions are not the result of agreement, which is what the term public choice appears to imply, but rather of coercion. Some people are able to use the coercive power of government to force others to comply. Second, a significant part of the literature has broken out of the comparative static methodology that characterizes much of economics and much of public choice to develop models of path dependency, where what happens in the present is not just a function of present conditions but is substantially influenced by historical developments. If these theories are descriptive of government growth, then they also must be descriptive of the political process underlying government growth. Thus, this literature on government growth suggests that public choice more generally could benefit from taking seriously the coercive nature of government and the path dependencies that may influence political action.

12. Looking Ahead

Some of the factors underlying government growth in the twentieth century have played themselves out, or even reversed. Income taxation, along with the institutional features that allow it to be collected – such as wage workers employed by corporations and withholding to extract taxes from those workers – helped government grow in the twentieth century, but those past changes will not cause government to continue to grow in the twenty-first century. With the end of the Cold War, and with advances in transportation and communication technology, the world economy promises to be more open in the twenty-first century than in the twentieth, and resource mobility takes away some of government's power to tax. Of course, new wars, including the "War on Terror", might intervene to restrict international resource mobility.

What about the huge unfunded liabilities – social security and health care entitlements – that regularly make the news in the early twenty-first century? If the size of government is determined by the amount of revenues government can extract from its citizens, then these programs will have to be restructured to fit within the government's budget constraint. That constraint may be loosened somewhat through the political process as the median voter ages, but it seems unlikely that transfer recipients will be able to extract enough from productive citizens to make good on all of government's current entitlement promises. Some citizens may be disappointed when they get less from government than they believe they were promised – but this would not be the first time that government disappointed someone.

The factors that propelled twentieth century government growth are unlikely to generate more growth in the twenty-first century, but government growth is difficult to reverse. Taking all factors into account, the best forecast for the twenty-first century may be for stabilized government, but not shrinking government. The era of big government will remain with us.

Notes

1. President Clinton declared in his 1995 State of the Union address that "The era of big government is over." He refined this idea further in a January 27, 1996 radio address, when he said, "The era of big government is over, but we can't go back to a time when our citizens were just left to fend for themselves."
2. For example, Barlow (1970), Borcherding and Deacon (1972), and Bergstrom and Goodman (1973) are three papers in top journals written around the time of the publication of Niskanen's (1971) book that used the median voter model to justify an assumption that the public sector produces what the median voter prefers.
3. As Buchanan and Lee (1982) explain, revenue-maximizing behavior by government may actually set taxes higher than the revenue-maximizing level in the long run.
4. For an interesting exchange on this topic, see Wittman (2002) and Niskanen (2002).
5. Even this rate was as high as it was in response to the crisis of the Great Depression. The highest marginal income tax rate was increased from 25% to 63% (for incomes above $1 million) in 1932, and then increased to 79% (for incomes above $5 million) in 1936.
6. These figures are from the US Census Bureau (US Department of Commerce, 1975, p. 1095).
7. This is discussed in more detail in Holcombe (2002, pp. 224–228).
8. For example, McChesney (1987, 1997) incorporates this element of compulsion into the rent-seeking literature to argue that rent-seeking is even more pernicious than previously recognized.
9. This was the famous thesis of Turner (1896).
10. These figures are taken from Table 3 of Holcombe and Lacombe (2001, p. 187), adjusted to 1990 prices.
11. This story would have been different if the US federal government had been able to levy property taxes, but political institutions prevented that, allowing the local governments' tax bases to grow more rapidly than the federal government's.
12. Niskanen (1975) has himself backed away from the pure budget-maximization hypothesis that serves as the foundation of his 1971 book.

References

Barlow, R. (1970). Efficiency aspects of local school finance. *Journal of Political Economy*, *78*(5), 1028–1040.

Baumol, W. J. (1967). Macroeconomics of unbalanced growth: The anatomy of urban crisis. *American Economic Review*, *57*(3), 415–426.

Becker, G. S. (1983). A theory of competition among pressure groups for political influence. *Quarterly Journal of Economics*, *98*(3), 371–400.

Becker, G. S., & Mulligan, C. B. (2003). Deadweight costs and the size of government. *Journal of Law and Economics*, *46*(2), 293–340.

Bergstrom, T. C., & Goodman, R. (1973). Private demand for public goods. *American Economic Review*, *63*(3), 280–296.

Borcherding, T. E. (Ed.). (1977). *Budgets and Bureaucrats: The Sources of Government Growth.* Duke University Press: Durham, NC.

Borcherding, T. E., & Deacon, R. T. (1972). The demand for services of non-federal governments. *American Economic Review*, *62*(5), 891–901.

Brennan, G., & Buchanan, J. M. (1980). *The Power to Tax: Analytical Foundations of a Fiscal Constitution.* Cambridge University Press: Cambridge.

Brennan, G., & Lomasky, L. (1993). *Democracy and Decision: The Pure Theory of Electoral Preference.* Cambridge University Press: Cambridge.

Buchanan, J. M., & Lee, D. R. (1982). Politics, time, and the laffer curve. *Journal of Political Economy*, *90*(4), 816–819.

Buchanan, J. M., & Wagner, R. E. (1977). *Democracy in Deficit: The Political Legacy of Lord Keynes*. Academic Press: New York.

Bueno de Mesquita, B., Smith, A., Siverson, R. M., & Morrow, J. D. (2003). *The Logic of Political Survival.* MIT Press: Cambridge, MA.

Caplan, B. (2001). Rational irrationality and the microfoundations of political failure. *Public Choice*, *107*(3–4), 311–331.

Caplan, B. (2003). The logic of collective belief. *Rationality and Society*, *15*(2), 218–242.

Diamond, P. A., & Mirrlees, J. A. (1971). Optimal taxation and public production: I and II. *American Economic Review*, *81*(March), 8–27, (June), 261–278.

Downs, A. (1960). Why the government budget is too small in a democracy. *World Politics*, *12*(4), 541–564.

Edelman, M. (1964). *The Symbolic Uses of Politics.* University of Illinois Press: Urbana.

Friedman, D. (1977). A theory of the size and shape of nations. *Journal of Political Economy*, *85*(1), 59–77.

Friedman, M. (1962). *Capitalism and Fredom.* University of Chicago Press: Chicago.

Gastil, R. D. (1978). *Freedom in the World: Political Rights and Civil Liberties, 1978.* Freedom House: New York.

Gwartney, J., & Lawson, R. (2003). *Economic Freedom of the World, 2003 Annual Report.* Fraser Institute: Vancouver, B.C.

Hayek, F. A. (1944). *The Road to Serfdom.* University of Chicago Press: Chicago.

Higgs, R. (1987). *Crisis and Leviathan: Critical Episodes in the Growth of American Government.* Oxford University Press: Oxford and New York.

Higgs, R. (1991). Eighteen problematic propositions in the analysis of the growth of government. *Review of Austrian Economics*, *5*(1), 3–40.

Holcombe, R. G. (1989). The median voter model in public choice theory. *Public Choice*, *61*(2), 115–125.

Holcombe, R. G. (1993). Are there ratchets in the growth of federal government spending? *Public Finance Quarterly*, *21*(1), 33–47.

Holcombe, R. G. (1994). *The Economic Foundations of Government.* New York University Press: New York.

Holcombe, R. G. (1996). The growth of the federal government in the 1920s. *Cato Journal, 16*(2), 175–199.

Holcombe, R. G. (2002). *From Liberty to Democracy: The Transformation of American Government.* University of Michigan Press: Ann Arbor.

Holcombe, R. G., & Lacombe, D. J. (2001). The growth of local government in the united states from 1820 to 1870. *Journal of Economic History, 61*(1), 184–189.

Holcombe, R. G., & Lacombe, D. J. (2004). Factors underlying the growth of local government in the 19th century united states. *Public Choice, 120*(3–4), 359–377.

Holcombe, R. G., & Mills, J. A. (1995). Politics and deficit finance. *Public Finance Quarterly, 23*(4), 448–466.

Kahneman, D. (2003). Maps of bounded rationality: Psychology for behavioral economics. *American Economic Review, 93*(5), 1449–1475.

Kahneman, D., Knetsch, J. L., & Thaler, R. H. (1991). Anomalies: The endowment effect, loss aversion, and status quo bias. *Journal of Economic Perspectives, 5*(1), 193–206.

Kau, J. B., & Rubin, P. H. (1981). The size of government. *Public Choice, 37*(2), 261–274.

Keynes, J. M. (1936). *The General Theory of Employment, Interest, and Money.* Harcourt, Brace & Company: New York.

Levi, M. (1988). *Of Rule and Revenue.* University of California Press: Berkeley.

Lott, J. R., Jr., & Kenny, L. W. (1999). Did women's suffrage change the size and scope of government? *Journal of Political Economy, 107*(6, part 1), 1163–1198.

Marx, K. (1906). *Capital.* Charles H. Kerr & Company: Chicago.

McChesney, F. S. (1987). Rent seeking and rent creation in the economic theory of regulation. *Journal of Legal Studies, 16*(1), 101–118.

McChesney, F. S. (1997). *Money for Nothing: Politicians, Rent Extraction, and Political Extortion.* Harvard University Press: Cambridge, MA.

Meltzer, A. H., & Richard, S. F. (1981). A rational theory of the size of government. *Journal of Political Economy, 89*(5), 914–927.

Mirrlees, J. A. (1971). An exploration in the theory of optimum income taxation. *Review of Economic Studies, 38*(2), 175–208.

Mueller, D. C. (2002). Interest groups, redistribution and the size of government. In Winer S. L. & Shibata H. (Eds.), *Political Economy and Public Finance: The Role of Political Economy in the Theory and Practice of Public Economics* (pp. 123–144). Edward Elgar: Cheltenham, UK and Northampton, MA, USA.

Niskanen, W. A. (1971). *Bureaucracy and Representative Government.* Aldine-Atherton: Chicago.

Niskanen, W. A. (1975). Bureaucrats and politicians. *Journal of Law and Economics, 18*(2), 617–643.

Niskanen, W. A. (2002). On the origin and identification of government failures. In Winer S. L. & Shibata H. (Eds.), *Political Economy and Public Finance: The Role of Political Economy in the Theory and Practice of Public Economics* (pp. 111–116). Edward Elgar: Cheltenham, UK and Northampton, MA, USA.

Olson, M., Jr. (1982). *The Rise and Decline of Nations.* Yale University Press: New Haven, CT.

Peacock, A. T., & Wiseman, J. (1961). *The Growth of Government Expenditures in the United Kingdom.* Princeton University Press: Princeton, NJ.

Peltzman, S. (1980). The growth of government. *Journal of Law and Economics, 23*(2), 209–287.

Persson, T., & Tabellini, G. (1999). The size and scope of government: Comparative politics with rational politicians. *European Economic Review, 43*(4–6), 699–735.

Persson, T., & Tabellini, G. (2003). *Economic Effects of Constitutions*. MIT Press: Cambridge, MA.

Posner, R. A. (1971). Taxation by regulation. *Bell Journal of Economics and Management Science*, *2*(1), 22–50.

Rassler, K. A., & Thompson, W. R. (1985). War making and state making: Government expenditures, tax revenues, and global wars. *American Political Science Review*, *79*(2), 491–507.

Romer, T., & Rosenthal, H. (1978). Political resource allocation, controlled agendas, and the status quo. *Public Choice*, *33*(4), 27–43.

Tullock, G. (1965). Entry barriers in politics. *American Economic Review*, *55*(2), 458–466.

Tullock, G. (1982). Why so much stability? *Public Choice*, *37*(2), 189–202.

Turner, F. J. (1896). The problem of the west. *Atlantic Monthly*, *78*(September), 289–297.

US Department of Commerce, Bureau of the Census. (1975). *Historical Statistics of the United States from Colonial Times to 1970*. Bureau of the Census: Washington, DC.

Usher, D. (1992). *The Welfare Economics of Markets, Voting, and Predation*. University of Michigan Press: Ann Arbor.

Wittman, D. A. (1989). Why democracies produce efficient results. *Journal of Political Economy*, *97*(6), 1395–1424.

Wittman, D. A. (1995). *The Myth of Democratic Failure*. University of Chicago Press: Chicago.

Wittman, D. A. (2002). Normative public finance without guilt: Why normative public finance is positive public finance. In Winer S. L. & Shibata H. (Eds.), *Political Economy and Public Finance: The Role of Political Economy in the Theory and Practice of Public Economics* (pp. 101–110). Edward Elgar: Cheltenham, UK and Northampton, MA, USA.

Yeager, L. B. (2001). *Ethics as a Social Science*. Edward Elgar: Cheltenham, UK and Northampton, MA, USA.

Public Choice (2005) **124:** 115–133
DOI: 10.1007/s11127-005-4749-9

Nineteenth-century voting procedures in a twenty-first century world

MICHAEL C. MUNGER
Departments of Political Science and Economics, Duke University, Durham, NC 27708, USA

Accepted March 2005

Abstract. Voting procedures nowadays are anachronistic on two counts: the technology of recording and counting votes often is outmoded and too much is expected from the mechanisms of democratic choice. Even if votes always and everywhere were counted perfectly, election outcomes would still be arbitrary since *no* collective choice process can divine the "general will". The crucial line in any state is the one dividing private decisions from collective decisions. Democracy is part of the package for nations freeing themselves from totalitarianism's grip, but it may be the last, rather than the first thing that should be added to the mix.

> It [is impossible] to separate the democratic idea from the theory that there is a mystical merit, an esoteric and ineradicable rectitude, in the man at the bottom of the scale – that inferiority, by some strange magic, becomes superiority – nay, the superiority of superiorities. What baffles statesmen is to be solved by the people, instantly and by a sort of seraphic intuition. This notion ... originated in the poetic fancy of gentlemen on the upper levels – sentimentalists who, observing to their distress that the ass was overladen, proposed to reform transportation by putting him in the cart. (Mencken [1926], 1982, p. 154.)

1. Introduction

What many people appear to mean by "democracy" is some combination of good government, protection of individual rights, extremely broad political participation, and widely shared economic prosperity. One might as well throw in ideal body mass index and a cure for influenza. It's all good, but meaningless. Democracy has no useful definition.

There is a definition people sometimes pretend to believe, though they back off quickly if you press them. It is much narrower, and goes like this: *If a group is constituted to decide as one, then any numerical majority of that group can make decisions. These decisions can be binding on all (majority rules the totality), or binding just on some class or group specified in decision itself (majority rules the minority).* While I have already said that this (or any other) definition is not really useful, this version seems to be the one that many people accept, or act like they accept.

The problem with the narrower definition is that no one could really believe it, at least not in isolation from lots of other assumptions. One is left to wonder whether democracy, in the sense of rule by the people, is a conceit or a fraud. As a conceit, it may be harmless enough. It may even be useful, because it celebrates the wisdom and good will of the common person. This sort of mythology has a calming, leveling effect on public discourse.

If a fraud, however, then we are in darker and more forbidding terrain. The pretense that we find rectitude in the multitude is dangerous. The public invocation of the public wisdom simply holds citizens down whilst we steal their purses, or send their children off to war.

There are two linked ideas about democracy, and it is important to keep them separate. The first is the *existence* of a good, of a right (best) thing for the society to do. This is a question that has both normative and positive elements. It may seem strange to question the existence of "the good" in politics, but in fact it is simply not obvious that a society can discover transcendent principles of the good through voting. This question is beyond my charter in this paper, though I will refer to it when necessary.

The second aspect of the democratic idea is the problem of choosing rules or institutions most likely to lead to the discovery of the good (assuming it exists). There are two very different approaches to the problem. The positive, ends-based approach emphasizes the properties of the voting or preference revelation techniques as if they were estimators. One can then apply quasi-statistical techniques, much as if an estimator were being subjected to Monte Carlo testing. That is, given a configuration of preferences in which some "good" alternative is embedded by construction, what are the relative frequencies with which different techniques discover it?

The other approach, normative and process-based, focuses on the fairness or legitimacy of rules themselves, as *means*. There is an obvious assumption in this approach, one that has led two generations of public choice scholars (see, for example, Riker, 1982) to question it, but it persists nonetheless. That assumption is that "fair" processes necessarily lead to "good" outcomes.

In this paper, I will balance the limited application of republican elections in the nineteenth century as a means of exerting control over elected officials against the expansive modern faith in, and practice of, democratic governance. My argument will be that rules, procedures, and the basic "machinery" of democratic choice have not kept up with the faith people seem to have in the wisdom of the majority. To some extent, this is the fault of officials in the states, who have failed to give enough thought to problems involved in implementing new paperless voting technologies. But the other problem, at least as important, is that the academic establishment in the United States has done a poor job making students understand the limitations and dangers of unlimited democratic choice. For both reasons, the mismatch between what we demand of democratic institutions and what they can reasonably deliver endangers the stability of our system of government.

While this danger may be most significant in the United States, I also describe briefly the consequences of the secular trend toward reliance on "democracy" as a means of reconciling disagreement in other nations. What social choice theory teaches us is that we cannot expect institutions to produce consensus in the face of disagreement, unless (a) certain arguments or positions are outlawed, or (b) choice is left up to a single individual, or dictator. People seem to believe in the value of consensus, but they do not appear to believe in either domain restrictions or dictatorship. The problem policymakers must face is that the failure of voting institutions to produce consensus is really two separate problems: we must bring voting technology into the 21th century, because we have come to accept much less than is possible. But we must also take voting ideology back to the 19th century, because we have come to expect much more than is possible.

2. I Want, You Want: What do *We* Want?

> Democracy is precisely the constitution out of which tyranny comes; from extreme liberty, it seems, comes a slavery most complete and most cruel. . . . When a democratic city gets worthless butlers presiding over its wine, and has drunk too deeply of liberty's heady draught, then, I think, if the rulers are not very obliging and won't provide plenty of liberty, it calls them blackguards and oligarchs and chastises them. . . . [A]nd any who obey the rulers they trample in the dust as willing slaves and not worth a jot. (Plato, *The Republic*, Book VIII, pp. 560A–564B)

2.1. *Domains and rules*

Collective choice has two aspects: (1) the proper *domain*, and (2) the proper *choice rules*. While this distinction has been made by a number of public choice scholars (see, for example, Holcombe, 1994, 2002; Munger, 2000 and the work they review), the clearest and sharpest distinction may be found in Buchanan and Congleton's *Politics by Principle, Not Interest* (1998).

Buchanan and Congleton claim that the basis of democratic governance is gains from exchange, with participation in the state benefiting each citizen. But then, they point out:

> In this conception of the political enterprise, there can be no normatively grounded limits on what can be done. Ultimate legitimization may be sought in some alleged correspondence between what is done and the "will of the people" generally, as was claimed by some Communist regimes, or

> in some democracy, which has come to be equated with majority electoral-decision processes in non-Communist settings. In the latter view, so long as political actions are determined by majoritarian coalitions, there are no grounds for complaint or concern on behalf of those persons or groups that may be differentially exploited. *There is, indeed, no constitutionally protected sphere of activity into which politics cannot potentially enter. In essence, majoritarian agreement is the ultimate source of value.* All and everything else is politicizable. (p. 19; emphasis added)

The problem is to decide over what activities it is legitimate for the state to exert collective control.

2.2. *Public decisions and collective decisions*

Many policy conflicts hinge on whether the public can tell individuals what to do. There is a subtlety that is often missed in policy debate: there is a difference between *public* decisions and *collective* decisions. As P.J. O'Rourke notes, the fact that a majority likes something doesn't mean that the majority should get to choose that something for everyone.

> Now, majority rule is a precious, sacred thing worth dying for. But – like other precious, sacred things, such as the home and the family – it's not only worth dying for; it can make you wish you were dead. Imagine if all of life were determined by majority rule. Every meal would be a pizza. Every pair of pants, even those in a Brooks Brothers suit, would be stone-washed denim. Celebrity diets and exercise books would be the only thing on the shelves at the library. And – since women are a majority of the population, we'd all be married to Mel Gibson. (O'Rourke, 1991, p. 5)

So, the starting point is to divide those things we decide collectively from those things we decide privately. The easiest way to appreciate this distinction is to consider Table 1. There

- public decisions are defined as those where my choices affect your welfare;
- private decisions are then choices that affect only my welfare.

This "affect welfare" standard may be subjective, of course. It may "affect my welfare" that you wear an ugly (in my opinion) tie, or use racial epithets, or enjoy pornographic films and books. In the extreme, "you have offended me" could be an almost universal excuse for forcing my will on others. Alternatively, the idea of "private" actions is hard to define, or sustain. One might argue that marriage is a private act. Yet the idea that gay men or lesbians may want to marry is an important political issue, because at present that right is

Table 1. Collective decisions and public decisions

	Individual Decision: I can choose, alone and without interference	Collective Decision: Choices are made by a group, and are binding on all
Private Decision: My choice has no consequence for your welfare	Liberty of the individual: • What socks should I wear? • Whom should I marry?	Tyranny of the majority: • Invasion of privacy • Theft of property rights
Public Decision: My choices affect your welfare	Underinvestment, or else theft by the minority: • Air or water pollution • Education	Liberty of the group • How much to spend on defense? • How to take care of the poor?

not established. In some ways, "public" decisions are just those that other people care a lot about, which is simply subjective. It is tempting to define "public" decisions as those that have objective nonzero externalities, but in fact it is difficult to restrict the political process this way.

On the other hand, the difference between individual and collective decisions (the columns of Table 1) can be defined in practical, measurable terms, as a question of the power to choose. This is the distinction that matters: can the state, either in its manifestation of the "will of the people" or the legislature that that "will" has selected, make choices enforceable on individuals?

As can be seen, there is a difference between the public-private activities, and individual-collective conceptions of choice. Certainly, many of the decisions a society faces fall along the main diagonal (top left and bottom right boxes) in Table 1: individuals make private decisions, and public decisions are made collectively. But that is not always true. There is *nothing* about the machinery of democracy that prevents private decisions from being made collectively. This result is usually identified as "tyranny of the majority" over an individual or smaller group.

Conversely, individuals may make public decisions: I may choose to pollute the air or the water, or I may undertake activities that affect others positively (such as seeking an education) without being able to capture the full gains from the activity. The final point worth noting about Table 1 is the fact that it identifies the path of rhetorical political strategy. In most cases, the default "policy" is the top left box: individual decisions made on private matters. The rhetoric of the debate will focus on the question of whether the problem is really more appropriately in the bottom right box: public decisions, collectively reached. So the crux of the debate is whether the decision should be made *collectively*, but the words of the debate will be a contest over whether the decision is *public*.

3. 19th Century Voting Procedures, 21st Century Technology

> The highest function of the citizen is to serve the state – but the first assumption that meets him, when he essays to discharge it, is an assumption of his disingenuousness and dishonor. Is that assumption commonly sound? Then the farce only grows more glorious. ... Is [democracy] extraordinarily wasteful, extravagant, dishonest? Then so is every other form of government: all alike are enemies to decent men. ... In the long run, it may turn out that rascality is an ineradicable necessity to human government, and even to civilization itself – that civilization, at bottom, is nothing but a colossal swindle. I do not know. I report only that when the suckers are running well the spectacle is infinitely exhilarating. But I am, it may be, a somewhat malicious man: my sympathies, when it comes to suckers, tend to be coy. What I can't make out is how any man can believe in democracy who feels for and with [common citizens], and is pained when they are debauched and made a show of. How can any man be a democrat who is sincerely a democrat? (Mencken [1926], 1982, pp. 167–168)

3.1. *Policy change – Preferences, or rules?*

Voting procedures, and technology, have been nearly immune to technological change in the United States. Some of the procedures for counting votes have been modified, for reasons of cost and "fairness". The technology of the counting machines used in Florida, and other US states, in 2000, is directly adapted from the IBM card reader machines of the 1960s and 1970s.

There is a certain appeal to this kind of "fair but arbitrary" rule for counting. If the machine (presumably nonpartisan, because inert[1]) can read a card as having a single, legal vote for one candidate in a race, then that vote counts. If for any other reason the card is not read as a legal vote, it can be sent through the reader again. If there is still no legal vote the machine can discern, then the ballot is pronounced spoiled.

Or, is it? In Florida in 2000 we were treated to the spectacle of unidentified state officials peering at cards, holding them up to the light. They were trying to divine the voter's "intent", by looking intently at the cards. This seemed to violate the whole point of the counting machines. Of course, time ran out and the Supreme Court cut off the whole process before it reached whatever end would have awaited it.

It is hard to know what the outcome would have been if the Supreme Court had not intervened. The most likely result is a victory for George W. Bush, in the House of Representatives (voting by state delegations). The sense that the election was "stolen" arises from the perception that the form of the ballot itself, and the counting procedure, influenced the outcome.

When most people consider the fairness of the voting procedure, however, they refer to the mechanism used to record and aggregate votes, not the techniques used to (re)count them. The distinction is perhaps not as sharp as I have tried to draw it. After all, the way we count ballots in a literal sense is always going to be related to the way that we take account of preferences in a more general sense. Voting procedures of any kind must somehow reconcile the fact that people want different things, but that a polity can only "want" one thing.

More simply, as is so often the case in public choice problems, the *way* we decide often affects *what* we decide. Plott (1991) succinctly summarized the problem, in his "fundamental equation of politics":

$$\text{Preferences} \times \text{Institutions} = \text{Outcomes}.$$

We might think of "preferences" as what individual voters want. "Institutions" are the rules and practices (be they systems such as majority rule, or particular conventions such as paper ballots or electronic touch-screen voting) through which collective preferences are registered. Plott's equation demonstrates that there are two very different sources of potential change in policy outcomes: change in what individuals want, and change in the rules for deciding.

- If *preferences change*, outcomes can change, even if *institutions remain constant.*
- If *institutions change*, outcomes can change, even if *preferences remain constant.*

The problem many had with the US election in 2000 was that the choice seemed arbitrary, because the counting procedure determined the outcome. But for the public choice scholar this is simply a new manifestation of the generic problem of arbitrary dependence of outcome on institution of choice, even holding preferences fixed. In fact, as Cox (1997, p. 70) argued, even small changes in some portions of ballot access or other institutional features of elections can change the effective competitiveness of such contests dramatically.

For those who are opposed to the policies of George Bush, one might wish for "President Gore". After all, if the Florida voting system had used electronic voting instead of paper "butterfly" ballots, it is entirely possible (though not obvious) that the outcome would have been different.[2] This seems arbitrary, and contrary to the logic of democracy as a means of discovering truth.

But the arbitrariness of the outcome is much more troublesome for people who *otherwise* believe in the moral force of majority rule. The *public choice* view, by contrast, is by and large that *all selection procedures will have an element of arbitrariness*. In this view, the majority preference is simply what most people happen to think. It has no moral force, other than as a means of resolving disputes. (For an elaboration of this view, founded in a theory of choice of constitutions and decision rules, see Buchanan & Tullock, 1962. For a review of the literature more broadly, see Mueller, 2003).

3.2. *The basis for obeying – The dictatorship of the median*

The principle that the median preference wins in majority rule elections was formalized by Duncan (1958):

> **Median Voter Theorem**: If *the issue space is a single-ordered dimension, and preferences are single-peaked, a median position cannot lose to any other alternative in a majority rule election.*

The MVT implies that the middle of the distribution of citizen preferences in a society holds a privileged position in political competition. Early in the development of the public choice literature, some attention was given to the moral force of the median in one or several dimensions (or the mean if the distribution of voters is continuous; see Davis & Hinich, 1968; Davis, DeGroot, & Hinich, 1972).

If preferences aren't single peaked, of course, then there can be cycles. The public choice literature uses the famous "Condorcet's Paradox" as a way of illustrating this problem.

> **Condorcet's Paradox**: Suppose all individual preferences are transitive, but not necessarily single-peaked. Then the social preference ordering under majority rule may be intransitive.

The "paradox" is that the aggregation of *individually* transitive preferences leads to an *aggregate* intransitivity.[3] Society finds itself in an endless cycle of "best" alternatives, none of which commands a majority against all other alternatives.

The problem of cycling is not widely understood, outside of the public choice literature. In particular, the "single-peaked" assumption is more restrictive than it seems. All that is really required is three choosers, three choices, and disagreement.

Consider an example. Suppose that the only three foods in the world were apples, broccoli and carrots. Each type of food is sold only in large crates. Consider three people who, if they cooperate, will have *just enough* money to buy one, but only one, crate of food. The preference profiles of the three people, Mr. 1 (who loves apples), Ms. 2 (who loves carrots) and Mr. 3 (who loves broccoli), are listed in Table 2.

Table 2. Preference "lists" of three voters over apples, broccoli, and carrots

	Person:		
Ranking:	Mr. 1	Ms. 2	Mr. 3
Best	Apples	Carrots	Broccoli
Middle	Broccoli	Apples	Carrots
Worst	Carrots	Broccoli	Apples

The premise of the example is that choice is *collective*: if they cannot agree on a food, all will go hungry, because no one has enough money to buy a crate alone. But the three people disagree about what to buy. So they decide to vote.

The problem is that the preferences profiled in Table 2 do not admit of a Condorcet winner. By majority rule, apples are preferred to broccoli is preferred to carrots are preferred to apples, always by 2 to 1 margins. There is no unique choice that is defensibly the "general will" of this group. The general will does not exist, or more accurately it cannot be discovered by any procedure that relies on decentralized "counting" of preferences, such as voting.

And, as is well known, Condorcet's paradox is no more than a simple example of a general class of paradoxes that all point toward two central conclusions: (1) The outcomes of *any* social choice mechanism will be either arbitrary or imposed. (2) The information voters give as inputs to social choice processes are not reliable, because all such rules are manipulable. Many political scientists have concluded that there is no sure way of making an ethically defensible collective choice, if a part of the definition of "ethically defensible" is that all citizens' preferences count. (A complete discussion of these paradoxes, or "impossibility theorems", is beyond my scope here; the interested reader should consult Mueller, 2003).

I have argued in this section that there is a difficulty with using majority rule outcomes as normative prescriptions. In the language I used earlier in this paper, there is little basis for claiming that the majority can choose for all, or that the majority can choose for the minority. Those who defend majority rule or "democracy" need some other basis for claiming moral legitimacy goes with majority will. There are two possibilities: forbearance and constitutional domain restriction.

Forbearance relies on the majority holding itself back from abusive or repressive policies. "To be governed by appetite alone is slavery, while obedience to a law one prescribes to oneself is freedom" (Rousseau, 1988, Book I, chapter 8). If the majority does not act on "appetites", but rather enacts only good laws, *the same policy would be chosen* by one person, by a group, or by the whole society, provided the choosers are wise, well informed, and well intentioned. Such an approach begs the question of collective choice by assuming the problem away: the collective is organic, not composed of many individuals with potentially different ideas.

Constitutional domain restrictions, on the other hand, put certain policies beyond the reach of the majority, or in fact beyond any collectively based regulation or interference. The difficulty with this approach is that it requires the consent of the majority in the first place: all must agree to accept the set of limits inherent in domain restrictions, such as the US Bill of Rights. But even after such constitutional restrictions are put in place, the majority must accept these limits as legitimate, and (once again) forebear changing or ignoring the rules, even though it would be in the majority's interest.

The problem, then, with both approaches (simple forbearance or constitutional domain restriction) is that the nation must hold distrust of majority rule as one of its core values. If citizens, parties and interest groups come to see democratic processes as a means to obtain and hold power, the separate norm of forbearance breaks down, and nothing can hold back the majority's tyranny. In this circumstance, majority rule is simply two wolves and one sheep deciding what to have for dinner.[4]

3.3. *An example: The Electoral College*

The system for choosing presidents and vice presidents in the United States is widely derided, but not widely understood. The Electoral College was a triumph of institutional design, at least in terms of the problems that it was intended to solve in the 1780s. It is important to recognize that the US chief executive was to be chosen from among 13 geographically distinct states of varying sizes. There were no communication networks, or even transportation systems, that could have allowed anything like modern political campaigns.

Perhaps even more important, it was believed that campaigns themselves were unseemly, and political parties were downright reprehensible. Madison's concern in Federalist No. 10 had been with the evils of "faction", but one might have substituted "party" and done little damage to Madison's central point. The system the framers of the US Constitution came up with was a compromise, an attempt to steer between the Scylla of popular opinion and the Charybdis of organized interests in the state legislatures or in the federal Congress. The idea of a separate "College of Electors", chosen in the states, by the citizens, but with each state controlling the means and process of selection of their own Electors, was finally settled upon by a committee of the Constitutional Convention, and accepted by the entire Convention in the final draft.[5]

It is useful to recall, however, why the idea of a pure democracy was a non-starter for the founders of the American republic. Consider this description, from *Federalist* No. 10:

> . . . a pure democracy, by which I mean a society consisting of a small number of citizens, who assemble and administer the government in person, can admit of no cure for the mischiefs of faction. A common passion or interest will, in almost every case, be felt by a majority of the whole; a communication and concert result from the form of government itself; and there is nothing to check the inducements to sacrifice the weaker party or an obnoxious individual. Hence it is that such democracies have ever been spectacles of turbulence and contention; have ever been found incompatible with personal security or the rights of property; and have in general been as short in their lives as they have been violent in their deaths. Theoretic politicians, who have patronized this species of government, have erroneously supposed that by reducing mankind to a perfect equality in their political rights, they would, at the same time, be perfectly equalized and assimilated in their possessions, their opinions, and their passions. (Madison, 1787, p. 5)

If the system by which the United States chooses presidents is not democratic, that is no accident. But is it workable? The Electoral College seems cumbersome, but in fact it has just three essential features. These features are (i) indirectness, (ii) overrepresentation of small states, and (iii) winner-takes-all selection of state Electors. It is useful to consider each of these separately.

3.3.1. *Indirectness*

The Electoral College is indirect in the sense that citizens of states don't really vote for one of the tickets that have been campaigning during the months leading up to Election Day. Instead, each vote goes toward electing an Elector, or a person selected by the state party apparatus to represent the party in the Electoral College in the event that the party wins the vote. Importantly, the vote is *truly* indirect; it is perfectly possible for electors, who are already in most cases *faceless* (because their identities are secret), also to be *faithless*, voting for a different candidate from that party, or even for a candidate from another party. This is a fundamentally republican (note the small "r") feature of the Electoral College, in the sense that citizens are selecting electors who will represent their interests, not choosing presidential candidates directly.

Most ballots now obscure the fact that votes are for electors, not candidates, but this was not always the case. For a century (or longer in some states) after the 12th Amendment in 1804 modified the Electoral College to its current format, the actual names of electors were listed on ballots. This led to some strange results. In addition to the problem of faithless electors, some states formally split their Electoral College delegations, most recently in West Virginia in 1916, which elected seven Republican electors and one Democrat (Kimberling, n.d., p. 6).

3.3.2. *Overrepresentation*

Each citizen in a "small" state casts a vote that counts more than a citizen in a large state. The reason is that power in the Electoral College is apportioned according to an affine transformation of population. Roughly speaking, the equation for determining a state's Electoral College votes is

$$\text{Electoral College Votes} = 2 + \text{Integer}(\text{State Population}/600,000) \quad (1)$$

Of course, the relationship in (1) is only approximate. Consider the two states of Wyoming and California as an extreme example. Wyoming has a population of about 500,000, and so gets 2 + Integer(500,000/600,000) = 3 Electoral College votes. (The "integer" operator generally rounds up; it always does so for a state's first US Representative, since all states get at least one, regardless of the state's population.) California has a population of 35.5 million, and if Equation (1) were perfectly accurate would have an Electoral College allocation of about 60 votes. But because so many other states are smaller than the 600,000 quota determined by House membership, the relationship is only approximate: California's actual Electoral College allocation is 55 votes.

What this means, of course, is that the ratio of California to Wyoming Electoral College votes is 55/3 = 18.33. But the California-Wyoming population ratio is 35.5/0.5 = 71. But then the conclusion is inescapable: each vote cast in Wyoming "counts" nearly 4 times as much (71/18.33 = 3.88) as any one vote in California. True, California is still the great prize of the Electoral College, representing 10% of the total electoral vote for the presidency. But California counts much less under the Electoral College than it would under a pure "one person, one vote" scheme.[6]

3.3.3. *Winner takes all*

The key feature of the Electoral College, in terms of most current efforts at reform, is its winner-takes-all aspect. The reason that Florida was so important in 2000 was that all 25 of the state's electoral votes hinged on the few hundred ballots whose "chads" were in question. If Florida's electoral vote were proportional, instead of winner takes all, the split would have been 12 for Bush, 12 for Gore, and one electoral vote in contest. But it would not have mattered much, because Gore would have had 278 electoral votes overall, and Bush would have had 258 votes. The awarding of the last remaining Florida Electoral College vote would have been of no consequence, as 12 of the 25 Florida votes would have put Gore over the required 270 electoral vote majority.

The impact, and value, of the winner-takes-all provision is hard to analyze. On one hand, in close races (such as Florida in 2000, or Ohio, Pennsylvania, or New Mexico in 2004), the value of each vote is magnified, possibly spurring higher turnout. On the other hand, in electorally "secure" states such as Texas,

North Carolina, California, Massachusetts, or New York, there is little question what the outcome will be, and so turnout may be attenuated.

There have been a variety of attempts to change the winner-takes-all provision recently. This may be because this is the only aspect of the Electoral College system that requires no constitutional changes at the federal level. Since states are fully in charge of how they choose electors, they can also decide if they want to diverge from the winner-takes-all norm. California has recently considered legislation that would implement a proportional system; Colorado recently rejected a proposed state constitutional amendment (Amendment #36), which would have made that state's Electoral Vote allocation proportional; and several other states have decided to study the issue.

Maine and Nebraska have already moved to a proportional system of a sort, awarding the two electoral votes associated with their US Senate delegations "at large", and then dividing the remaining Electoral College votes according to which presidential candidate wins the popular vote in each congressional district. This latter approach is, frankly, a terrible idea. Congressional districts are so gerrymandered in the United States that House races in well over 90% of these districts are not competitive.

It seems probable that the larger movement, to go to a proportional system rather than a congressional district system, will also soon fizzle out. The author was on a radio show recently with the Governor of Colorado, William Owens, who compared this proposal (in his case, the then-pending Amendment #36) to "unilateral disarmament".

Consider an example to see why this is so. In California, the vote totals are always in the 55–44%, or 53–45%, range. If California went to a proportional system, that would mean that, in a typical election, 30 Electoral College votes would go to the winning presidential candidate and 25 votes would go to the loser. But this is an election, so only net votes matter. What that means is that California transforms itself from the 800-pound gorilla of the Electoral College, with 55 votes, to a five-net-vote (30–25) weakling.

A different proposal would be to change the allocation of Electoral College votes for entire nation, but that would require a constitutional amendment. And the net effects are hard to estimate, either for voter participation or for the perceived legitimacy of elections. On the plus side, it would be practically impossible for the popular vote and the Electoral College vote to differ. On the downside, it would be possible to win the election with large majorities in just a few large states, since both candidates would pick up at least some votes from every states, rather than being shut out.

The point is this: for all its flaws, and complexities, the Electoral College withstands scrutiny remarkably well. Its amended form, dating from the 19th century, answers a number of needs of the 21st century far better than any alternative system that has been proposed. The reason is that the Electoral College is explicitly designed to require a winning candidate to appeal to large geographic areas, rather than just to voters in the population centers on the coasts. The criticisms of the institutions of the Electoral College, based on an assumption that there is a mystical "will of the people" that can be divined through elections, are misguided. There is no better system for controlling political excesses, and forcing presidential candidates to represent the entire nation, than that created out of the original wisdom and compromises of the early 19th century.

4. *Chancengleichheit* and Process

The German word *chancengleichheit* means something like "equality of opportunities".[7] Any argument for the moral force of the majority's view must rest on an extreme form of *chancengleichheit.* Suppose that the society has come to agreement on the domain of public choice, so that the only things decided collectively are those questions that are public, and even then the range of alternatives is circumscribed by constitutional or other super-legal means.[8]

Our 19th century institutions at one time ensured *chancengleichheit*, but now are an important means by which equality of opportunity can be restricted. The most central of these is the political party. Parties *were* the means by which the collective action problem, and the collective choice problem, could be simultaneously and credibly overcome (Aldrich, 1995). People whose sense of ambition led them to careers in politics could use parties to achieve those ambitions. Voters who wanted a brand name that allowed a partial solution to the cheap talk, or "lemons", problem (Akerlof, 1970; Hinich & Munger, 1994, chapter 4) again looked to parties as the answer.

But the advent of mass media campaigning, and particularly television ads, created very large barriers to entry. The economies of scale that had always characterized a national party organization were now nearly insurmountable. No candidate could possibly run "on his own", for the presidency or even for a senatorial or gubernatorial seat, because the amount of money required to run a campaign was enormous.

Not surprisingly, rent-seeking officials in the two major parties saw in these natural entry barriers an opportunity to use government power to cartelize politics even further. Over the last century, a series of ballot access restrictions (Winger, 1994) have reified and institutionalized the major US parties, magnifying the effects of the technical economies of scale. As Rosenstone, Behr and Lazarus (1986, p. 16) point out:

> The rules that govern elections in the United States are far from neutral. They form barriers that block the emergence and discourage the growth

of more than two parties. These biases help ensure that the Democrats and Republicans retain their position of dominance. The founding fathers created some of these barriers; the two major parties have helped erect others.

One could argue, of course, that "third" parties are not really important actors in the modern political process. But their "popular" planks are quickly adopted by the major parties (Stone & Rapaport, 2001). And as many as half of all voters vote strategically, casting their votes for one of the two major parties, even though their honest first choice is one offered by the "third" parties (Abramson et al., 1995; Herrnson & Green, 2003).[9] The combination of rising economies of scale in advertising and brand name creation over the television era has fortified the existing institutional barriers, insulating the parties from competition from new entrants. The problem is that, because of the institutionalization of the parties and the political system as a rent-seeking business, economies have become increasingly politicized (Ekelund & Tollison, 1997).

And there's the rub. As our economies move toward the 22nd century, our insulated duopolistic political institutions are in danger of returning us politically to a time of mercantilism. The process of counting votes is simply the tip of the iceberg.

5. Conclusion

Political choice is perhaps the most important type of choice by a society. The way we choose collectively helps define what kind of society we are. Democratic societies, which allow their citizens to feel a sense of ownership of government, and participation in the process of decision, are more stable and more prosperous than societies with other forms of government. Since the middle 1980s, the world has seen a quiet revolution, with more and more nations embracing the idea, and in some cases the practice, of democracy.

But there are two problems with 19th century institutions in a 21st century world, which I have tried to explain here. The first is the problem of archaic institutions. Our electoral system and institutionalized two-party system are simply incapable of carrying the weight of expectations of rapid, accurate and fair accounting of votes. These institutions need to be brought forward to the 21st century.

The other problem is more subtle, but hardly less important. Elections may not have the capacity to satisfy all the hopes we have for them. What appears to be an institutional design problem turns out to be a problem of expectations: no electoral system can produce truth, or morality. The problem isn't hard; it's impossible. The fact is that neither citizens nor public officials can be counted on to act in the best interests of the larger society. Political systems that require this kind of altruism, or other-regarding action, are open to manipulation by factions of voters or coalitions of elected officials.

I will close with one other quote, again attributed to H. L. Mencken. It is intended jokingly, but in fact it really does reveal the danger of expecting too much, and investing too little, in republican institutions, of which elections are the most visible. "Under democracy one party always devotes its chief energies to trying to prove that the other party is unfit to rule – and both commonly succeed – and are right."

Acknowledgments

The author thanks William Shughart and Robert Tollison for their comments and suggestions, and thanks the editors of *Public Choice* for the opportunity to express these views. And thanks also to Duke University's MicroIncentives Research Center, whose sponsorship of this research made it possible. All errors are the sole responsibility of the author.

Notes

1. To be fair, some partisans are mentally inert, also.
2. For recent results in this literature, see Wand et al. (2001); Herron and Sekhon (2003, 2004); and Mebane and Sekhon (2004). On the other hand, see Lott (2003, 2004).
3. It is possible to question whether the "individually transitive, collectively intransitive" contradiction is a genuine paradox. Buchanan (1954), Tullock (1967) and Plott (1972) argue that the "paradox" simply results from an indefensible insistence on the ability to construct an organic notion of the good out of individual preference building blocks. For a review, see Mueller (2003, pp. 585–591).
4. This saying supposedly originated with Benjamin Franklin, though the attribution is almost certainly apocryphal. (For one thing, "lunch" is anachronistic). The entire quote is: "Democracy is two wolves and a lamb voting on what to have for lunch. Liberty is a well-armed lamb contesting the vote!"
5. Kimberling (n.d., p. 2) argues that the Electoral College bears some important resemblances to the Roman system of the Centurial Assembly, with "many of the same advantages and disadvantages."
6. On the other hand, as Rabinowitz and MacDonald (1986) argue, the winner-takes-all aspect of the Electoral College swamps the overrepresentation aspect, and gives a few large states disproportionate power.
7. For more explanation, and details on how the German system does, and does not, satisfy this standard, see Pulzer (2001).
8. A simple legal restriction will not do, as a new law can change the law, and so some super-legal (probably constitutional) constraint is required.
9. The strategic voting problem is complex, because the truly "strategic" choice would appear to be abstention: votes have next to no probability of influencing the outcome. There have been questions about whether the Electoral College helps or hurts this process, but the answer

is contingent. Beck (1975) found that ties are extremely unlikely if one candidate is even slightly favored. Since the number of polls taken and reported has increased enormously in the past two decades, this would imply that voters are unlikely (rationally) to expect that their vote would influence the outcome.

Margolis (1977) tried to correct Beck's analysis by making a subjective perceptions claim. First, not all individuals view election outcomes the same way. Second, all voters make their forecasts with a degree of uncertainty, both because polls have sampling error and information sets differ across citizens. But this means, according to Margolis, that even if polls show one candidate receiving 53%, or even 55%, of the vote, the subjective probability of a tie in conditions of uncertainty is still high enough that voting may be rational.

Chamberlain and Rothschild (1981) generalized these studies to find that the probability of a tie is on the order of $1/N$, where N is the number of voters. In any reasonably sized electorate, even a state, this probability is only slightly larger than winning the lottery.

It is important to point out that these analyses assumed simple plurality voting, whereas US presidential elections are decided in the Electoral College. Ehrlich (2001) analyzes the probability of a recount (triggered by outcomes in a fixed closeness threshold). He finds that, perhaps against common intuition, the institution of the Electoral College actually makes recounts less likely, and reduces their scope by requiring only state-level, rather than national level, counts. Thus, in one important sense at least, the Electoral College actually preserves stability and props up the legitimacy of our voting institutions by reducing the incentives for, and therefore the appearance of, corruption.

On the other hand, as Abramson et al. (1995) demonstrate, eliminating the Electoral College would almost certainly enhance the chances of third parties, and at a minimum would reduce the barriers to entry of any party with national aspirations.

References

Abramson, P. R., Aldrich, J. H., Paolino, P., & Rohde, D. W. (1995). Third party and independent candidates in American politics: Wallace, Anderson, and Perot. *Political Science Quarterly*, *110*(3), 349–367.

Akerlof, G. A. (1970). The Market for "Lemons": Quality uncertainty and the market mechanism. *Quarterly Journal of Economics*, *84*(3), 488–500.

Aldrich, J. H. (1995). *Why Parties? The Origin and Transformation of Political Parties in America*. University of Chicago Press: Chicago.

Black, D. (1958). *The Theory of Committees and Elections*. Cambridge University Press: Cambridge and New York.

Beck, N. (1975). A note on the probability of a tied election. *Public Choice*, *23*(3), 75–79.

Buchanan, J. M. (1954). Individual Choice in Voting and the Market. *Journal of Political Economy*, *62*(4), 334–343.

Buchanan, J. M., & Congleton, R. D. (1998). *Politics by Principle, Not Interest: Toward Nondiscriminatory Democracy*. Cambridge University Press: Cambridge and New York.

Buchanan, J. M., & Tullock, G. (1962). *The Calculus of Consent: Logical Foundations of Constitutional Democracy*. University of Michigan Press: Ann Arbor.

Chamberlain, G., & Rothschild, M. (1981). A note on the probability of casting a decisive vote. *Journal of Economic Theory*, *25*(1), 152–162.

Cox, G. W. (1997). *Making Votes Count: Political Economy of Institutions and Decisions*. Cambridge University Press: Cambridge and New York.

Davis, O., DeGroot, M., & Hinich, M. (1972). Social preference orderings and majority rule. *Econometrica*, *40*(January), 147–157.

Davis, O., & Hinich, M. (1968). On the power and importance of the mean preference in a mathematical model of democratic choice. *Public Choice*, *5*(Fall), 59–72.

Ehrlich, S. (2001). The Probability of Recounts under Differing Electoral Laws. Paper presented at the Annual Meetings of the American Political Science Association. URL: http://www-personal.umich.edu/~ehrlichs/probability-of-recounts.pdf.

Ekelund, R. B., Jr., & Tollison, R. D. (1997). *Politicized Economies: Monarchy, Monopoly, and Mercantilism*. Texas A&M University Press: College Station.

Herrnson, P., & Green, J. C. (Eds.). (2003). *Responsible Partnership? The Evolution of American Political Parties in the Post-War Era*. University of Kansas Press: Lawrence.

Herron, M. C., & Sekhon, J. S. (2003). Overvoting and representation: An examination of overvoted Presidential ballots in Broward and Miami-Dade counties. *Electoral Studies*, *22*(1), 21–47.

Herron, M. C., & Sekhon, J. S. (2004). Black candidates and black voters: Assessing the impact of candidate race on uncounted vote rates. *Journal of Politics*, *67*(1), forthcoming.

Hinich, M., & Munger, M. (1994). *Ideology and the Theory of Political Choice*. University of Michigan Press: Ann Arbor.

Holcombe, R. G. (1994). *The Economic Foundations of Government*. Macmillan: London.

Holcombe, R. G. (2002). *From Liberty to Democracy: The Transformation of American Government*. University of Michigan Press: Ann Arbor.

Kimbering, W. C. (n.d.). The Electoral College. Federal Election Commission, Office of Election Administration: Washington, DC.

Lott, J. R., Jr. (2003). Non-voted ballots and discrimination in Florida. *Journal of Legal Studies*, *32*(January), 181–220.

Lott, J. R., Jr. (2004). Documenting Unusual Declines in Republican Voting Rates in Florida's Western Panhandle Counties in 2000. http://ssrn.com/abstract=276278.

Madison, J. (1787). The Utility of the Union as a Safeguard against Domestic Faction and Insurrection (continued). *Daily Advertiser*, Thursday, November 22. Reprinted as *Federalist No. 10*, http://www.constitution.org/fed/federa10.htm.

Margolis, H. (1977). Probability of a tie election. *Public Choice*, *31*(Fall), 135–138.

Mebane, W., & Sekhon, J. S. (2004). Robust estimation and outlier detection for overdispersed multinomial models of count data. *American Journal of Political Science*, *48*(2), 392–411.

Mencken, H. L. ([1926] 1982). *Notes on Democracy*. Knopf: New York. Reprinted in *A Mencken Chrestomathy*. Vintage Books: New York.

Mueller, D. C. (2003). *Public Choice III*. Cambridge University Press: Cambridge and New York.

Munger, M. C. (2000). *Analyzing Policy: Choices, Conflicts, and Practices*. Norton: New York.

O'Rourke, P. J. (1991). *Parliament of Whores*. Atlantic Monthly Press: New York.

Plato (1956). *Republic*. In E. H. Warmington & P. G. Rouse (Eds.), *Great Dialogues of Plato*, trans. by W. H.D. Rouse. New English Library (Mentor): New York.

Plott, C. R. (1972). Ethics, social choice theory and the theory of economic policy. *Journal of Mathematical Sociology*, *2*(2), 181–208.

Plott, C. R. (1991). Will economics become an experimental science? *Southern Economic Journal*, *57*(April), 901–919.

Pulzer, P. (2001). Votes and resources: Political finance in Germany. *German Politics and Society*, 19(1), 1–36.

Rabinowitz, G., & MacDonald, S. E. (1986). The power of the states in U.S. Presidential Elections. *American Political Science Review*, *80*(1), 65–87.

Riker, W. H. (1982). *Liberalism against Populism*. W.H. Freeman: San Francisco.

Rosenstone, S. J., Behr, R. L., & Lazarus, E. H. (1986). *Third Parties in America*, 2nd ed. Princeton University Press: Princeton, NJ.

Rousseau, J.-J. (1988). *On Social Contract or Principles of Political Right*. In A. Ritter & J. Conaway Bondanella (Eds.), *Rousseau's Political Writings*. Norton: New York.

Stone, W., & Rapoport, R. (2001). It's Perot, stupid! The legacy of the 1992 Perot Movement in the major-party system, 1992–2000. *Political Science and Politics*, *34*(2), 49–58.

Tullock, G. (1967). The general irrelevance of the general impossibility theorem. *Quarterly Journal of Economics*, *81*(2), 256–270.

Wand, J. N. A., Shotts, K. W., Sekhon, J. S., Mebane, W. R., Jr., Herron, M. C., & Brady, H. E. (2001). The butterfly did it: The aberrant vote for Buchanan in Palm Beach County, Florida. *American Political Science Review*, *95*(4), 793–810.

Winger, R. (1994). The importance of ballot access. *Long Term View* (*University of Massachusetts Law Journal*), 2(2), 40–45.

Public Choice (2005) **124:** 135–156
DOI: 10.1007/s11127-005-4750-3

Some talk: Money in politics. A (partial) review of the literature

THOMAS STRATMANN
Department of Economics, George Mason University, Fairfax, VA 22030 USA
(E-mail: tstratma@gmu.edu)

Accepted March 2005

Abstract. The financing of political campaigns is an area of active scholarly study. I review some of the recent literature and discuss important methodological issues that arise in empirical research on campaign expenditures and campaign contributions. The effects of campaign expenditures and advertising on candidate and ballot-measure elections are summarized, as are the impacts of contributions on contributors' welfare. Many states have changed their campaign finance laws in the past few years, and I describe work that exploits variations in these laws. A discussion of the strategies used by interest groups to allocate their campaign contributions provides insights into contributors' motives.

1. Introduction

In the past decade, campaign contributions and campaign expenditures have been growing rapidly. In 1996, the race for the White House cost President Bill Clinton and Republican challenger Senator Robert Dole $80 million altogether. Four years later, candidates George W. Bush and Albert Gore spent $307 million campaigning for the presidency and in 2004 the expenditures of incumbent Bush and his Democratic opponent, Senator John Kerry, summed to more than $550 million.[1] The last figure does not include spending by advocacy groups and political parties; including them raises total spending in the 2004 US presidential election to $1.2 billion.[2] The growth in spending is less dramatic, but still worthy of notice, in races for the US Congress. In the 1989–1990 election cycle, candidates running for the US Senate and the US House of Representatives spent $283 million, whereas they spent $670 million in 2003–2004. In real dollar terms, this translates into a 64% increase in congressional campaign spending over a 14-year period. Across all US elections in 2004, the grand total spent is estimated to be about $4 billion.

Patterns of campaign contributions and campaign spending differ sharply between incumbents and challengers. The 404 US House incumbents running for reelection in 2004 collected, on the average, $1.1 million in campaign contributions in the 2003–2004 election cycle. About 54% of those contributions come from individuals and about 42% came from Political Action Committees (PACs) and other political committees not formally associated with political party organizations.[3] Challengers, in contrast, raised an average of $260,000 with about 65% of these contributions coming from individuals and about 16% from other, non-party sources.

In this paper, I review some of the scholarly literature that explores the causes and consequences of money in politics. Much work has been done in this area; space constraints allow me to focus only on a few studies.

2. Campaign Expenditures in Candidate Elections

A number of theoretical models incorporate campaign contributions and campaign expenditures into theories of elections and generate testable predictions. While earlier models of campaign finance did not specify precisely how the sources and uses of money affect voters' choices (for example, see reviews by Morton & Cameron, 1992; Austen-Smith, 1987), recent theoretical work attempts to be explicit about those links. In these models, candidates provide voters with information or signals through their advertisements. In some models, campaign advertising reduces voter uncertainty regarding a candidate's policy position (Austen-Smith, 1987; Hinich & Munger, 1989; Bailey, 2002). In other models, campaign advertising informs voters about candidate quality (Ortuno-Ortin & Schultz, 2000; Coate, 2004a), or transmit signals about candidate quality or policies (Potters, Sloof & van Winden, 1997; Prat, 2002a, b; Wittman, 2004a, b). Recent work by Abrajano and Morton (2004) analyzes conditions under which candidates prefer to advertise "substance" (i.e., supply information about their own record or the record of the opponent), as opposed to "style", which includes non-policy valence issues.

A nice feature of some of these models is that they incorporate interest groups and the possibility of quids pro quo between candidates and contributors. When a candidate's ideological position is assumed to be fixed, one motivation for interest groups to contribute is the expectation of policy favors from the candidate if elected (Coate, 2004b). When a candidate's position is flexible, interest groups may contribute because they want to move the office-seekers's platform closer to their own position (Coate, 2004a; Ashworth, 2003; Prat, 2002a). These models predict that voters are less responsive to campaign messages when they believe that candidates have obtained campaign funds by promising policy favors to contributors. As one might expect, the results in the theoretical campaign finance models depend on assumptions regarding the objectives of candidates, the rationality of voters, the type of electoral competition, the goals of contributors, and the role of advertising in inducing voters to change their voting behavior. Empirical work can help inform this work as to which assumptions are most useful and which ones are not.

It has been found, for instance, that campaign spending has little, if any, effect on vote shares at the national level (Levitt, 1994; Palda & Palda, 1998). Set in the context of some of the recent theoretical models, this empirical result may imply that "the informational benefit of spending is offset by the policy bias needed to raise contributions" (Prat, 2002a, p. 182).

Experimental results by Houser and Stratmann (2005) support the implication of Coate's (2004a) model that voters' evaluations of candidates are influenced by the sources of the candidate's campaign funds. They find that voters in a Coate-type environment elect the high-quality candidate substantially less often when campaigns are financed by special interests. Moreover, while the incremental change in the margin of victory due to an additional advertisement in publicly financed campaigns is positive and roughly constant, Houser and Stratmann find that it is positive but decreasing in special interest campaigns. The reason for this difference is that voters become skeptical that candidates in privately financed campaigns are engaged in substantial favor-trading.

The Coate and Prat models also imply that the marginal product of contributions is higher when contributions are limited. Stratmann (2004a) reports evidence consistent with this prediction. Exploiting variations in state contribution limits across states and over time, he finds that the marginal product of campaign spending is higher in states that limit contributions than in states with unlimited spending.

The empirical literature on campaign spending in candidate elections is dominated by work that examines whether spending affects the identity of the winning candidate. While incumbents and challengers spend much time on fund-raising and appear to believe that money is an important ingredient for winning elections, academic researchers for the most part have trouble establishing a causal and quantitatively important connection between spending and vote shares. This is reflected in Moon's (2002) view that one of the major puzzles in the campaign finance literature is the apparent ineffectiveness of incumbent campaign spending in congressional elections. To date, no consensus has been reached regarding the effectiveness of campaign spending on vote shares (Milyo, 1999).

With good measures of candidate quality and constituency preferences the regression equation

$$\begin{aligned} \text{incumbent vote \%} = \alpha &+ \beta \text{ incumbent spending} + \gamma \text{ challenger spending} \\ &+ \delta \text{ candidate characteristics} \\ &+ \theta \text{ constituency preferences} + \epsilon \end{aligned} \tag{1}$$

correctly identifies the marginal impact of campaign spending for both candidates. Lacking good variables for candidate characteristics and district constituency preferences, starting with Jacobson (1978), and with few exceptions, scholars have used incumbents' vote shares in the previous election as a proxy for those missing variables. The findings from OLS estimates show that incumbent spending by US House incumbents does not have a positive and statistically significant effect – and sometimes even has a negative effect – on their vote shares (see, for example, Feldman & Jondrow, 1984; Ragsdale & Cook, 1987; Levitt, 1994). However, challenger spending in US House elections increases challengers' vote shares.[4]

In contrast, most empirical work on the US Senate finds that incumbent spending has a positive and statistically significant effect on incumbents' vote shares (see, for example, Abramowitz, 1988; Grier, 1989; Moon, 2002). However, similar to the estimates for the House, the marginal product of challenger campaign spending in Senate elections is larger than that of incumbent spending.

From the beginning, scholars have noted that incumbents' vote shares and spending are simultaneously determined: while spending influences the vote share, the expected vote share may influence spending. For example, incumbents who expect a competitive race may spend more to win reelection than incumbents who face no significant challenge. In this case, incumbents' vote shares and spending are negatively correlated, which may lead to the potentially erroneous conclusion that more campaign spending leads to smaller vote shares. One of the causes of this negative correlation between incumbent spending and their vote shares is the failure to control for unobserved incumbent and challenger quality.

Put differently, not including important incumbent characteristics and district partisanship in the regression equation results in an omitted variable bias. For example, a strong constituency preference for a Republican incumbent will lead contributors to donate less money to that incumbent's campaign since he or she is likely to win, regardless of the amount spent in the campaign. In this case, failing to fully control for district partisanship leads to an underestimation of the coefficient on incumbent spending. Similarly, some incumbents may receive high vote shares because they are of high quality, because they are trustworthy, or because they expend a lot of effort on constituency service, all of which raise their chances of winning. If such incumbents decide to spend little on campaign advertising because they are likely to be reelected regardless of advertising, then incumbents' campaign advertising and their vote shares will be negatively correlated. However, without good measures of incumbent quality, trustworthiness, and effort, the effect of incumbent spending on votes is underestimated. Unobserved or omitted variables also impart a downward bias to the estimated challenger spending coefficient.

This bias appears to be larger in regressions for the House than for the Senate, since the impact of incumbent spending is positive and often statistically significant in the Senate, while it is zero and sometimes negative in the House. The difference in the findings between the two chambers may suggest that quality differences between challengers and incumbents are smaller in the US Senate. This could be due to challengers in the Senate typically having longer track records in public office than challengers for seats in the House. If so, voters are better informed about the quality of Senate candidates than they are about of the quality of House challengers. This informational asymmetry may explain why the omitted variable bias in House races is more severe than in Senate races.

To correct for the omitted variable bias, two stage least square (TSLS) estimation, panel estimation, and better control variables have been proposed.[5] One example of the last approach is the work by Abramowitz (1991), who includes a measure of elite expectations in the regression model. This variable is meant to control for the possibility that the expectation of an incumbent winning leads to low incumbent spending and a large percentage of the popular vote for that incumbent. However, even when this variable is included, incumbent spending in the US House remains statistically insignificant (Abramowitz, 1991). Another example of better controls is the work by Green and Krasno (1988), who introduce an eight-point scale to measure challenger quality. However, the introduction of this quality measure does not change the conclusion regarding House incumbent spending's lack of effectiveness.

To remove a potential bias in challenger and incumbent spending estimates, and to implement a two-stage least squares (TSLS) estimation, one needs to identify a variable that is correlated with incumbent spending along with another one that is correlated with challenger spending, but that has no direct effect on the incumbent's vote share. Green and Krasno (1988) used lagged spending as the instrument for current incumbent spending and found that both incumbent and challenger coefficients have the anticipated signs and are statistically significant. Analyzing US Senate elections, Gerber (1998) instruments for both incumbent and challenger spending, using state population and candidate wealth, and finds that Senate incumbent spending and challenger spending are equally productive.[6]

Recent work on US Senate elections shows that the productivity of spending by incumbents and challengers is equal in contested races, but that the productivity of incumbent spending is larger than that of challengers in races where incumbents' seats are safe (Moon, 2002). One possible explanation for this finding is that a contested race is a race where both candidates are of equally high quality. As such, examining races where both candidates have similar quality attributes addresses the omitted variable bias.

Levitt (1994) has questioned the methodology of some of these studies and casts some doubt on whether they have convincingly established a causal effect. He suggests employing a different method that is not sensitive to the validity of the chosen instruments. To control for unobserved candidate characteristics, Levitt suggests examining races where the same candidates meet more than once, calling such contests "repeat-challenger races". Focusing the analysis in this way, one can control for candidate quality by introducing a candidate-pair indicator variable. Applying this technique, Levitt finds no statistically significant relation between incumbent campaign spending and incumbent vote shares, and a weak relation for challengers. Moreover, the point estimates are so small that, even if the estimates were statistically significant, extra spending would have a negligible effect on vote shares.

If the effect of money is small, one is left to wonder why candidates appear to invest a great deal of effort in raising funds. Perhaps there is so much fund raising because the cost of raising funds relative to the gain from winning office is low, or because candidates confuse correlation with causation (Levitt, 1994). An alternative view is that scholars should develop a different research design to uncover the effect of campaign spending in races for elective office.

The productivity of campaign spending is an important research question, and answers to this question become even more important when it is observed that incumbency reelection rates are at record highs. One cannot help but wonder whether the fact that incumbents outspend challengers on average by a margin of more than three to one contributes to their apparent electoral advantages. Moreover, the productivity of campaign spending is a critical issue for the campaign finance reform debate. If incumbent spending is ineffective in increasing their vote shares, while challenger spending is effective in reducing incumbents' vote shares, the argument of some reform advocates that limits on spending level the playing field between advantaged incumbents and disadvantaged challengers does not apply.

The previously mentioned studies assume that the same campaign dollar buys the same amount of advertising whether it is spent in a low-advertising cost or high-cost area. In Montana, the cost-per-point for a 30-second, prime-time television spot that reaches the entire constituency is less than $100, while the equivalent message would cost more than $1,500 in the Los Angeles area (Stratmann, 2004b). Thus, total spending may not be an accurate measure of how much candidates are effectively campaigning. The same amount of campaign spending buys a different number of television advertisements in different regions of the country, and differences in costs per point across jurisdictions lead to different amounts of advertising even though candidates may spend the same total amount.

Stratmann (2004b) adopts Levitt's (1994) methodology of examining a sample of repeat-challenger races, but instead of looking at the effects of total campaign expenditures on vote shares, he employs a measure of television advertising. Using this new measure, campaign advertising has a qualitatively and quantitatively important effect for both challengers and incumbents. In one of the specifications, a 15% increase in incumbent advertising relative to the mean increases the incumbent's vote share by 1.2 percentage points and a 43% increase in challenger advertising relative to the mean increases the challenger's vote share by 2.1 percentage points.

One promising avenue to a better understanding of campaign advertising involves examining the types of messages candidates send. Abrajano and

Morton (2004) analyze whether candidates' television advertising emphasizes valence issues, something they call "style", or whether they instead send truthful, credible policy messages, something they call substance. Analyzing data from the 2000 US House elections, they find evidence for strategic advertising. When a candidate's position is close to that of the median voter, candidates reveal substance about their records. The farther their policy positions are away from the median voter's ideal point, the more likely candidates are to emphasize style issues in their television advertising.

3. Campaign Spending on Ballot Measures

When one does not control for the endogeneity of candidate spending in elections, most studies find that spending by one side is effective, while spending by the other side is not. This finding has a parallel in the campaign finance literature on ballot initiatives. Here, when not controlling for the endogeneity of advertising, most studies also find an asymmetry in its effectiveness.[7]

As in elections involving candidates for political office, campaign spending on ballot initiatives has been steadily rising. In 1992, $117 million was spent in 21 states by groups supporting and opposing various ballot measures; in 1998, interest groups spent close to $400 million in 44 states. California led the nation in this regard. Interest groups spent $522 million between 1992 and 1998 on that state's ballot measures, including $256 million in 1998 alone. As for more recent years, Stratmann (2005) documents that in California between the 2000 primary and the 2004 primary, interest groups spent $494 million on passing or defeating ballot measures (in real March 2004 dollars). Of this total, the supporting side spent $344 million and the opposing side spent $149 million.

The older literature on the effects of campaign spending on initiatives looked at whether the side that spent more also was more likely to obtain a majority vote for its cause. Lowenstein (1982), for example, examines ballot measures with "spending on either the affirmative or the negative side that exceeds $250,000 and that is at least twice as high as the spending on the opposing side." Using this selection criterion, he finds that the supporting side was successful in passing 67% of the measures on which they outspent opponents, whereas the opposing side succeeded in defeating measures 90% of the time when they outspent supporters.

This asymmetry holds up when regression techniques are employed. In her empirical analysis, Gerber (1998) finds that contributions from economic groups lower the probability that a measure will pass, but that contributions from citizen groups have no impact on passage rates. Taking these results literally, economic interest groups could improve a measure's chances of passing by not spending anything. Related work by Bowler and Donovan (1998) reports that campaign expenditures have little effect on voters' opinions regarding ballot measures. Asymmetry in the effectiveness of spending is also found in the regressions of Garret and Gerber (2001). They report that total expenditures by supporters have a positive but statistically insignificant effect on ballot measure vote shares, whereas opponents' total expenditures have a negative and statistically insignificant effect. These results pose some puzzles. Why would the supporting side spend money when it is ineffective and sometimes even reduces voter support (Matsusaka, 2000)? This question raises the issue of whether previous studies have accounted for all of the relevant factors that determine spending on ballot measures and election outcomes.

Endogeneity may plague regressions designed to explain the impact of ballot initiative advertising on passage rates, just it does in the case of candidate vote shares. If an interest group that opposes a ballot measure knows that voters prefer the status quo and thus also are opposed to the measure's passage, the group may spend few resources campaigning against it. This is because the group expects the measure to be defeated even if little effort is made to push its point of view. In this case the effect of negative advertising is overestimated. However, the supporting side nevertheless may spend large sums to inform voters about the benefits of supporting the measure; thus, unobserved or unmeasured voter preferences favoring the status quo will lead to an underestimation of the effect of spending by supporters.

One way of addressing this causality issue is to estimate a regression that has controls for individual propositions and for the geographic area in which voters cast their ballots (Stratmann, 2005). In Stratmann's paper, the unit of observation is the vote share in a county for a ballot measure, and this vote share is linked to the degree of voter exposure to ballot initiative advertisements on television. This approach captures unobserved voter preferences in a county as well as statewide preferences for or against a particular initiative. Stratmann further divides initiatives into those favored by liberal voters and those favored by conservative voters and allows county preferences to differ for both initiative types. The results from this study differ from the findings in previous studies. Using this research design, the estimates show that supporting spending is at least as productive as opposition spending. For example, in examining the effect of advertising on the percentage of votes favoring passage, 100 extra supporting television advertisements increases the ballot's vote share by 1.2 percentage points, and the same number of opposition advertisements decreases this share by 0.6 percentage points. If one calculates the magnitude of these effects based on the actual number of advertisements, the impact of advertising does not appear to be large. For example, to obtain a 1.2 percentage point increase in the fraction of voters favoring passage, the supporting side has to increase its advertising by 23% relative to the mean. The opposing side must increase its advertising by 53% to obtain a 0.6 percentage point reduction in voter support.

4. Campaign Contributions and Policy Decisions

Do incumbents who receive money from special-interest groups cater to their wishes because they received campaign contributions, or do they receive contributions because they were already committed to the interest group's point of view? In the latter case, groups contribute to assure their preferred candidate's reelection and to show their appreciation for the incumbent's positions.

Many theoretical models assume or predict that interest groups buy policy favors with their campaign contributions (see, for example, Grossman & Helpman, 1994, 1996, 2001). The evidence for this prediction appears mixed.[8]

As in the other areas of campaign finance research, there is the issue whether campaign contributions are endogenous. A simple correlation between contributions and voting behavior does not help to address whether the causality goes from incumbent's positions to contributions, or from contributions to incumbent's positions. Ordinary least square estimates will overestimate the effect of contributions on voting behavior if interest groups donate to their friends. These estimation techniques also underestimate the effect when interest groups focus their contributions on potential foes. Thus, it is difficult to determine whether OLS estimates are biased downwards or upwards.

Recent research shows that campaign contributions have not had much of an effect on legislative voting behavior, as summarized by popular voting indexes, such as those produced by the AFL-CIO's Congress on Political Equality (COPE), the liberal Americans for Democratic Action (ADA), and the defense-industry oriented National Security Council (NSC). Bronars and Lott (1997) examine whether retiring legislators, who are not threatened by retaliation in the next election cycle, change their voting behavior, measured as a change in voting score, when there is a change in contributions from relevant PACs. They find only modest evidence that changes in these contributions change voting behavior. Ansolabehere, de Figuieredo and Snyder (2003) examine the effect of labor and corporate contributions on voting scores assigned by the US Chamber of Commerce and likewise find no evidence that contributions affect voting in the predicted directions once one allows for member or district fixed effects, or uses instrumental variables estimation.

One way of analyzing the link between campaign contributions and legislative votes is to examine votes that occur repeatedly in Congress and to ask whether changing contributions are associated with changing legislative voting behavior. If the underlying constituency characteristics do not change (i.e., if voter preferences do not change), then it can be argued that if contributions from a special-interest group increase between the first and the second vote and legislators switch from opposing to favoring the group's interests, then this change in voting behavior constitutes evidence that the interest group influenced legislation with its campaign contributions.

Stratmann (2002) conducts such an analysis by examining two pieces of financial services legislation at different points in time. In 1991, the US House of Representatives took a vote on a bill to repeal the Glass-Steagall Act. The 1991 bill was defeated, and another vote on the same issue was taken in 1998. The House passed the latter measure. Banking interests favored repeal, while the insurance and securities industries opposed it. Stratmann (2002) regresses the change in a representative's vote from 1991 to 1998 on the changes in contributions from those three groups. He finds that these contribution changes have a statistically significant effect on a representative's voting decision. In particular, Stratmann finds that an extra $10,000 in banking contributions increases the likelihood of a House member voting in favor of repeal by approximately eight percentage points. Stratmann also finds that the influence of campaign contributions on voting decisions was larger for junior members of the House than for their more senior colleagues.

The timing of interest group contributions can provide some clues as to whether special-interest groups attempt to influence legislative voting behavior. Stratmann (1998) investigates whether roll call votes on agricultural subsidies in the US House of Representatives and significant actions by the House Agriculture Committee coincide with an influx of contributions from agricultural interests. He finds that the number of agricultural contributions spike around these events and that few contributions are made when the House is in recess. In addition to spikes around important events in Congress, Stratmann (1998) also documents an increase in contributions in the two months prior to the general election. One interpretation of these results is that contributions and votes are exchanged on a spot market.[9]

To examine whether this pattern of giving also holds for groups other than agricultural PACs, I collected data on the number of weekly roll votes and number of weekly contributions between the 1991–1992 and the 2000–2001 election cycle. I summed the votes, by week, over all six election cycles. Figure 1 shows the results of this exercise. The overall correlation coefficient between number of votes and number of contributions is 0.48 and it is 0.40 for votes and contribution amounts. Using the PAC classification of the Federal Election Commission, the highest correlation between votes and number of contributions is for corporate and trade PACs (0.50), and the lowest correlation is for ideological PACs (0.38), defined as PACs that are neither corporate, trade, or labor PACs. This finding is in similar spirit as the paper by Snyder (1992), who argues that some PACs focus on influencing elections, while others focus on influencing outcomes in the legislature.

One little explored channel of influence is the effect of contributions on the behavior of bureaucracies. Gordon and Hafer (2005) build a model predicting that large contributors are less likely to comply with regulations than smaller ones. This prediction is based on the assumption that contributions are a signal of a firm's willingness to fight an agency. Using plant-level

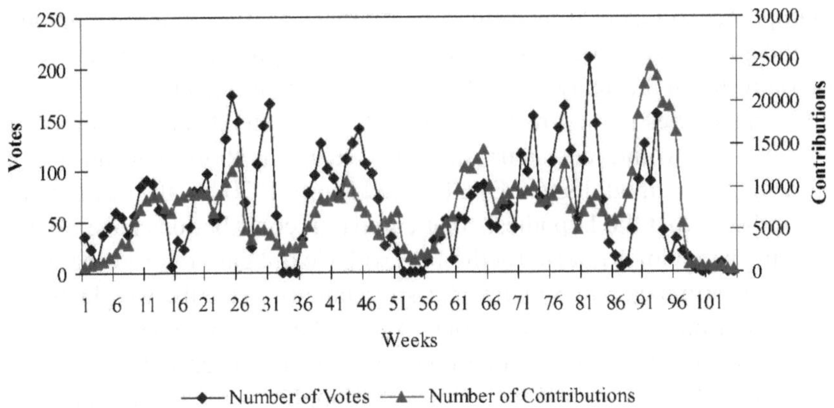

Figure 1. Weekly votes and weekly contributions: 1991–1992 to 2001–2002.

data from the Nuclear Regulatory Commission, they find support for their prediction.

Ansolabehere, de Figuieredo and Snyder (2003) surveyed articles in the economics and political science literatures that estimated the effects of campaign contributions on roll call votes. Of the nearly 40 articles surveyed, they find that the estimated contribution coefficients are either statistically insignificant or have the wrong sign in roughly 75% of the cases. If one were to ask whether money influences votes based on whether the median contribution coefficient shows a statistically significant effect, one would be forced to conclude that it does not.

Djankov and Murrell (2002) suggest using meta-analysis to determine whether an effect of money on legislative voting behavior is supported by the weight of the evidence. This type of analysis considers the sign and significance level of each of the coefficients that have been reported in the literature. Specifically, "it is readily apparent that a set of analyses with small positive *t*-statistics could be significant in the aggregate even with non-significance in each individual analysis" (Djankov & Murrell, 2002, p. 749).[10] Using their methodology, I have conducted a meta-analysis of the papers surveyed in Ansolabehere, de Figuieredo and Snyder (2003).

Those articles vary as to how coefficient estimates are reported and whether predictions are made concerning the direction of the effects of the included campaign contribution variables. I omitted coefficients for which authors made no prediction as to the expected sign. Kau and Rubin (1981), for example, estimate the effect of campaign contributions on passage of minimum wage legislation, and include separately contributions from agricultural, environmental, and other interests. Since they use these variables as controls, they made no a priori predictions for them; accordingly, these coefficients are not included in my meta-analysis. Also not included are estimates where I could not impute a t-statistic. Some authors report that a coefficient is insignificant or significant, but do not state the level of statistical significance. These selection criteria result in the analysis of 265 contribution coefficients.

Giving studies that corrected for the simultaneous determination of contributions and voting decisions the same weight as those that did not, and following the methodology in Djankov and Murrell (2002), the meta-analysis tests indicate that the hypothesis that campaign contributions have no effect on voting behavior is rejected at the 1% level. Next, I gave the 196 coefficients that were estimated by correcting for simultaneity twice the weight as those that did not include such corrections. Again, the null hypothesis is rejected, lending support to the claim that contributions affect legislative voting behavior. Finally, I examined the studies that applied simultaneity techniques separately and the null hypothesis likewise is rejected.[11]

This meta-analysis reverses the finding reported in existing studies that campaign contributions have no effect on legislative voting behavior. The meta-analysis performed here suggests that money does indeed influence votes. However, one needs to be careful in not overstating this result. Whether one believes that contributions matter depends on whether one also believes that all of the studies underlying the meta-analysis properly have controlled for the potential simultaneous determination of contributions and votes. Future meta-analyses could drop some of the studies that one deems to be lacking in this respect.

One of the few studies that examine the effect of campaign contributions by corporations on the fortunes of the contributing firms is the innovative work by Jayachandran (2004). Using the unexpected departure of Senator Jim Jeffords from the Republican party in May 2001, resulting in a shift in the Senate majority, Jayachandran examines the effect of this change on the market value of firms contributing soft money to the Republican and Democrat parties. This event study shows that in the week after Jeffords switched, firms lost 0.8% of market capitalization for every $250,000 contributed to Republicans. The stock price gain to firms with Democratic contributions is smaller, but not statistically different in magnitude.

5. Determinants of Campaign Contributions

Theory predicts that contributors give money to candidates whose position is closest to their own, to those who are likely to change their position to the one preferred by the contributor, and to those candidates who have a high probability of winning (Mueller, 2003). Further, the predicted determinants of contributions differ, depending on the assumptions regarding contributor objectives. Do contributors consider contributions as pure consumption, as investment in policy, as a means of gaining access to the legislator, or as a way of influencing elections?

One of the most robust findings in the literature is that money flows to incumbents in close races (see, for example, Poole & Romer, 1985; Kau, Keenan & Rubin, 1982; Jacobson, 1985; Stratmann, 1991).[12] There is much evidence supporting the proposition that groups donate to their friends in Congress. This can also be readily seen in the pattern of contributions by labor unions and organizations such as the National Rifle Association. Systematic evidence for this hypothesis is provided by Poole and Romer (1985), who find that conservative PACs tend to contribute most to conservative candidates and that liberal PACs contribute most to liberal candidates. Many other studies have supported these findings (see, for example, Kau, Keenan & Rubin, 1982; Grier & Munger, 1991; Kroszner & Stratmann, 1998).

Snyder (1992) documents persistence in giving and suggests such behavior is consistent with the hypothesis that PACs establish long-run investments relationship with legislators. McCarty and Rothenberg (1996) point to the commitment problems that make establishing a long-term relationship between contributors and legislators difficult. They report a less than 50% probability that PACs donating to federal legislators in 1977–1978 were still supporting the same legislators in 1985–1986. Kroszner and Stratmann (2000, 2005) suggest that long-run relations can be sustained by reputation. They examine whether politicians who follow a strategy of developing reputations for reliability are rewarded with high levels of corporate campaign contributions. Clear and consistent policy positions could help reduce uncertainty about a candidate and lead to high campaign contributions from favored interests. Alternatively, such clarity could alienate those from disfavored interests and hinder the politician from raising contributions from groups on both sides of an issue. Using data on corporate PAC contributions to members of the US House during the seven election cycles from 1983–1984 to 1995–1996, Kroszner and Stratmann (2005) find that high reputational development is rewarded with more generous PAC contributions.

A number of studies have documented that incumbents serving on powerful congressional committees raise more funds (see, for example, Grier & Munger, 1991; Romer & Snyder, 1994; Milyo, 1997). One interesting avenue of work investigates changes in the pattern of giving when legislators switch committees. Romer and Sndyer (1994) examine changes in a representatives's committee and leadership assignments on changes in PAC contributions. One of the advantages of examining changes in contributions, as opposed to levels, is that this helps control for other factors. Their careful examination of the data shows that PACs reallocate their contributions when legislators move off or move onto a committee. Their data show that PAC giving is about representatives' committee assignments as well as their committee experience.

Also focusing on committees in the US Congress, Kroszner and Stratmann (1998) examine the contribution behavior of PACs from competing segments of the financial services industry, namely commercial and investment banks, securities firms, and insurance companies. Their empirical investigation is guided by the theory of a long-run exchange relationship between committee members and interest groups. Consistent with their model, Kroszner and Stratmann find that these PACs contribute most to members on the House banking committee and that each group concentrates its contributions on particular committee members. They also document that contributions to banking committee members fall when their committee service ends and that members who are not successful in raising large contributions from interested groups tend to leave the committee.

Suppose that the goal of PACs is to influence legislative outcomes. Stratmann (1992) tests this by conjecturing that agricultural PACs want to assemble a congressional majority favoring farm subsidies, and to investigate the implications of this hypothesis. Given that agricultural PACs have limited funds, they may not find it worthwhile to contribute to incumbents representing farm districts in North Dakota or Montana, who predictably would support agricultural subsidies regardless of the amount received. Instead, the PACs will contribute to legislators with only a few farmers in their district or those who are undecided. Stratmann (1991) documents this pattern of giving by showing that the largest farm contributions flow to the legislators with the median rural constituency. Strategic giving also gains support when it is observed that liberal PACs give most to conservative Democrats and that conservative PACs give most to liberal Democrats (Stratmann, 1996). This evidence suggests that failing to find a significant correlation between contributions and voting behavior does not mean that PACs are not successful in influencing legislator's actions.

Much of the observed pattern of political giving is consistent with the motive of buying access as well as with the motive of influencing votes. Legislators may be more willing to listen to lobbyists representing large contributors than small ones. The motive of purchasing access is reinforced by the finding that large contributors also invest heavily in lobbying activities (Wright, 1990; Asolabehere, Snyder & Tripathi, 2002).

One of the few attempts to explain the growth of campaign expenditures is by Lott (2000). He takes the view that rent seeking is an interest group's primary motive for contributing to political campaigns and hypothesizes that when more rents are available, groups have stronger incentives to invest resources in obtaining them. Using state government size as a proxy for rent availability, he finds that campaign expenditures are higher in states where governments are bigger, ceteris paribus.

A different line of research has examined the characteristics of contributors. Pittman (1988), Zardkoohi (1988), and Grier, Munger and Roberts (1994) examine the characteristics that determine whether an industry has established a PAC and how much each contributes. They find that industry size, concentration, and whether it faces government regulations helps explain variations in both measures of business political activity. Using firm-level data from the high-tech sector, Hart (2001) finds that larger sales or being regulated by the government increases the probability that a firm forms a PAC.

6. Campaign Finance Reform

Money's growing importance in politics led, at least in part, to recent federal campaign finance reform legislation, the Bipartisan Campaign Reform Act (BCRA) of 2003. Differences in campaign finance laws at the state level usefully can be employed to study the effects of regulating money in politics. State reforms have included the introduction of contribution limits, a tightening of existing limits on contributions by individuals, corporations, labor unions, PACs, and parties, as well as the adoption of public financing combined with expenditure limits. The variation in the data allows one to analyze how a number of political outcomes are affected by changes how campaigns are financed.

Theoretical work by Che and Gale (1998) suggests that, in a rent-seeking environment, contribution caps can increase aggregate effort levels by making a larger number of races more competitive, and that there are reasons to expect overall contributions to increase after a cap is imposed. Riezman and Wilson (1997) present a theoretical model exploring the effects of campaign finance reform on lobby formation. Drazen, Limao and Stratmann (2004) show that a not-too-stringent limit on contributions can improve interest groups' bargaining positions relative to politicians, thus increasing the payoff from contributing. In this case the limit increases the equilibrium number of contributors. Testing the bargaining model with data on contribution limits adopted at the state level from 1986 to 2000, Drazen, Limao and Stratmann report empirical evidence indicating that caps have increased the number of lobbies between 7% and 8%.

The Coate (2004a) model generates testable implications regarding the effects of campaign contribution limits on the closeness of elections. Although contribution limits result in less campaign spending and reduce voters' information about their voting options, limits may decrease the number of favors candidates promise to contributors. In particular, the probability that a voter will switch his vote to the advertising candidate will increase with limits if the beneficial effects of limits (i.e., fewer policy favor promises) outweigh their negative effects (i.e., the information loss). This reasoning implies further that if campaign contributions are only position-induced, then contribution limits lead to a narrowing of the margin of victory. However, if contributions are also service-induced – there is a quid pro quo – limits on contributions can increase the margin of victory. In the latter case, limits reduce the amount of favors promised and thus voters find the advertising messages of high quality candidates to more credible, leading to larger margins of victory.

Using variation over time and controlling for state-specific effects, Stratmann and Aparicio-Castillo (2005) examine electoral competitiveness in legislative elections across 45 states from 1980 to 2000. Panel data techniques reduce the possibility that omitted variables are correlated with observed party competitiveness and with a state's decision to adopt a campaign finance law or to modify an existing one. Stratmann and Aparicio-Castillo find that stricter limits on individuals, corporations, labor unions, and PACs are associated with narrower margins of victory and a greater number of candidates in elections. These findings are consistent with those of Besley and Case (2002), who report that the existence of corporate campaign contribution limits lead to more vigorous party competition in state legislatures.

The Coate (2004a) model also predicts that, relative to privately financed campaigns, public financing increases the high-quality candidate's chances of winning an election. Publicly financed advertising is the case of purely informative advertising: no promises need be made to contributors when campaign messages are paid for by the taxpayers. Guided by this prediction, Houser and Stratmann (2005) find that the high-quality candidate is elected more frequently and his margin of victory is larger in publicly financed campaigns. Specifically, Houser and Stratmann report that the high-quality candidate wins one-third less often when campaigns are financed by special interests. They also study contribution caps and matching funds, finding that the right candidate (in terms of voter welfare) is elected more frequently in the matching treatment than under private financing and no matching.[13]

While the incremental change in the margin of victory due to an additional publicly financed advertisement is positive and roughly constant, the margin is positive but decreasing in special-interest campaigns. In view of the Coate (2004a) model, the reason for this asymmetry is that voters become skeptical that high-quality, but power-hungry candidates in privately financed campaigns are engaged in substantial favor-trading. One way to circumvent this belief is to cap the amount of private funds that can be raised.

Arizona and Maine are among some of the states that recently have enacted campaign finance reform laws that provide for public financing. Public funds accounted for over half of the total amount spent in legislative races in those two states in 2002. Examining trends in political outcomes in Arizona and Maine, it appears that the reelection rates of incumbents drop when public financing is significant (Mayer, Werner & Williams, 2004). Public funding also appears to increase the number of candidates seeking election and the likelihood that an incumbent faces a competitive race. On the other hand, analyzing cross-sectional data, Malbin and Gais (1998) find no evidence that public funding with spending limits makes elections more competitive.

Another interesting avenue along which to study campaign finance reform is to examine its effects on voter participation (Milyo, Primo & Groseclose, 2002) and on political efficacy and trust (Primo & Milyo, 2004). Using data from National Election Studies, Primo and Milyo find little evidence that state laws mandating public disclosure of political contributions and limiting contributions from organizations are associated with increased efficacy, while public financing decreases efficacy.

7. Conclusion

Among other changes, the recent federal campaign finance reform (McCain-Feingold) eliminated "soft money" and doubled the allowable individual contribution for the 2004 election from $1,000 to $2,000 per candidate per election cycle. (Primary and general elections count as separate elections.) Since challengers rely more on party contributions than incumbents, and since incumbents have an advantage in fund-raising, this law has probably benefitted the current office holders relative to their potential challengers. Getting rid of soft money has accelerated the rise of so-called 527 groups, groups that spend money on campaign advertising independent of candidates. Little academic work has been done to date analyzing the effects and the allocation of these funds. In particular, it would be interesting to see if these groups spend monies in similar markets as the candidate they support or oppose, or whether they instead tend to advertize in different markets. Further, detailed data on the timing of candidate advertising and advertising of independent groups allows for the study of strategic interactions, and how polls respond to advertising.

Not all campaign finance reform necessarily benefits incumbents. In many states voters have used ballot initiatives to limit contributions to candidates in state elections. These contribution limits seem to have the effect of making elections more competitive (Stratmann & Aparico-Castillo, 2005). One possible explanation for this finding is that limits are primarily binding for incumbents, but not for challengers, resulting in an improvement in challengers' relative positions.

Little academic work has been done on in-kind contributions, such as "volunteers" distributing campaign literature, telephoning voters and contacting them in person. Clearly these volunteers can serve as substitutes or complements to funds expended in campaigns. Volunteers may enhance the credibility of a campaign and thus cause campaign spending to become more productive. Endorsements represent another area of research where little empirical work has been done. Like in-kind contributions, endorsements of candidates by the local media, celebrities or other political figures can have a direct or indirect effect on election outcomes.

Notes

1. Data for the 1996 campaign were obtained from http://www.fec.gov/ pres96/presmstr.htm# disbursements; data for the 2000 and 2004 campaign were obtained from http://www.fec.gov/finance/disclosure/srssea.shtml.

2. See http://www.opensecrets.org/pressreleases/2004/04spending.asp.
3. http://www.fec.gov/press/press2004/20050103canstat/overviewpost2004.pdf.
4. Milyo (2001) suggests that these findings are consistent with the view that incumbents are intertemporal utility-maximizers.
5. One alternative approach is to employ covariance restrictions, as in Erikson and Palfrey (1998).
6. For studies examining the effect of incumbents' war chests on deterring entry by challengers see, for example, Epstein and Zemsky (1995), Box-Steffesmeier (1996), and Goodliffe (2001).
7. Contributions to committees supporting or opposing initiatives or referenda are not subject to spending limits, while contributions to candidates in elections are limited. The legal motivation for the difference in treatment is that the Supreme Court sees the potential for quids pro quo between candidates and contributors, but that this option is not available when groups contribute to committees whose goals are to pass or defeat ballot initiatives.
8. Only a few studies examine how contributions influence the allocation of time by legislators. One example is the work by Hall and Wayman (1990). This is surely an interesting avenue for future research. Time is a scarce good and there are many political actors competing for a legislator's time.
9. A benign interpretation of this result is that interest groups either immediately reward a legislator after having cast a vote or, if a legislator announces a favorable position prior to a vote, that the interest group expresses its gratitude immediately by contributing to the legislator's campaign. However, even under this benign view, some observers will interpret the observed patterns of giving as suggesting at least the appearance of corruption. Stratmann (1995) finds that contributions that are given in the election cycle when a roll call vote is taken, in addition to contributions from the previous election cycle, have independent and a statistically significant influence legislators' voting behavior.
10. This is one of the reasons why meta-analysis may be useful. For example, ten predicted signs, each of them statistically insignificant, may nevertheless be statistically significant in aggregate. Thus, pooling the information in a systematic manner may give additional information regarding the effectiveness of campaign contributions.
11. These conclusions are unaffected when the results from the labor and corporate PAC coefficient estimates reported in Ansolababere, de Figuieredo and Snyder (2003) are included.
12. These studies typically do not address whether contributors give more in close races because they hope to influence the outcome, or because participation in the political process is more rewarding when a race is tight, just as sports events seem to draw larger audiences when the teams are more evenly matched. Future work may also want to examine whether more contributions make races closer or if closer races draw more contributions.
13. Experimental work in the area of campaign finance limits is rare. One exception is Cadigan (2004), who does not examine the effects of limits directly, but draws inferences based on experimental data. He suggests that BCRA 2002 is likely to make elections less competitive.

References

Abrajano, M., & Morton, R. (2004). All style and no substance? The strategic calculus of campaign advertising. Working paper, New York University.

Abramowitz, A. (1988). Explaining senate election outcomes. *American Political Science Review*, *82*(June), 385–403.

Abramowitz, A. (1991). Incumbency, campaign spending, and the decline of competition in U.S. house elections. *Journal of Politics*, *53*(February), 34–56.

Ansolabehere, S., de Figueiredo, J., & Snyder, J. Jr. (2003). Why is there so little money in U.S. politics? *Journal of Economic Perspectives*, *17*(1), 105–130.

Ansolabehere, S., Snyder, J. Jr., & Tripathi, M. (2002). Are PAC contributions and lobbying linked? New evidence from the 1995 Lobby Disclosure Act. *Business and Politics*, *4*(2), 131–155.

Ashworth, S. (2003). Campaign finance and voter welfare with entrenched incumbents. Mimeo, Harvard University.

Austen-Smith, D. (1987). Interest groups, campaign contributions and probabilistic voting. *Public Choice*, *54*(2), 123–139.

Bailey, M. (2002). Money and representation: An exploration in multiple dimensions with informative campaigns. Mimeo, Georgetown University.

Besley, T., & Case, A. (2003). Political institutions and policy outcomes: Evidence from the United States. *Journal of Economic Literature*, *41*(1), 7–73.

Bowler, S., & Donovan, T. (1998). *Demanding Choices: Opinion and Voting in Direct Democracy*. Ann Arbor: University of Michigan Press.

Box-Steffesmeier, J. (1996). A dynamic analysis of the role of war chests in campaign strategy. *American Journal of Political Science*, *40*(2), 352–372.

Bronars, S., & Lott, J. Jr. (1997). Do campaign donations alter how a politician votes? Or, do donors support candidates who value the same things that they do? *Journal of Law and Economics*, *40*(2), 317–350.

Cadigan, J. (2004). Asymmetric rent seeking and the bipartisan campaign reform act: Theory and experimental analysis. Working paper, American University.

Che, Y., & Gale, I. (1999). Caps on political lobbying. *American Economic Review*, *88*(3), 643–651.

Coate, S. (2004a). Pareto improving campaign finance policy. *American Economic Review*, *94*(3), 628–655.

Coate, S. (2004b). Political competition with campaign contributions and informative advertising. *Journal of the European Economic Association*, *2*(5), 772–804.

Djankov, S., & Murrell, P. (2002). Enterprise restructuring in transition: A quantitative survey. *Journal of Economic Literature*, *40*(September), 739–792.

Drazen, A., Limao, N., & Stratmann, T. (2004). Political contribution caps and lobby formation: Theory and evidence. NBER working paper, Washington, DC.

Epstein, D., & Zemsky, P. (1995). Money talks: Deterring quality challengers in congressional elections. *American Political Science Review*, *89*(2), 295–308.

Erikson, R., & Palfrey, T. (1998). Campaign spending and incumbency: An Alternative simultaneous equations approach. *Journal of Politics*, *60*(May), 355–373.

Feldman, P., & Jondrow, J. (1984). Congressional elections and local federal spending. *American Journal of Political Science*, *28*(1), 147–164.

Garret, E., & Gerber, E. (2001). Money in the initiative and referendum process: Evidence of its effects and prospects for reform. In M. Waters (Ed.), *The Battle Over Citizen Lawmaking* (pp. 76–82). Durham, NC: Carolina Academic Press.

Gerber, A. (1998). Estimating the effect of campaign spending on senate election outcomes using instrumental variables. *American Political Science Review*, *92*(2), 401–411.

Goodliffe, J. (2001). The effect of war chests on challenger entry in U.S. house elections. *American Journal of Political Science*, *45*(4), 830–844.

Gordon, S., & Hafer, C. (2005). Flexing muscle: Corporate political expenditures as signals to the bureaucracy. *American Political Science Review*, forthcoming.

Green, D., & Krasno, J. (1988). Salvation for the spendthrift incumbent: Re-estimating the effects of campaign spending in house elections. *American Journal of Political Science*, *32*(November), 884–907.

Grier, K. (1989). Campaign spending and senate elections, 1978–1984. *Public Choice, 63*(3), 201–220.

Grier, K., & Munger, M. (1991). Committee assignments, constituent preferences, and campaign contributions. *Economic Inquiry, 29*(January), 24–43.

Grier, K., Munger, M., & Roberts, B. (1994). The determinants of industrial political activity, 1978–1986. *American Political Science Review, 88*(4), 911–926.

Grossman, G., & Helpman, E. (1994). Protection for sale. *American Economic Review, 84*(4), 833–850.

Grossman, G., & Helpman, E. (1996). Electoral competition and special interest politics. *Review of Economic Studies, 63*(2), 265–286.

Grossman, G., & Helpman, E. (2001). *Special Interest Politics*. Cambridge, MA: MIT Press.

Hall, R., & Wayman, F. (1990). Buying time: Moneyed interests and the mobilization of bias in congressional committees. *American Political Science Review, 84*(3), 797–820.

Hart, D. (2001). Why do some firms give? Why do some firms give a lot? High-tech PACs, 1977–1996. *Journal of Politics, 63*(4), 1230–1249.

Hinich, M., & Munger, M. (1989). Political investment, voter perceptions, and candidate strategy: An equilibrium spatial analysis. In P. Ordeshook (Ed.), *Models of Strategic Choice in Politics* (pp. 49–68). Ann Arbor: University of Michigan Press.

Houser, D., & Stratmann, T. (2005). Selling favors in the lab: Experiments on campaign finance reform. Working paper, George Mason University.

Jacobson, G. (1978). The effects of campaign spending on congressional elections. *American Political Science Review, 72*(June), 469–491.

Jacobson, G. (1985). Money and votes reconsidered: Congressional elections 1972–1982. *Public Choice, 47*(1), 7–62.

Jayachandran, S. (2005). The Jeffords Effect. Working paper. University of California, Los Angeles.

Kau, J., & Rubin, P. (1981). The impact of labor unions on the passage of economic legislation. *Journal of Labor Research, 2*(1), 133–45.

Kau, J., Keenan, D., & Rubin, P. (1982). A general equilibrium model of congressional voting. *Quarterly Journal of Economics, 97*(2), 271–293.

Kroszner, R., & Stratmann, T. (1998). Interest group competition and the organization of congress: Theory and evidence from financial services political action committees. *American Economic Review, 88*(5), 1163–1187.

Kroszner, R., & Stratmann, T. (2000). Congressional committees as reputation-building mechanisms: Repeat PAC giving and seniority on the house banking committee. *Business and Politics*, 2(April), 35–52.

Kroszner, R., & Stratmann, T. (2005). Corporate campaign contributions, repeat giving, and the rewards to legislator reputation. *Journal of Law and Economics*, forthcoming.

Levitt, S. (1994). Using repeat challengers to estimate the effects of campaign spending on election outcomes in the U.S. house. *Journal of Political Economy, 102*(August), 777–798.

Lott, J. Jr. (2000). A simple explanation for why campaign expenditures are increasing: The government is getting bigger. *Journal of Law and Economics, 43*(2), 359 –393.

Lowenstein, D. (1982). Campaign spending and ballot propositions: Recent experience, public choice theory and the first amendment. *UCLA Law Review, 29*(505), 505–641.

Malbin, M., & Gais, T. (1998). *The Day After Reform: Sobering Campaign Finance Lessons from the American States*. Albany, NY: Rockefeller Institute Press.

Matsusaka, J. (2000). Elisabeth R. Gerber, *The Populist Paradox: Interest Group Influence and the Promise of Direct Legislation* (book review). *Public Choice, 104*(3–4), 394–397.

Mayer, K., Werner, T., & Williams, A. (2004). Do public financing programs enhance electoral competition? Working Paper. Department of Political Science, University of Wisconsin-Madison.

McCarty, N., & Rothenberg, L. (1996). Commitment and the campaign contribution contract. *American Journal of Political Science*, *40*(August), 872–904.

Milyo, J. (1997). The electoral and financial effects of changes in committee power: GRH, TRA86, and money committees in the U.S. house. *Journal of Law and Economics*, *40*(April), 93–112.

Milyo, J. (1999). The political economics of campaign finance. *Independent Review*, *3*(4), 537–547.

Milyo, J. (2001). What do candidates maximize (and why should anyone care)? *Public Choice*, *109*(1–2), 109–139.

Milyo, J., Primo, D., & Groseclose, T. (2002). The effects of campaign finance regulation on turnout, Electoral competition, and partisan advantage in gubernatorial elections, 1949–1998. Working paper, University of Chicago.

Moon, W. (2002). The paradox of less efficient incumbent spending: Theory and tests. Working paper, University of California, Los Angeles.

Morton, R., & Cameron, C. (1992). Elections and the theory of campaign contributions: A survey and critical analysis. *Economics and Politics*, *4*(March), 79–108.

Mueller, D. (2003). *Public Choice III*. Cambridge and New York: Cambridge University Press.

Ortuno-Ortin, I., & Schultz, C. (2000). Public funding for political parties. CESifo working paper no. 368.

Palda, F., & Palda, K. (1998). The impact of campaign expenditures on political competition in the french legislative elections of 1993. *Public Choice*, *94*(1–2), 157–174.

Pittman, R. (1988). Rent-seeking and market structure: Comment. *Public Choice*, *58*(2), 173–185.

Poole, K., & Romer, T. (1985). Patterns of political action committee contributions to the 1980 campaigns for the U.S. house of representatives. *Public Choice*, *47*(1), 63–112.

Potters, J., Sloof, R., & van Winden, F. (1997). Campaign expenditures, contributions, and direct endorsements: The strategic use of information and money to influence voter behavior. *European Journal of Political Economy*, *13*(February), 1–31.

Prat, A. (2002a). Campaign advertising and voter welfare. *Review of Economic Studies*, *69*(4), 999–1018.

Prat, A. (2002b). Campaign spending with office-seeking politicians, rational voters, and multiple lobbies. *Journal of Economic Theory*, *103*(1), 162–189.

Primo, D., & Milyo, J. (2004). Campaign finance and political efficacy: Evidence from the states. Working paper, University of Rochester.

Ragsdale, L., & Cook, T. (1987). Representatives' actions and challengers' reactions: Limits to candidate connections in the house. *American Journal of Political Science*, *31*(February), 45–81.

Riezman, R., & Wilson, J. (1997). Political reform and trade policy. *Journal of International Economics*, *42*(February), 67–90.

Romer, T., & Snyder, J. Jr. (1994). An empirical investigation of the dynamics of PAC contributions. *American Journal of Political Science*, *38*(August), 745–769.

Snyder, J. Jr. (1992). Long-term investing in politicians: Or, give early, give often. *Journal of Law and Economics*, *35*(April), 15–43.

Stratmann, T. (1991). What do campaign contributions buy? Deciphering causal effects of money and votes. *Southern Economic Journal*, *57*(3), 606–620.

Stratmann, T. (1992). Are contributors rational? Untangling strategies of political action committees. *Journal of Political Economy*, *100*(3), 647–664.

Stratmann, T. (1995). Campaign contributions and congressional voting: Does the timing of contributions matter? *Review of Economics and Statistics*, *77*(1), 127–136.

Stratmann, T. (1996). How reelection constituencies matter: Evidence from political action committees' contributions and congressional voting. *Journal of Law and Economics*, *39*(2), 605–635.

Stratmann, T. (1998). The market for congressional votes: Is timing of contributions everything? *Journal of Law and Economics*, *41*(1), 85–114.

Stratmann, T. (2002). Can special interests buy congressional votes? Evidence from financial services legislation. *Journal of Law and Economics*, *45*(2), 345–374.

Stratmann, T. (2004a). Contribution Limits and the Effectiveness of Campaign Spending. Working paper, George Mason University.

Stratmann, T. (2004b). How prices matter in politics: The returns to campaign advertising. Working paper, George Mason University.

Stratmann, T. (2005). Is interest group pressure to preserve the status quo more effective than to change it? Evidence from ballot measures. Working paper, George Mason University.

Stratmann, T., & Aparicio-Castillo, J. (2005). Competition policy for elections: Do campaign contribution limits matter? Working paper, George Mason University, forthcoming in Public Choice.

Wittman, D. (2004a). Candidate quality, pressure group endorsements, and the nature of political advertising. Working paper, Department of economics department, University of California, Santa Cruz.

Wittman, D. (2004b). Pressure groups and political advertising: How uninformed voters can use strategic rules of thumb. Working paper, Department of economics, University of California, Santa Cruz.

Wright, J. (1990). Contributions, lobbying, and committee voting in the U.S. house of representatives. *American Political Science Review*, *84*(June), 417–438.

Zardkoohi, A. (1988). Market structure and campaign contributions: Does concentration matter? A reply. *Public Choice*, *58*(2), 187–191.

Public Choice (2005) **124:** 157–177
DOI: 10.1007/s11127-005-4760-1

The eclipse of legislatures: Direct democracy in the 21st century

JOHN G. MATSUSAKA
Marshall School of Business and Law School, University of Southern California, Los Angeles, CA 90089-1427, USA
(E-mail: matsusak@use.edu)

Accepted March 2005

Abstract. Demographic, political, and technological trends are fueling an unprecedented growth in direct democracy worldwide. If the trends continue, direct democracy threatens to eclipse legislatures in setting the policy agenda. This article reviews existing scientific knowledge about the initiative and referendum – the main institutions of direct democracy – and highlights key issues for the future.

> A democracy [is] the only pure republic, but impracticable beyond the limits of a town.
>
> – Thomas Jefferson

> Direct democracy, under almost any decision-making rule, becomes too costly in other than very small political units when more than a few isolated issues must be considered.
>
> – James Buchanan and Gordon Tullock (1962, p. 213)

1. Introduction

Direct democracy has been almost an afterthought in the study of public choice. It was considered empirically unimportant, impractical for any meaningful governments in the seminal contributions in the field (for example, Buchanan & Tullock, 1962; Downs, 1957; Black, 1958). The founders focused instead on the institutions of representative democracy, primarily legislatures and political parties. The subsequent literature has by and large followed the pattern set down at the beginning. A rough classification of the last 20 issues of *Public Choice* reveals more than 50 articles on elected representatives compared to only four on direct democracy.

The thesis of this article is that the neglect of direct democracy will soon come to an end if current trends hold. Demographic and technological developments are fueling an unprecedented expansion of direct democracy that is likely to continue into the foreseeable future. Legislatures are gradually being eclipsed as the primary creators of public policy, and in some states they already have assumed a secondary role. To continue to speak meaningfully about public decisionmaking, the study of public choice will have to grapple with the new institutions of direct democracy.

The article begins by documenting the rise of direct democracy, and then discusses how direct democracy is changing public policy. Recent research gives reasons to view direct democracy as a positive innovation in democratic institutions. A review of existing theory and critical research questions follows.

2. Forms of Direct Democracy

Direct democracy, as conceived in much public choice work, is something like a town meeting. All members of a polity assemble in a legislature of the whole to make public decisions. Seen in this way, direct democracy is a substitute for representative democracy, and is obviously impractical for large states.

In practice, direct democracy has taken a different form. Statutes or constitutional amendments are proposed and placed before all the voters in an election. The proposal becomes law if a majority of the electorate votes in favor of it. Unlike town meetings, this sort of direct democracy can be and is implemented on a national scale. And it is not a complete substitute for the legislature.

Direct democracy takes a variety of forms. The most high powered is the *initiative*: ordinary citizens propose a law, qualify their proposal for the ballot by collecting a predetermined number of signatures from fellow citizens, and the final decision is made by a vote of the electorate as a whole. More common, but less prominent, are *referendums*.[1] Referendums are laws that originate with the legislature before going before the voters for approval. In some cases, the legislature chooses to put the law before the voters in order to sample public opinion, called an *advisory referendum*. An example is national votes on European integration. In other cases, the legislature is required to place a measure before the voters, for example, when it comes to amending the constitution or issuing bonds, called a *legislative referendum*. Yet a third type of referendum is placed on the ballot by citizen petition in order to reverse a decision of the legislature, called a *petition referendum*.

3. The Rise of Direct Democracy

Direct democracy has roots in ancient Greece and the Swiss have used it for centuries, but its modern efflorescence can be traced to California's tax-cutting Proposition 13 in 1978. Figure 1 shows the number of statewide initiatives by decade dating back to 1905. As can be seen, initiative use accelerated in the late 1970s and has continued to grow decade after decade for 30 years. The last 10 years saw over 360 measures, a record.

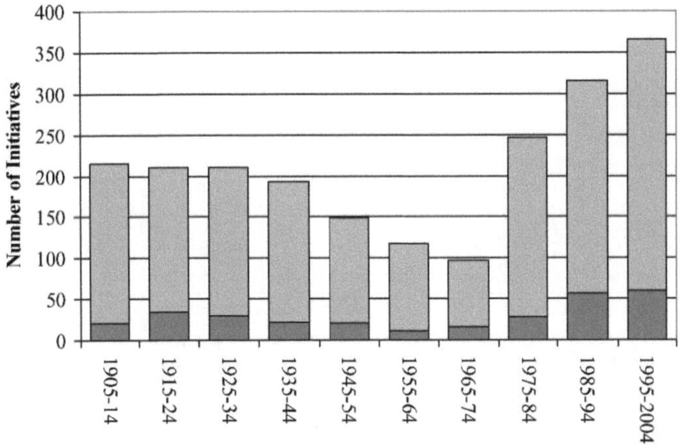

Figure 1. Number of statewide initiatives by decade (*Note*: The number of initiatives in California is shown with dark shading. Data source: Initiative and Referendum Institute).

Prop. 13 was one of the signal political events of the later 20th century and its passage reverberated across the country. In the years immediately following Prop. 13, some thought the country was in the midst of a passing infatuation with direct lawmaking, but by now it seems more likely that we are undergoing a more permanent shift in how policy decisions are made.

Referendums have always been part of American democracy. Massachusetts held a referendum to approve its new constitution in 1780. Rhode Island in 1842 became the first state to require popular approval for constitutional amendments. By the middle of the nineteenth century it was becoming standard practice across the nation to hold a referendum when amending a state constitution. Today, only one state (Delaware) does not require constitutional amendments to be put before the voters. Referendums have long been used to authorize bonds as well. The requirement that the people approve bond issues grew out of a wave of defaults in the nineteenth century by state and local governments that had borrowed to finance railroads, turnpikes, and canals. Currently 21 states require a popular vote before state bonds can be issued (Kiewiet & Szakaly, 1996).

Perhaps the most important innovation in direct democracy was the development of the initiative because it broke the legislature's monopoly over the agenda. South Dakota was the first state to adopt the initiative in 1898. A burst of adoption activity followed associated with the Progressive movement; by 1918, 20 states had adopted the process.[2] Since then, states have adopted the process at a rate of about one per decade. Figure 2 shows the American states that currently provide for the initiative and (in parentheses) the date of adoption.

A popular misconception about the initiative process is that it is primarily a Californian or regional phenomenon. Figure 1 shows the number of initiatives

Figure 2. States with the initiative in 2004 (adoption year in parentheses).

that appeared on the California ballot (dark shading). California is obviously important, but it is only one part of a broader movement. Figure 2 reveals that the initiative is particularly popular west of the Mississippi River, but it appears in all regions of the country, from the Northeast (Maine, Massachusetts) to the South (Arkansas, Florida, Mississippi) to the central states (Michigan, Ohio). The initiative is not fully national yet, but it would be misleading to view it as only a regional or California-specific phenomenon.

The initiative process appeared in American cities at about the same time it appeared at the state level. California counties were given initiative rights in 1893, and the first cities to adopt the initiative process were San Francisco and Vallejo in 1898. By 1910, all or substantially all municipalities in 10 states had been granted initiative rights, and individual cities in at least nine other states had the process. Comprehensive information on current initiative availability in cities is not available, but the best estimate is that half of all US cities now have the initiative, including 15 of the 20 largest cities. As with the state-level initiative, the local initiative is most popular in the West, available in 77% of cities. But it is also available in 47% of Northeast cities, 35% of Southern cities, and 49% of cities in the central states. Again, it would be misleading to view the initiative as a purely regional phenomenon.[3]

Comprehensive information on local initiative activity is hard to come by, but the available data suggest intense use. Gordon (2004) found there were 474 municipal and 58 county initiatives in California during the period 1990–2000. Figure 3 reports the number of ballot propositions of all types (initiatives+referendums) for all levels of government (counties+cities+special districts)

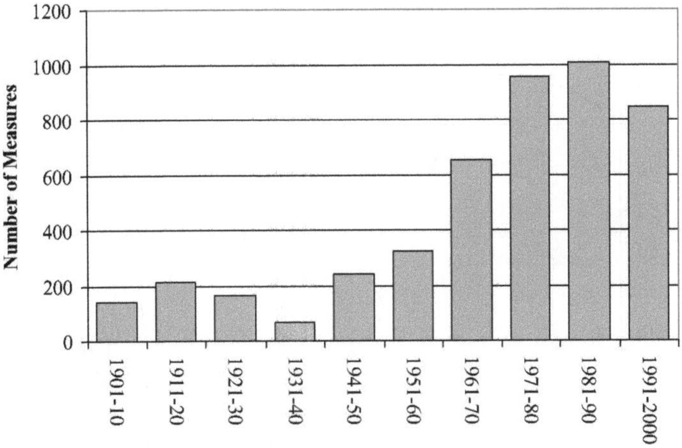

Figure 3. Number of Local Ballot Measures in Four California Counties (*Note*: The figure reports the number of ballot measures (initiatives+referendums) for all levels of government (counties, cities, school districts, and special districts) in the counties of Los Angeles, Orange, Riverside, and San Bernardino. The numbers are not comprehensive, especially before 1950. Data source: *Preserving the Record of Direct Democracy in Southern California: An Archive Completed by the University of California, Santa Cruz, Environmental Studies Department*, by Daniel Press, August 2001).

in four Southern California counties since 1901. The numbers over the past several decades are staggering: more than 1,000 measures came before the voters in 1981–1990 alone! The data are incomplete going back in time, but it is nevertheless clear that the number has gone up over the last 30 years, roughly paralleling the state-level trend seen in Figure 1.

This article focuses on the United States, which is at the leading edge of the direct democracy movement, but it is worth noting that the trend toward popular decisionmaking extends across the world. In Europe, 10 countries allow initiatives (as do six of the post-Soviet states), and the constitution of the European Union includes both the initiative and referendum. Twenty-nine referendums have been held on European integration alone, and it is now almost expected in many countries that such matters will be put before the voters. In the Far East, Taiwan uses referendums for local issues, and in 2003 the government adopted national initiatives and referendums.[4]

4. The Eclipse of Legislatures

All of this indicates that direct democracy is spreading. It is also becoming increasingly important in deciding the broad directions of state and local policy. To get a sense of this, consider some of the high-profile issues that emerged through the initiative process over the last decade or so: affirmative action, illegal immigration, lotteries and casinos, medical marijuana, school

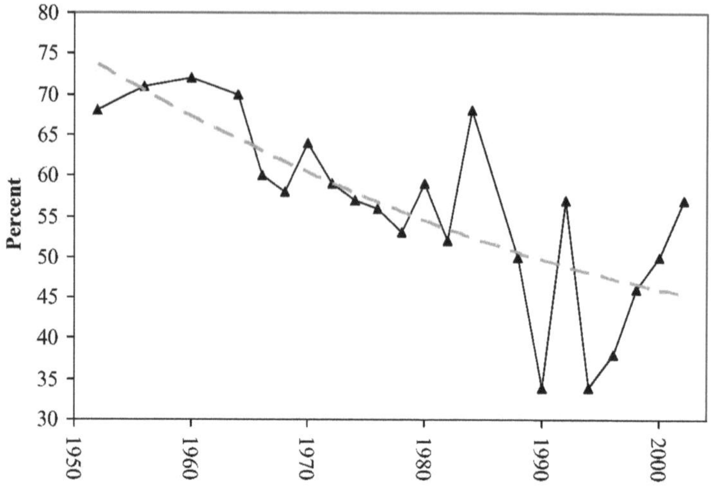

Figure 4. Percent agreeing that "people have a say in what government does", 1952–2002 (*Note*: The gray dashed line is a polynomial trendline. Data source: National Election Studies).

vouchers, tax limits, and term limits. Now try to compose a comparable list of important policy developments that emanated from legislatures; it is difficult to identify more than a handful. Legislatures in initiative states are increasingly focused on budgeting and responding to policy trends that originate from ballot propositions. It does not seem an exaggeration to say that policy innovation is now being driven as much by voter initiatives as by legislatures and governors.

The eclipse of legislatures by direct democracy goes hand in hand with a general meltdown in public confidence regarding legislatures (and government in general) over the last four decades. A variety of public opinion data document an erosion of popular support for elected officials beginning in the late 1960s, following a period of relative stability. Figure 4 is a representative example, taken from the National Election Studies. Respondents were asked if they believe people "have any say about what government does". The figure reports the percentage of respondents who believe people do have a say. Public opinion is somewhat volatile but the gradual downward trend is evident. The modern term limits movement that spread across the nation in the 1990s is a vivid symptom of the growing dissatisfaction with legislatures.

The upshot of the decline of confidence in legislatures is that direct democracy has taken a privileged place in the minds of Americans when it comes to policymaking. A recent national survey conducted for the Initiative & Referendum Institute asked:[5]

> All other things being equal, which do you think is most likely to produce laws that are in the public interest: when the law is adopted by the legislature or when the voters adopt the law?

Sixty-six percent of respondents selected "voters" compared to 20% that selected "the legislature". The pattern held for men and women, across all age groups, and for whites, blacks, and other ethnic groups.

5. Causes

While the trends are fairly clear – a growing role for direct democracy and a gradual eclipse of legislatures – the causes are less apparent. What seems clear is that the causes run deep: the trends have been developing for decades now and are appearing in democracies across the world.

Somewhat speculatively, I would like to suggest that two main forces are at work, one demographic and the other technological. The demographic force is the growing amount of education among the population. Across a variety of metrics, Americans have become more and more educated over the last 40 years. For example, in 1960 high school graduates were 41% of the adult population; today they are 84% of the population. Similarly, 8% of adults were college graduates in 1960, compared to 27% today.[6] The technological force is the ongoing revolution in communication technology: the Internet and World Wide Web, blogs, media transmitted via satellite, cable and fiber optics, videotext and fax machines, digital data, and so on. The digital revolution has made more information available to ordinary citizens at a lower cost than at any time in human history.

These two forces together – rising education and falling information costs – are dramatically reducing the knowledge advantage that elected officials once had over ordinary citizens. A century ago, many citizens may have felt that important policy decisions ought to be left to legislatures, with their superior education and access to information. Now many ordinary citizens feel competent to make policy decisions themselves and no longer believe that elected officials are smarter, wiser, or better-informed. As a result, pressure has mounted to shift important policy decisions from legislatures to the people.

A possible concern with this interpretation of the trends is that it is not clear that citizens are becoming more informed *about policy*. Indeed, survey evidence suggests that citizens are fairly ignorant about many of the details of policy, as they have been for decades. Such ignorance is entirely rational, as explained by Downs (1957) long ago.

There are two ways to reconcile these observations. First, it should be recognized that broad policy decisions do not require a deep knowledge of institutions, economics, or policy. Think of moral issues such as whether to allow gay marriage or physician-assisted suicide. Many budgetary policies have the same flavor; they are mainly about establishing spending priorities and do not require a great deal of expertise to form an opinion.

Second, current research concerning voter decisionmaking suggests that substantive knowledge may not be necessary to make competent decisions in the first place. A citizen can cast a vote in his or her interest without understanding the details of a measure by relying on information cues – advice and endorsements from trusted friends, public figures, or groups. For example, an environmentalist may be able to vote his interest on an environmental proposition simply by learning whether it is supported or opposed by the Sierra Club. There is growing evidence that reliance on information cues allows citizens to vote their interests just as effectively as substantive knowledge does (Lupia, 1994; Lupia & McCubbins, 1998; Bowler & Donovan, 1998).

Voters have long used such cues (especially party labels) when deciding which candidate to support for an office. The demographic and technological trends discussed above are likely to increase the effectiveness of cues. More education and lower information costs make it easier for citizens to search out information cues and determine their reliability. Returning to the example above, an educated environmentalist might be more sophisticated at identifying environmental groups that most closely share his or her views, and the Internet makes it a simple matter to determine the issue positions of those groups.

Finally, when thinking about the knowledge necessary to make wise policy decisions, it is useful not to place the legislature on too elevated a platform. Professional legislators also rely on cues when making many of their decisions whether to support a bill or not. The California legislature sent Governor Arnold Schwarzenegger more than 1,200 bills during his first year in office, 954 of which he signed into law. Plainly, neither the legislators nor the governor read the language of every bill personally. They made their voting decisions (or veto decisions in the case of the governor) based on advice from trusted aides, fellow legislators, representatives of interest groups, and so on. The business of modern government is simply too complicated for any person to keep track of all the details; the use of information cues is inevitable. Whether legislators are more skilled at tapping the relevant information than the electorate is an open question, but the gap is surely narrowing.

6. Policy Consequences

What does the growth of direct democracy augur for public policy? Recent public choice research has sketched the contours of an answer.

6.1. *For the many or the few?*

A central question is whether the initiative and referendum bring about policies favorable to the majority or instead provide a way for wealthy, organized special interests to subvert the majority. The primary justification for the initiative and referendum has always been to empower the majority, and allow "the public" to counteract the perceived disproportionate influence of "special interests" in the legislature. However, some thoughtful observers believe that the initiative and referendum have the opposite effect. In the words of David Broder (2000, p. 243), "the experience with the initiative process at the state level in the last two decades is that wealthy individuals and special interests – the targets of the Populists and Progressives who brought the initiative a century ago – have learned all too well how to subvert the process to their own purposes."

At first glance, this presents something of a puzzle: how can the initiative and referendum hurt the majority if it takes a majority of voters to pass a measure? There are several possibilities. First, if some groups are better at mobilizing their members to go to the polls then they can prevail on Election Day even if their policies are harmful to the majority. The idea that public policies may not reflect the majority view because some groups are better at delivering votes than others is a central theme of the interest group theory developed by Stigler (1971), Peltzman (1976) and Becker (1983). Second, deceptive advertising might lead some citizens to cast votes against their own interests. A third and more subtle possibility, discussed below, is that the presence of the initiative or referendum may cause the legislature to adopt policies that are worse for the majority than if the processes were not available.

Whether direct democracy serves the many or the few is ultimately an empirical question. The early research was anecdotal in nature and inconclusive. Only recently has the question been addressed using modern theory and empirical methods. Game theory is especially important in structuring the analysis. It might seem reasonable, at first glance, to measure the effect of the initiative on policy by examining the content and success of measures that appear on the ballot, what might be called the "direct" effect of the process. However, game theory tells us that the initiative will also have an "indirect" effect. The *threat* provided by the initiative can cause the legislature to alter its policy decisions even if the threat is not carried out (Romer & Rosenthal, 1979; Gerber, 1996). Therefore, examination of the actual measures (the direct effect) will only capture part of the consequences of the initiative, and will be biased in unpredictable ways.

One way to measure the full (direct+indirect) effect is to search for differences between states/cities that have the initiative and referendum and those that do not, controlling for other determinants of policy. A full-length study along these lines is my book *For the Many or the Few* (FMF) (Matsusaka, 2004). FMF examines several dimensions of the fiscal policy of state and local governments throughout the twentieth century. The main results concern tax and spending policies since 1970. FMF documents three significant differences between initiative and noninitiative states over the last 30 years: (1) combined spending of all governments (state and local) in initiative states was less than noninitiative states; (2) spending was more decentralized from state to local government in initiative than noninitiative states; and (3) initiative states relied less on taxes and more on user fees and charges for services than noninitiative states. All three effects appear after controlling for conventional variables, such as income, population, urbanization, region, and partisan control of the government. Evidence is also provided showing that the effects are not the spurious result of unobserved ideology: initiative states were not spending less simply because their citizens were more conservative to begin with.[7] FMF concludes that the initiative *caused* the policy changes.

FMF then compares the policy changes brought about by the initiative with the preferences of the people as expressed in opinion surveys. Opinion data were collected for each policy, (1)–(3). The main finding is that all three policy changes brought about by the initiative were moving policy in the direction favored by a majority of voters: a majority of people expressed a desire to reduce government spending, shift spending from state to local government, and switch revenue out of general taxes and into fees. Evidence supporting the idea that the initiative brings about policies opposed by the majority, as the special interest subversion view maintains, was almost entirely absent. In short, the initiative seems to work for the many and not the few.

Evidence from studies of non-fiscal policies points in the same direction. Gerber (1996, 1999) examined state death penalty and abortion policies. She found that initiative states are more likely than noninitiative states to allow capital punishment and to require parental notification of abortions by minors. She also showed that a majority of voters in all states favor these policies, implying that the initiative makes majority outcomes more likely. Another example is term limits. Polls show majorities in favor of legislative term limits across the country. Congressional or state legislative term limits have been adopted in 22 of 24 initiative states but in only two of 26 noninitiative states. Initiative states are also more likely than noninitiative states to have adopted gubernatorial term limits (Matsusaka, 2005).

The existing empirical evidence to date is fairly consistent in concluding that the initiative tends to bring about policies that the majority wants. This finding does not warrant a strong normative conclusion, however. On the one hand, majority rule is a fundamental premise of democracy, so there is something to be said for bringing it about. On the other hand, the majority's choice is not necessarily the "wisest" policy, and the majority might abuse its power, what has been called the "tyranny of the majority". The "quality" of decisions under direct democracy and the threat to minority rights will be taken up next.

6.2. *Economic performance*

There is no universally accepted metric for judging whether a public policy is good or bad. Accordingly, many attempts to evaluate the quality of public decisions under direct democracy end up revealing more about the researcher's preferences than anything else. A handful of studies, however, employ metrics familiar from economics.

The first statistical study appears to have been Pommerehne's (1983) examination of trash collection in Swiss municipalities. He found that cities with direct democracy collected trash at a lower cost than cities without direct democracy, all else equal. How this came about was not explained. In a similar vein, Feld and Savioz (1997) estimated aggregate production functions for Swiss cantons (equivalent to American states) and found greater total factor productivity in cantons with more direct democracy. Again, the mechanism was not explained, but higher productivity could be evidence of more productive public sector investments. Blomberg, Hess and Weerapana (2004) fit a growth model to data from American states over 1980–2000, and found that states with the initiative process grew more quickly and had higher output per capita than noninitiative states, again holding constant other factors such as the capital stock.

Evidence of a different sort comes from Frey and Stutzer (2000). They used survey data in which individuals reported their "subjective well-being", called "happiness" for short. Frey and Stutzer found that people living in Swiss cantons reported higher levels of happiness when there was more direct democracy available.

Finally, there is evidence on how initiatives affect public budgeting. One symptom of dysfunctional budgeting would be sustained or excessive deficits. It is sometimes argued that direct democracy creates deficits by allowing myopic voters to appropriate spending while cutting taxes. The evidence, however, shows that initiative states are no more likely to borrow than noninitiative states, and mandatory referendums on debt issues actually reduce borrowing, if anything (Matsusaka, 1995; Bohn & Inman, 1996; Kiewiet & Szakaly, 1996; Feld & Kirchgassner, 2001). Another argument is that so many initiatives dedicate public funds to certain uses and prevent tax increases that legislatures do not have enough degrees of freedom left to budget responsibly. However, estimates for California (where this claim is typically made and is most plausible) indicate that at most 32% of the state budget is tied up by initiatives (and only about 2% is locked into programs that would not otherwise be funded) and that initiatives do not prevent tax increases, except on property, to any significant degree (Matsusaka, forthcoming).

It should be emphasized that none of these metrics is sufficient for establishing that direct democracy leads to good policy decisions. However, it is striking that direct democracy does seem to bring about "good" outcomes using conventional economic criteria (and one unconventional measure).

6.3. *Minority rights*

Numerous authors have raised the specter of majority tyranny. In an oft-cited passage of *Federalist* No. 51, Madison observed:

> It is of great importance in a republic, not only to guard the society against the oppression of its rulers; but to guard one part of the society against the injustice of the other parts. Different interests necessarily exist in different classes of citizens. If a majority be united by a common interest, the rights of the minority will be insecure.

Unfortunately, there is little rigorous empirical work on this issue, and the work that does exist rests on flawed methodologies (see Matsusaka, 2004, Ch. 8).

On an anecdotal level, there are instances of initiatives that violated the basic rights of minorities. In 1910 Oklahoma voters approved an initiative depriving black citizens of their voting rights, and in 1920 California voters approved an initiative that restricted the property rights of Japanese. But no form of government is perfect: minority rights have been undermined repeatedly by legislatures, most egregiously in the South, where blacks were systematically deprived of their voting and civil rights. The internment of Japanese citizens during World War II is another example. Seen in this light, the initiative does not appear to be any worse than the alternative. The fact that large majorities of Asian, black, and Latino voters support the initiative reinforces the conclusion that the initiative may not pose a great threat to minority rights. But more work is certainly called for on this question.

7. Theory

In some respects, the empirical literature has jumped ahead of the theoretical literature. We now have plenty of evidence that the initiative process brings about significant changes in policy, but our understanding of how this comes about is more limited. Several theoretical approaches seem promising.

7.1. *Internal-external costs and logrolling*

The foundation of public choice is the internal-external cost model of Buchanan and Tullock (1962). In that model, public decisions expose individuals to two kinds of costs. *Internal* (or "decisionmaking") costs are the time and effort that individuals expend when they participate in the public choice process. Included are the costs of becoming informed and of negotiating with other parties. *External* costs arise when public decisions are harmful to a person's interests. An optimal public choice process in this framework would minimize the sum of the two costs.

Direct democracy is worse than representative democracy in terms of internal costs. Direct democracy involves the entire population in the policymaking process, incurring large decisionmaking costs. Representative democracy, which delegates decisions to a relatively small group of elected officials, economizes on decisionmaking costs.

On the other hand, direct democracy outperforms representative democracy when it comes to external costs. For one thing, representatives may not be fully accountable to their constituents (there may be agency problems, in modern jargon) and may choose policies that are harmful to many of them. A great deal of theory and evidence now suggests that elected officials are less than perfect agents of the voters.[8]

Another external cost arises when legislatures engage in logrolling, trading votes on one project to secure approval of another. Buchanan and Tullock note that such legislative bargains can be efficient when the minority on some issue has more intense preferences than the majority. However, they also observe that logrolls are vulnerable to a fiscal externality arising from the fact that taxes are spread over the population at large, not tailored to benefits received. A legislator is willing to approve a project with particularistic benefits for his constituents that would fail normal benefit-cost tests because his constituents have to absorb only a fraction of the costs. In principle, then, logrolls can be a good or bad thing, but a fair amount of evidence has accumulated in favor of the fiscal-externalities view that logrolls drive up spending to inefficient levels.[9]

Voters can use the initiative and referendum to unbundle legislative logrolls by stripping out and deciding individual issues. To the extent that inefficient logrolls are prevented or undone, external costs are lower under direct democracy than representative democracy.

The conventional conclusion is that the internal cost of direct democracy outweighs the external cost of representative democracy:

> Direct democracy, under almost any decision-making rule, becomes too costly in other than very small political units when more than a few isolated issues must be considered. The costs of decision-making become too large relative to the possible reduction in expected external costs that collective action might produce. (Buchanan & Tullock, 1962, p. 213)

The conclusion seems warranted if we think of direct democracy as a town meeting. The costs would surely be prohibitive to convene an assembly of all citizens to make policy decisions in any reasonably sized polity.

The conclusion fits less well when we think of direct democracy as the initiative and referendum. The internal/decisionmaking costs of these processes would seem to be of the same magnitude as the costs of representative democracy. First, the cost of locating cues to become informed would not seem too different for candidate elections versus referendum elections. In the internal-external costs model, the most important component of decisionmaking costs is the cost of *reaching agreement* (Buchanan & Tullock, 1962, Ch. 8). If agreement had to be reached by a process of negotiation between all the interested parties, the cost would surely be astronomical when the group size is large. However, negotiation is not required to make a decision with initiatives and referendums. The only thing necessary is for a majority of citizens to vote in favor of a measure. Thus, the tradeoff between representative democracy and (these forms of) direct democracy hinges primarily on a comparison of the external costs, which as we have seen, cuts in favor of citizen lawmaking.

7.2. *Agenda control*

Romer and Rosenthal (1979) introduced another important idea into the theory of direct democracy: agenda control. Their model of legislative referendums highlighted the importance of the power to make proposals. Without direct democracy, legislatures have a monopoly over what issues are to be decided, in what order, and in what form. With the initiative, the monopoly is broken, and ordinary people are allowed to make proposals.

A central insight from the agenda control literature is that fragmenting the agenda control tends to bring policy closer to the position of the median voter than when policy is monopolized by representatives. To see the intuition, consider a spatial model in which the median voter, the legislature, and an interest group have ideal points along the real line and single-peaked preferences. The game begins with the legislature establishing an initial policy that becomes the status quo. The interest group then has the option to propose an alternative policy, in which case the voter makes the final choice between the two options. Now suppose the legislature would choose some policy x if the initiative is not available. If the initiative is available, outside groups propose an alternative policy y. The median voter will adopt the alternative y if it is closer (measured in terms of utility) to his or her ideal point than x, and reject it otherwise. The voter is never worse off from having a choice, and can be better off.

Then there is the indirect effect: the legislature may respond to the threat of an outside proposal by modifying its initial policy. The legislature will only pay attention to groups that threaten a policy closer to the median than x because only such a policy could gain voter approval. In order to deter the group from qualifying an initiative, the legislature must move away from x and either adopt a policy that the median voter finds more attractive than y, or a policy that the outside group finds sufficiently appealing to forego its own proposal. In either case, an effective response requires the legislature to adopt a policy closer to the median than x. Thus, both the direct and indirect effect of direct democracy push policy closer to the position of the median voter. This setup also implies that the initiative and referendum can have an effect on policy even if they are not used, an implication that is central for empirical research, as discussed above.

This pro-median-voter result poses something of a mystery: why isn't direct democracy more common if it can only help the median voter? A partial answer to this question can be found by extending the basic model to incorporate asymmetric information. With asymmetric information, direct democracy can push policy to an extreme, away from the median position. For example, if legislators are uncertain about voter preferences, they may respond to the threat of an extreme initiative by meeting the interest group halfway. By accommodating the group, the extreme measure never reaches the ballot and there is no risk that voters will actually adopt it. Such behavior can make voters worse off when the initiative is available than when it is unavailable (Gerber & Lupia, 1995; Matsusaka & McCarty, 2001). Another situation is where voters have less information about a policy's effect than legislators have. When this is the case, voters will look at the policy chosen by the legislature and use it to make inferences about the underlying quality of the project. Knowing this, a legislature facing a referendum may choose an inefficient policy in order to signal or hide its information from the voters. If this happens, the voters may be worse off with a referendum than if the decision had been fully delegated to the legislature (Marino & Matsusaka, 2005).

7.3. *Information*

The preponderance of research views direct democracy as a way of reining in unfaithful agents. The initiative and referendum are seen as last resorts, useful only when elected officials fail to perform adequately. A somewhat new vein of research focuses on how direct democracy affects the quality of information used to make public decisions. The value of direct democracy depends on whether it increases or reduces the quality of information.

Much depends on what is assumed about the nature of the relevant information. One view is that the information necessary to make "good" policy decisions is centralizable and can be obtained from specialists (legislatures, government bureaucrats, academics). Under this assumption, direct democracy typically leads to worse outcomes than purely representative government because ordinary citizens lack access to the expert opinion that is available to legislators (Maskin & Tirole, 2004). Even worse, regular use of ballot propositions may reduce the incentive of public officials to collect information, further degrading the quality of decisions (Kessler, forthcoming).

An alternative view, following Hayek (1945), is that the relevant information is widely dispersed and inherently unknowable by any small group of experts. For example, the best occupational safety regulation might depend on specific facts known by employers and employees concerning their private benefits and costs under any given regulatory regime. Moreover, some issues may not have a "right" decision, particularly issues involving values. For example, the decision whether to allow physician-assisted suicide is to a large degree a matter of a community defining its standards rather than a search for an objectively optimal policy. For such issues, the opinions of the community at large may be more relevant for choosing policy than the information of legislators or experts.

When the information necessary to make the right decision is dispersed, elected officials will find themselves without the relevant information, and may make poor policy decisions inadvertently, what could be called "honest mistakes". According to this view of information, direct democracy is a way of tapping the dispersed information of the electorate. Direct decisionmaking can outperform representative decisionmaking if voters have better or more relevant information than experts (Matsusaka, 1992).

Direct decision-making can also be better when voters have no more or even worse information than legislators, following the logic of the "Condorcet Jury Theorem". By the law of large numbers, aggregating the opinions of a million voters can give a very accurate estimate of an underlying parameter even if each individual's chance of knowing the parameter is small. Aggregation can make the decision of a poorly informed mass more accurate than the decision of a small group of highly informed experts (Lupia, 2001).

In contrast to the agency view, direct democracy is not a last resort from an information perspective. It may well be a first resort. Some issues may be so dependent on dispersed information or community values that they are better resolved by popular vote than by legislative action, even if legislatures are entirely faithful public servants.

The information view helps explain why successful initiatives in one state sometimes trigger similar policy changes in other states, such as Prop. 13. A successful measure reveals information about voter preferences and perceived benefits and costs of policies. Once revealed, this information will affect decisions by policy makers in other states who want to adjust their policies to accommodate voter preferences.

The information view implies that initiatives and referendums are most valuable when it is difficult for legislators to determine voter preferences. This could be one reason why large cities are more likely than small cities to allow and use initiatives (Matsusaka, 2004; Gordon, 2004): it is harder for representatives to keep in touch with their constituents when the population is large. The same line of reasoning would suggest that initiatives are used more often in heterogeneous cities than in homogeneous cities. The evidence on this is mixed: Matsusaka and McCarty (2001) found more initiatives in states that are ethnically and income diverse. Gordon (2004) found more initiatives in cities with unequal income, but fewer in ethnically diverse cities.

Whether the information necessary to make good policy decisions is centralizable or widely dispersed probably varies from issue to issue. There are some issues, such as detailed standards governing water quality, that are best left to experts, and others, such as whether to allow capital punishment, where experts have no obvious informational advantage. The information view suggests that legislatures should focus on technical issues and initiatives should be used to resolve issues involving values where representatives have no information advantage. Some evidence suggests that this is what happens in practice (Matsusaka, 1992).

8. Future Directions

Research to date has focused on comparing representative with direct democracy, largely with an eye toward determining which is better in some sense. The preponderance of evidence suggests that direct democracy is no worse than representative democracy along a variety of dimensions. As time goes by, the broad question of what form of democracy is superior will likely diminish in importance: direct democracy is here to stay, and all indicators suggest it will play an ever larger role in setting public policies. The key research questions for the 21st century will involve understanding how direct democracy fits into and changes the institutions of representative democracy. Among them are the following.

8.1. *What is the optimal division of labor between representative and direct democracy?*

The initiative and referendum will not make representatives obsolete. Modern government is too large and complicated to be managed with periodic ballot propositions. The specialization arguments for a class of government experts will only become stronger over time.

The question is what tasks should be performed by direct and what by representative democracy in the future? The emerging pattern appears to be that initiatives and referendums are used to resolve broad policy issues, while implementation details and overall budgeting are left to legislatures. For example, Matsusaka (1992) shows that initiatives are more likely to address broad distributional and moral issues while technical regulatory and government administration issues are left to the legislature.

Along the same lines, what polities are better suited for direct democracy? To take a concrete example, are the initiative and referendum more valuable in big cities or small cities? At least two factors suggest a higher value for direct democracy in large cities. First, agency problems are likely to be more severe in large cities than in small cities because free rider problems make it less likely that constituents will monitor their representatives in large cities. Second, elected officials are less likely to understand the preferences of their constituents in large than small cities. Empirically, large cities are more likely than small cities to have and use the initiative, as noted above, suggesting that institutions might be evolving in an efficient way.

8.2. *How does direct democracy change representative government?*

Direct democracy is likely to change the role and behavior of elected representatives. As noted above, the threat of an initiative can cause the legislature to revise its policy decisions. And, also as noted above, to the extent that initiatives take the lead in setting spending priorities and determining the broad direction of policy, legislatures will find their role redefined to focus on implementation of policy priorities set by the people, both in terms of writing supporting legislation and in terms of budgeting. This may change the nature of skills required in elected officials, the desirability of term limits, the role of political parties, and so on.

Buchanan and Tullock (1962) stressed that logrolling was a central feature of legislatures. Initiatives and referendums tend to undermine legislative logrolls. The question of how this will affect the functioning of legislatures is largely unexplored. Besley and Coate (2003) focus on the bundling of issues in candidates, and show how the presence of initiatives can lead to more efficient candidate elections. Matsusaka (2005) shows how unbundling can allow voters to deliver stronger sanctions at the polls, by reducing the number of issues elected officials are accountable for. No research to date has explored how unbundling will affect the internal organization and procedures of legislatures.

There is also the question of how the initiative will affect the executive branch. Direct democracy, by overriding the legislature, would seem to shift the balance of power toward the governor and away from the legislature. Indeed, governors not infrequently make use of the initiative when their policy goals are stymied by the legislature. The median voter model suggests that governors on average will be more closely aligned with the median voter than the legislature (especially when legislative seats are gerrymandered). The governor should therefore be able to threaten initiatives with some credibility, further tipping the scales in his favor. However, initiatives also provide an avenue around the executive's veto, which could weaken his bargaining position. Exactly what the implications are for the strengthening of the executive vis-à-vis the legislative merits serious investigation.

9. Conclusion

This essay began by describing a variety of political, demographic, and technological trends that pointed to an eclipse of legislatures in the 21st century, and the rise of direct democracy as the first choice for making broad policy decisions. If the trends do play out the way I speculate they might, current evidence suggests that it should not be a cause for alarm. Indeed, the quality of governance may well improve in some respects. The initiative and referendum seem to bring about greater majority rule without undermining the rights of minorities, and lead to policies that improve economic performance.

While direct democracy takes away some of the functions of legislatures, it does not do away with representative government. Indeed, the benefits of economic specialization create strong pressure for the delegation of many public functions to professionals. A critical challenge for public choice scholarship will be to understand how direct democracy impacts and changes the functioning of legislatures. Among the important changes brought about by direct democracy is the unbundling of legislative logrolls, which threatens to create havoc in the heart of the legislative enterprise.

Acknowledgments

I would like to thank Scott Altman for raising a number of issues that forced me to think through the argument more carefully. USC provided financial support and some data were provided by the Initiative & Referendum Institute at USC. Parts of this essay are based on my book, *For the Many or the Few: The Initiative, Public Policy, and American Democracy* (Matsusaka, 2004).

Notes

1. I use referendum*s* instead of referend*a* following the *Oxford English Dictionary*, most mainstream media, and the emerging scholarly convention.
2. Mississippi adopted in 1916 but the initiative was struck down by a court ruling in 1922.
3. The information in this paragraph is from Matsusaka (2003, 2004).
4. For information on legal provisions and histories in the United States and Europe, see Waters (2003) and the web sites of the Initiative & Referendum Institute (www.iandrinstitute.org) and IRI-Europe (www.iri-europe.org).
5. The survey was conducted by Portrait of America. It can be found in Waters (2003) and on the web site of the Initiative & Referendum Institute (www.iandrinstitute.org).
6. From *Statistical Abstract of the United States*, US Department of Commerce (2003, Table No. 227).
7. It is worth noting that although the initiative has tended to push policy in a conservative direction over the last several decades, it pushed policy in a liberal direction in the early twentieth century (Matsusaka, 2000, 2004). Thus, the initiative does not have an inherent conservative bias.
8. See the symposium on "shirking" in the June 1993 issue of *Public Choice*.
9. Gilligan and Matsusaka (1995, 2001), Bradbury and Crain (2001) and Baqir (2002) test the "Law of $1/n$" implication of the theory identified by Weingast, Shepsle and Johnsen (1981). DelRossi and Inman (1999) provide direct evidence from congressional votes.

References

Baqir, R. (2002). Districting and government overspending. *Journal of Political Economy, 110*(6), 1318–1354.

Becker, G. S. (1983). A theory of competition among pressure groups for political Influence. *Quarterly Journal of Economics, 98*(3), 371–400.

Besley, T., & Coate, S. (2003). Issue unbundling by citizen initiatives. Working Paper, London School of Economics, London, UK.

Black, D. (1958). *The Theory of Committees and Elections*. Cambridge: Cambridge University Press.

Blomberg, S. B., Hess, G. D., & Weerapana, A. (2004). The impact of voter initiatives on economic activity. *European Journal of Political Economy, 20*(1), 207–226.

Bohn, H., & Inman, R. P. (1996). Balanced budget rules and public deficits: Evidence from U.S. states. *Carnegie-Rochester Conference Series on Public Policy, 45*(1), 13–76.

Bowler, S., & Donovan, T. (1998). *Demanding Choices: Opinion, Voting, and Direct Democracy*. Ann Arbor, MI: The University of Michigan Press.

Bradbury, J. C., & Crain, W. M. (2001). Legislative organization and government spending: Cross country evidence. *Journal of Public Economics, 82*(3), 309–325.

Broder, D. S. (2000). *Democracy Derailed: Initiative Campaigns and the Power of Money*. New York: Harcourt.

Buchanan, J. M., & Tullock, G. (1962). *The Calculus of Consent: Logical Foundations of Constitutional Democracy*. Ann Arbor: University of Michigan Press.

DelRossi, A. F., & Inman, R. P. (1999). Changing the price of pork: The impact of local cost sharing on legislators' demands for distributive public goods. *Journal of Public Economics, 71*(2), 247–273.

Downs, A. (1957). *An Economic Theory of Democracy*. New York: Harper & Row.

Feld, L. P., & Kirchgassner, G. (2001). Does direct democracy reduce public debt? Evidence from Swiss Municipalities. *Public Choice, 109*(3–4), 347–370.

Feld, L. P., & Savioz, M. R. (1997). Direct democracy matters for economic performance: An empirical investigation. *Kyklos, 50*(4), 507–538.

Frey, B. S., & Stutzer, A. (2000). Happiness, economy and institutions. *Economic Journal, 110*(466), 918–938.

Gerber, E. R. (1996). Legislative response to the threat of popular initiatives. *American Journal of Political Science, 40*(1), 99–128.

Gerber, E. R. (1999). *The Populist Paradox: Interest Group Influence and the Promise of Direct Legislation*. Princeton, NJ: Princeton University Press.

Gerber, E. R., & Lupia, A. (1995). Campaign competition and policy responsiveness in direct legislation Elections. *Political Behavior, 17*(3), 287–306.

Gilligan, T. W., & Matsusaka, J. G. (1995). Systematic deviations from constituent interests: The role of legislative structure and political parties in the states. *Economic Inquiry, 33*(3), 383–401.

Gilligan, T. W., & Matsusaka, J. G. (2001). Fiscal policy, legislature size, and political parties: Evidence from the first half of the Twentieth Century. *National Tax Journal, 54*(1), 57–82.

Gordon, T. M. (2004). *The Local Initiative in California*. San Francisco: Public Policy Institute of California.

Hayek, F. A. (1945). The use of knowledge in society. *American Economic Review, 35*(4), 519–530.

Kessler, A. S. (forthcoming). Representative versus direct democracy: The role of information asymmetries. *Public Choice*.

Kiewiet, D. R., & Szakaly, K. (1996). Constitutional limitations on borrowing: An analysis of state bonded indebtedness. *Journal of Law, Economics, and Organization, 12*(1), 62–97.

Lupia, A. (1994). Shortcuts versus encyclopedias: Information and voting behavior in california insurance reform elections. *American Political Science Review, 88*(1), 63–76.

Lupia, A. (2001). Dumber than chimps? An assessment of direct democracy voters. In L. J. Sabato, H. R. Ernst, & B. A. Larson (Eds.), *Dangerous Democracy? The Battle over Ballot Initiatives in America* (pp. 66–70). Lanham, MD: Rowman & Littlefield.

Lupia, A., & McCubbins, M. D. (1998). *The Democratic Dilemma: Can Citizens Learn What They Need to Know?* Cambridge and New York: Cambridge University Press.

Marino, A. M., & Matsusaka, J. G. (2005). Decision processes, agency problems, and information: An economic analysis of capital budgeting procedures. *Review of Financial Studies, 18*(1), 301–325.

Maskin, E., & Tirole, J. (2004). The politician and the judge: Accountability in government. *American Economic Review, 94*(4), 1034–1054.

Matsusaka, J. G. (1992). Economics of direct legislation. *Quarterly Journal of Economics, 107*(429), 541–571.

Matsusaka, J. G. (1995). Fiscal effects of the voter initiative: Evidence from the last 30 years. *Journal of Political Economy, 103*(3), 587–623.

Matsusaka, J. G. (2000). Fiscal effects of the voter initiative in the first half of the 20th century. *Journal of Law and Economics, 43*(2), 619–648.

Matsusaka, J. G. (2003). I&R in American cities: Basic patterns. In M. D. Waters (Ed.), *Initiative and Referendum Almanac* (pp. 31–36). Durham, NC: Carolina Academic Press.

Matsusaka, J. G. (2004). *For the Many or the Few: The Initiative, Public Policy, and American Democracy*. Chicago: University of Chicago Press.

Matsusaka, J. G. (2005). Direct democracy and the executive. Working Paper, USC Marshall School of Business, Los Angeles, CA.

Matsusaka, J. G. (forthcoming). Direct democracy and fiscal gridlock: Have voter initiatives paralyzed the california budget? *State Politics and Policy Quarterly*.

Matsusaka, J. G., & McCarty, N. M. (2001). Political resource allocation: Benefits and costs of voter initiatives. *Journal of Law, Economics, and Organization, 17*(2), 413–448.

Peltzman, S. (1976). Toward a more general theory of regulation. *Journal of Law and Economics, 19*(2), 211–240.

Pommerehne, W. W. (1983). Private versus Oeffentliche Muellabfuhr – Nochmals Betrachtet. *Finanzarchiv, 41*(2), 466–475.

Romer, T., & Rosenthal, H. (1979). Bureaucrats versus voters: On the political economy of resource allocation by direct democracy. *Quarterly Journal of Economics, 93*(4), 563–587.

Stigler, G. J. (1971). The theory of economic regulation. *Bell Journal of Economics and Management Science, 2*(Spring), 3–21.

Waters, M. D. (2003). *Initiative and Referendum Almanac*. Durham, NC: Carolina Academic Press.

Weingast, B. R., Shepsle, K. A., & Johnsen, C. (1981). The political economy of benefits and costs: A neoclassical approach to distributive politics. *Journal of Political Economy, 93*(4), 642–664.

Public Choice (2005) **124:** 179–204
DOI: 10.1007/s11127-005-4761-0

Corporations, collective action and corporate governance: One size does not fit all

J. HAROLD MULHERIN
Department of Economics, Claremont McKenna College, Claremont, CA 91711, USA
(E-mail: harold.mulherin@claremontmckenna.edu)

Accepted March 2005

Abstract. A review of the theory and evidence on corporate governance indicates several related themes. First, corporate governance is multidimensional. Second, corporate governance is an endogenous response to a firm's economic environment. Third, the role of different governance mechanisms varies across industries. New analysis of a sample of 1235 US corporations from 40 different industries in the year 2000 confirms the empirical regularities reported in prior research. The central policy implication of the prior research and new supporting evidence is that one size does not fit all in corporate governance.

1. Introduction

The modern corporation is a complex organizational form that coordinates the activity of a variety of interests. The number of shareholders and employees of a corporation can reach into the millions. Corporations also interact with creditors, suppliers, customers, financial advisors and other parties. Hence, the operation of the corporation represents a multidimensional collective action process. Given the many dimensions of conflicts of interest that are inherent in the corporation, a fundamental question posed by Alchian (1977b) is: how has such an organizational form managed to survive?

The answer to this question is known in modern parlance as "corporate governance". Corporate governance can be defined as the set of mechanisms directing the collective action process of the corporation. Narrowly considered, corporate governance refers to internal organizational devices such as inside ownership and the board of directors. From a broader perspective, such as the model provided by Jensen (1993), corporate governance also encompasses the legal, political and regulatory system as well as product and capital markets.

Recent events have raised the question as to whether there are serious defects in the corporate governance system in the United States. The ongoing list of scandals reported in the media nearly spans the alphabet, including corporations such as Adelphia, Enron and Tyco. Corporate executives seem more likely to be pictured in handcuffs than to be announcing dividend increases or new products.

In the wake of these scandals, a fall guy appears to be the corporate director. As outlined by Lowenstein (2003), corporate boards of directors have been viewed as being too passive in their monitoring of corporate executives. To remedy such governance defects, Congress passed the Sarbanes-Oxley Act in 2002 to increase board independence and thereby improve corporate responsibility. The New York Stock Exchange has developed new standards that also aim at improving the performance of the boards of its listed firms. Calls for further changes revisit proposals earlier made by Jensen (1993) to separate the positions of board chairman and chief executive officer and to reduce the sizes of boards.

The purpose of this paper is to weigh such calls for governance reform against the body of theory and empirical research on corporate governance and to offer new evidence pertinent to the current governance debate. As cautioned by Stigler in 1964, recommendations as to the reform of securities regulation are often made without a systematic evaluation of testable hypotheses and instead follow a process in which rhetoric replaces reason. In a similar vein, as a response to current governance proposals, Warren Buffet criticizes the reformers for following "checklists on proper corporate governance rather than thinking their positions through" (quoted in Klein, 2004).

In juxtaposing the calls for reform with the empirical evidence, a general question to address is: does corporate governance matter? This question itself can be subdivided into two distinct inquiries: first, does corporate governance vary systematically with firm and industry characteristics and, second, does corporate governance have causal effects on performance? Much of the prior research has focused on the first question and has provided evidence on the cross-sectional variation in corporate governance. In contrast, the interest of policymakers often focuses on the second question as to whether governance causes performance.

Because of the interest in inferring causal effects, a primary concern with the calls for change in governance is that they often offer a one-size-fits-all approach to governance reform. But would we expect the appropriate governance structure for a firm such as Wal-Mart, with several hundred thousand shareholders and more than a million employees, to be the same as for a firm such as Tiffany & Co., with 2500 shareholders and 5000 employees? Would we expect the governance structure at an electric utility to be the same as at an Internet company, or that of a commercial bank to be the same as that of a semiconductor firm?

A review of the theory and evidence on corporate governance indicates that governance does indeed vary predictably across firms. In particular, governance is multidimensional and varies systematically across industries. The multidimensional nature of corporate governance indicates that the focus in many reform proposals on a narrow set of mechanisms ignores the substitutability and complementarity provided by the broad set of forces operating on the corporation. The systematic variation in governance across industries indicates that an attempt to mandate change at all firms may distort the endogenous process through which governance evolves. As a whole, the research on corporate governance cautions against a one-size-fits-all approach that appears to be inherent in most reform proposals.

To present these ideas, the remainder of the paper proceeds as follows. Section 2 lays out Jensen's (1993) model of the forces operating on the corporation and reviews the pertinent theoretical and empirical research on corporate governance. Section 3 considers in detail the research on one particular component of corporate governance, ownership, as a means of illustrating how the endogenous nature of corporate governance affects conclusions as to the causal effects of a single governance mechanism. Section 4 offers new evidence from a recent sample that confirms and extends prior findings of systematic regularities in governance across industries. Section 5 summarizes the paper and offers some suggestions for future research.

2. The Control Forces Operating on the Corporation

Corporate governance can be viewed as the set of control devices that arise in response to the many potential conflicts of interest that are inherent in the modern corporation. For example, Becht, Bolton and Roell (2002) define corporate governance as the various mechanisms that resolve the collective action problem of the corporation (see Garvey & Swan, 1994; Shleifer & Vishny, 1997 for related discussions).

Consistent with the broad view of corporate governance, Jensen (1993) sketches a model in which there are four key control forces operating on the corporation: the legal, political and regulatory system; product and factor markets; capital markets; and internal control systems. This section reviews the theory and evidence on the role of these four governance factors. An outline of the theoretical and empirical research is provided in Table 1. Many of the empirical papers in Table 1 are collected in Mulherin (2004).

2.1. *The legal, political and regulatory environment*

The underlying legal, political and regulatory environment is an important aspect of corporate governance. As emphasized by Coase (1960) and Alchian (1977a), the strength of property rights affects the potential gains from trade that can be attained in a particular economic system. La Porta et al. (1998) provide international evidence of the effects of the variation in the legal system across countries.

Much of the empirical research on the effects of the external legal, political and regulatory environment on corporations has dealt with privatization and deregulation. As surveyed by Megginson and Netter (2001), privatization in Europe and elsewhere appears to work, in the sense that firms perform better after the government sells its stake in the enterprise. Related research

Table 1. The control forces operating on the corporation

Control force	Device	Theoretical research	Empirical research
Legal/political/ regulatory	Corporate law	Coase (1960)	La Porta, Lopez-de-Silanes, Shleifer and Vishny (1998)
	Privatization/ deregulation	Alchian (1977a)	Megginson and Netter (2001)
		Jensen and Meckling (1979)	Winston (1988)
			Kole and Lehn (1999)
			Mulherin, Netter and Stegemoller (2004)
			Andrade, Mitchell and Stafford (2001)
Product and factor markets	Competition	Coase (1937)	Mitchell and Mulherin (1996)
	Technological change	Fama (1980)	Mulherin and Boone (2000)
Capital markets	Takeovers and proxy contests	Manne (1965)	Mitchell and Lehn (1990)
	Corporate debt	Jensen (1986)	Mulherin and Poulsen (1988)
	Dividend policy	Easterbrook (1984)	Smith and Watts (1992)
		Williamson (1988)	
Internal control	Stock ownership	Alchian and Demsetz (1972)	Demsetz and Lehn (1985)
	Board of directors	Jensen and Meckling (1976)	Yermack (1996)
		Fama and Jensen (1983)	Lehn, Patro and Zhao (2003)
		Jensen (1993)	Agrawal and Knoeber (1996)
		Hermalin and Weisbach (1998)	Gillan, Hartzell and Starks (2003)

This table sketches the four control forces operating on the corporation as discussed in Jensen (1993) and lists selected theoretical and empirical research.

summarized by Winston (1998) reports similar evidence for deregulation in the United States.

An outstanding question is: how exactly do privatization and deregulation improve performance? One possibility is that privatization and deregulation more fully expose corporations to the survivorship mechanism modeled by

Alchian (1950). Evidence consistent with this line of thought is provided by Kole and Lehn (1999), who find that deregulation in the airline industry was followed by a gradual change in the governance structure at the representative airline and that surviving airlines more rapidly adapted their governance structures than non-survivors.

Another important feature of the private-sector corporation that has been emphasized in theoretical research is the transferability of shares. Jensen and Meckling (1979) note that the alienability of shares facilitates organized markets that regularly monitor the performance of corporations. More generally, Alchian (1977a) argues that the transferability of shares enables assets to flow to higher valued uses. Consistent with this argument, Mulherin, Netter and Stegemoller (2003) report that privatization in industries such as banking, electric utilities and telecommunications has been followed by heightened merger activity that arguably has enabled the privatized firms to better adapt firm size and organizational structure to a new economic environment. Andrade et al. (2001) report similar effects of deregulation on merger activity in the United States.

2.2. *Product and factor markets*

A second force that impinges on corporate governance is the strength of competition faced in product and factor markets. These competitive forces not only guide production decisions, such as plant size, and marketing decisions, such as the prices charged for the firm's products, but also affect the breadth of the production activities within a single firm (Coase, 1937) and the managerial labor market (Fama, 1980). Consistent with the effect of factor markets on organizational form, Mitchell and Mulherin (1996) find that merger activity during the 1980s clustered in energy-sensitive industries. For a sample of firms from the 1990s, Mulherin and Boone (2000) report that both mergers and divestitures cluster by industry and portray these patterns in corporate restructuring as responses to changes in the underlying economic environment.

Competition often interacts with other factors such as the legal, political, and regulatory system. Indeed, one of the reasons that privatization and deregulation have been associated with improved performance is that particular privatization programs and deregulation events often facilitate entry. In their analysis of airline deregulation, for example, Kole and Lehn (1999) report that competition from new entrants provided inducements for governance changes at industry incumbents.

As discussed in Weston, Mitchell and Mulherin (2004, pp. 188–194), the more vigorous competition associated with privatization and deregulation is often tied to technological change. For example, the timing of the privatization of telecommunications markets in Europe and the break-up of AT&T in the United States can be explained in large part by the lessening of the natural monopoly characteristics of wire lines produced by innovations in wireless and satellite communications. This combination of technological change and heightened competition is one reason why both privatization and deregulation are often followed by merger activity. Indeed, the impetus for privatization and deregulation in the first place is often an endogenous response to technological change.

2.3. *Capital markets*

A third set of corporate governance mechanisms comes from the capital markets. One component of this mechanism is the market for corporate control. As modeled by Manne (1965), the possibility of a corporate takeover provides a strong incentive for incumbent management to operate the firm in the interest of shareholders. Symmetrically, firms in which management fails to act in the interests of shareholders are likely to become vulnerable to takeover or proxy contests. Consistent with Manne's model, Mitchell and Lehn (1990) find that firms that make poor acquisition decisions become takeover targets themselves. Similarly, Mulherin and Poulsen (1998) find that poorly performing firms are often the object of a proxy contest and that senior managers at such firms are likely to be replaced following the contest.

Another aspect of the governance feature of capital markets comes from debt and equity markets. As modeled by Jensen (1986), the use of corporate debt monitors corporate performance by requiring regular payments and inducing a periodic return to lenders for more capital. Easterbrook (1984) makes similar arguments about the regular payment of dividends.

Williamson (1988) points out, however, that the choice of debt versus equity will respond to asset characteristics. Consistent with this argument, Smith and Watts (1992) find that financing policies and dividend payment schedules vary across industries. Firms in industries with tangible assets and few growth options have a greater fraction of debt in their capital structures and are more likely to pay dividends, while firms in industries with intangible assets and greater growth potential use proportionately more equity and are less likely to pay dividends. Hence, although debt and dividends may serve as corporate governance devices, their role is likely to vary with asset characteristics across industries.

2.4. *Internal control*

The fourth set of forces operating on the corporation is the body of internal control mechanisms, such as stock ownership and the board of directors. The underlying theory of internal control mechanisms can be traced to Alchian and Demsetz (1972). In studying the modern corporation, they isolated the essence of corporate governance with the provocative query, "who monitors the monitor?" Their answer was that residual claimancy in the form of stock ownership is a powerful incentive device for corporate managers. Jensen and Meckling (1976) extended this conceptual analysis by modeling the factors that affect the relative mixes of inside ownership, outside equity and outside debt that corporations tap for financing. Demsetz and Lehn (1985) provide a cogent analysis of the causes and effects of corporate ownership. A more detailed review of the empirical research in this area is provided in Section 3.

Subsequent analysis has considered the role of other internal mechanisms that complement the use of ownership as an incentive device. Fama and Jensen (1983) model how the structure of the board of directors, such as the fraction of inside and outside directors, can monitor the performance of corporations. Hermalin and Weisbach (1998) model the membership of the board and the monitoring of management as an endogenous process that is affected by firm performance and monitoring costs.

While the bulk of the theoretical analysis of internal control devices adopts a positive approach, much of the empirical analysis on internal governance is more normative in content. An example is research by Yermack (1996) on the effects of board size on corporate value. For a sample of 452 large industrial firms in the 1984 to 1991 period, Yermack finds that Tobin's q – the ratio of market value of assets to replacement cost – is inversely related to board size. He interprets the results as consistent with Jensen's (1993) conjecture that large corporate boards impede corporate performance.

A variety of evidence on internal corporate governance, however, raises concerns with such normative assertions of causality between board structure and corporate performance. Lehn, Patro and Zhao (2003) study a sample of 81 corporations over the 1935 to 2000 period and find that the size of corporate boards is endogenously determined by factors including firm size and growth opportunities. Agrawal and Knoeber (1996) jointly study the interdependence of a number of internal governance mechanisms for a sample of 383 firms in 1987 and conclude that the simple analysis of a single mechanism can produce misleading results. Gillan et al. (2003) study the governance structure for a sample of 2341 firms in the 1997 to 2000 period and find that governance is an endogenous response to industry characteristics such as growth opportunities and information environment.

2.5. *Summary*

This section has reviewed the various governance factors that operate on the modern corporation. As prescribed in Jensen's (1993) model, corporate governance is multidimensional and includes both external forces such as product and capital markets as well as internal devices such as ownership and the board of directors. A central theme that emanates from this review is that governance is an endogenous response to the environment faced by a corporation. A related theme is that the particular governance structure that evolves often varies across industries. This evidence suggests that corporate governance should not be treated with a once-size-fits-all approach. The following section expands on these themes by covering in detail the prior research on the causes and effects of corporate ownership.

3. Corporate Ownership: Does one Size Fit All?

The prior section has sketched the variety of control forces that govern the operation of the corporation. This section studies in detail the role of stock ownership as a governance device. This particular governance mechanism is chosen both because the apparent separation of ownership and control in modern corporations has long been a policy concern and because there is a substantial body of research on the topic. A review of this research illustrates how the endogeneity of governance structure raises cautions about a one-size-fits-all approach to corporate governance.

3.1. *Early research on corporate ownership and performance*

The analysis of the effects of corporate ownership on performance can be traced to Berle and Means's (1932) seminal work, *The Modern Corporation and Private Property*. Defining control as the power to select the board of directors, Berle and Means reported that the ownership of many major US corporations had become so dispersed that the firms were under management control rather than owner control. They expressed concern that such trends created a divergence of interests between owners and managers. As noted by Katz (1960, p. 75), however, in a review of Berle and Means's analysis, "No showing was made that stockholders in corporations with widely dispersed ownership had actually fared worse than those in corporations with concentrated ownership."

The mere existence of dispersed shareholdings is inherent in a major corporation and does not have any obvious policy implications. As noted by Alchian (1977b, p. 229), "Surely the music about the separation of ownership and control requires more lyrics than that stockholding is dispersed among many stockholders." Alchian (1977b) called for research on both the causes and the effects of the dispersion of ownership in modern corporations.

Taking up this charge, the early empirical research on ownership and performance focused on whether corporate ownership was positively associated with corporate performance. In such analyses, a performance measure, such as accounting return on equity, was the dependent variable. Borrowing from the classifications of Berle and Means, ownership was proxied by a dummy variable or set of dummies based on a preset level of ownership

Table 2. Early research on corporate ownership and performance

Study	Sample period	Sample size	Performance measure	Effect of ownership on performance?
Kamerschen (1968)	1959–64	200	Return on equity	No
Monsen, Chiu and Cooley (1968)	1952–63	432	Return on net worth	Yes
Palmer (1973)	1961–65 1966–69	500	Return on net worth	Yes
Sorensen (1974)	1948–66	60	Return on new worth	No
Stano (1976)	1963–72	354	Stock return	Yes
Stigler and Friedland (1983)	1928–38	90	Accounting profits	No

This table summarizes some of the initial research of the effect of corporate ownership on performance. The general approach of this research analyzes whether a measure of performance, such as accounting profit, differs between owner-controlled and manager-controlled firms, as suggested by Berle and Means (1932).

concentration, such as 20%, to indicate whether a given firm was owner-controlled or management-controlled.

Table 2 summarizes some of the early work on ownership and performance. While the studies vary somewhat in time period, sample size, and performance measures, they all ask the same basic question, does ownership affect performance? The answer to this question is evenly mixed across the six studies – three conclude that ownership affects performance and three conclude that it does not.

3.2. *More recent research on ownership and performance*

A later contribution by Demsetz and Lehn (1985) offers reasons why the prior research produced mixed results on the relation between ownership and performance. As noted by these two authors, the ownership level in a given industry is an endogenous response to the economic environment faced by the firm. Hence, the proper estimation of the effect of ownership on performance should control for the factors that cause ownership in the first place.

Demsetz and Lehn perform such an analysis on a sample of 511 firms from 1980. Their measure of ownership is the holdings of the five largest shareholders. Consistent with the endogenous determination of ownership, Demsetz and Lehn find that ownership is related to factors such as risk and size. They also detect significant industry patterns in ownership, finding below-average ownership concentration in the regulated utility and financial sectors and above-average ownership concentration in the publishing and media sectors that have high amenity potential. After controlling for such factors, Demsetz and Lehn observe no significant relation between ownership and performance.

Following Demsetz and Lehn, a number of other studies have addressed the relation between ownership and performance. These studies are summarized in Table 3. As noted in the table, of the five other studies, the three that control for the endogeneity of corporate ownership fail to detect a relation between ownership and performance. As a whole, the recent research is consistent with the view of Demsetz (1983, p. 386) that "the ownership structure likely to maximize the value of the firm's assets depends on the technology of the tasks required of the firm's labor force, on the desired scale of operation, and on the managerial ability of the potential owners of the firm. No single ownership structure is suitable for all situations if the value of the firm's assets is to be maximized." In other words, when it comes to corporate ownership, one size does not fit all.

4. Some Further Evidence of Industry Variation in Corporate Governance

The theory and evidence reviewed in Sections 2 and 3 indicate that corporate governance is a multidimensional process. Moreover, the importance of particular governance mechanisms, such as the capital market, varies across industries. Furthermore, the internal governance mechanisms at a given firm enogenously evolve in response to changes in the firm's economic environment. As a complement to the prior research, this section studies cross-sectional regularities in corporate governance for a recent sample of a broad set of firms. In particular, this section addresses the cross-sectional variation in governance variables tied to financial policy, ownership and board size.

4.1. *The data*

To add further insights on the cross-sectional variation in corporate governance, a dataset is developed on a large sample of firms from a recent time period. The starting point is the universe of firms listed on the Value Line Investment Survey in the first quarter of 2000. Value Line serves as a useful sampling source because of the accurate industry classifications provided by the survey. As noted by Kole (1995), Value Line also provides accessible information on data such as inside ownership.

From the total base of 1643 Value Line listings, all non-US firms are deleted. To enable accurate estimates of the characteristics of an industry, industries with less than 15 firms also are deleted. The resulting sample contains 1235 firms from 40 industries.

Table 4 reports the industry distribution of the sample. The 40 industries range from Aerospace Defense to Telecom Services. Eight hundred and

Table 3. More recent research on corporate ownership and performance

Study	Sample period	Sample size	Ownership measure	Mean ownership	Performance measure	Control for endogeneity?	Effect of ownership on performance?
Demsetz and Lehn (1985)	1980	511	5 largest holders	25%	Return on equity	Yes	No
Morck, Shleifer and Vishny (1988)	1980	371	Directors	10.6%	Tobin's q	No	Yes
McConnell and Servaes (1990)	1976, 1986	1173	Insiders	13.9%	Tobin's q	No	Yes
Cho (1998)	1991	326	Directors	12%	Tobin's q	Yes	No
Himmelberg, Hubbard and Palia (1999)	1982–92	600	Insiders	16%	Tobin's q	Yes	No
Demsetz and Villalonga (2001)	1980	223	5 largest holders, insiders		Tobin's q return on equity	Yes	No

This table summarizes recent research of the effect of ownership on performance. The research regresses measures of performance, such as accounting returns or Tobin's q, on levels of ownership by the largest stockholders, corporate insiders, or both.

Table 4. Sample of industries from the value line investment survey

Industry	Number of firms
Aerospace defense	15
Air & trucking transport	29
Apparel & textile	26
Auto parts	21
Bank & thrift	65
Building materials	15
Cable TV & entertainment	17
Chemical	60
Computer & peripherals	30
Computer software & services	43
Drug	37
Electric utility	78
Electrical equipment	17
Electronics	30
Financial services	46
Food processing	43
Grocery & drug store	18
Household products	16
Industrial services	29
Insurance	36
Internet	18
Machinery	48
Medical services	30
Medical supplies	54
Natural gas distribution	24
Natural gas diversified	19
Newspaper & publishing	26
Office equipment & supplies	20
Oilfield services	18
Paper & forest products	23
Petroleum	31
Precision instrument	24
Recreation	19
Restaurant	29
Retail special lines	66
Retail Store	18
Semiconductor	26
Steel	16
Telecom equipment	19
Telecom services	36
Total number of firms	1235

This table identifies the 40 industries and the corresponding number of firms in the sample taken from the Value Line Investment Survey in the first quarter of 2000.

Table 5. Variable definitions and sources

Variable	Definition	Source
Continuous variables		
Size	Value of common stock	Value line
Age	Age based on incorporation year	Moody's manuals
P/E ratio	Price to earnings ratio	Value line
Dividend yield	Dividend per Share/ Price	Value line
Fraction debt	% Debt in capital structure	Value line
Inside ownership	% Ownership by officers and directors	Value line
Directors	Number of directors	Moody's manuals
Industry dummy variables		
Utility	Electric utility natural gas distribution	Value line
Financial	Bank & thrift financial services insurance	Value line
Media	Cable TV & entertainment newspaper & publishing	Value line

This table reports variable definitions and sources.

ninety-four of the sample firms are listed on the New York Stock Exchange, 320 are listed on the NASDAQ and 21 are listed on the American Stock Exchange. The firms in the sample are large, publicly traded corporations. The total equity value of the sample firms is $12 trillion.

To analyze the relation between corporate governance and firm and industry characteristics, a number of variables are collected from Value Line and other sources. The variables and sources used in the analysis are reported in Table 5. Size is estimated from the equity value of a firm's common stock. Age provides one proxy for the growth potential of a firm. Another such proxy is the price-earnings (P/E) ratio, which is often used in corporate finance as an estimate of growth options (Ross, Westerfield, & Jaffe, 2005, p. 125). Measures of financial policy are dividend yield and the fraction of debt in a firm's capital structure. Governance variables are inside ownership and the number of directors on the board. Following the analysis of Demsetz and Lehn (1985), dummy variables designate firms in the Utility, Financial, and Media sectors.

4.2. *Industry characteristics*

The analysis of the data is performed at the industry level. For each variable, averages are computed across industries. As suggested by Stigler (1958), such aggregation captures the differences in the economic environment faced by the sample firms.

Table 6 reports the estimates of average firm characteristics by industry. For all of the variables, there is a wide variation across industries. Average firm size is $10 billion, but ranges from $39 billion in the Computer and

Table 6. Average firm characteristics by industry

Industry	Size ($bil.)	Age	*P/E* ratio	Dividend yield	Fraction debt
Aerospace defense	4.8	44	12	1.6%	38%
Air & trucking transport	4.0	36	13	0.7%	42%
Apparel & textile	0.7	43	10	1.5%	40%
Auto parts	1.7	47	10	2.0%	42%
Bank & thrift	11.0	30	12	3.4%	44%
Building materials	1.6	61	11	2.3%	35%
Cable TV & entertainment	23.8	35	37	0.3%	42%
Chemical	4.0	51	15	2.3%	40%
Computer & peripherals	39.0	29	30	0.0%	17%
Computer software & services	24.0	19	32	0.1%	14%
Drug	25.6	32	34	0.5%	20%
Electric utility	3.2	58	12	5.8%	48%
Electrical equipment	34.3	74	19	1.8%	25%
Electronics	5.1	40	33	0.2%	29%
Financial services	16.7	27	14	1.8%	37%
Food processing	3.4	55	15	1.9%	44%
Grocery & drug store	6.1	55	20	1.2%	34%
Household products	15.0	57	19	1.4%	46%
Industrial services	1.8	28	20	0.9%	21%
Insurance	4.9	33	16	2.3%	21%
Internet	22.4	8	34	0.0%	19%
Machinery	1.6	59	14	1.8%	35%
Medical services	2.8	19	14	0.1%	42%
Medical supplies	6.2	32	22	0.6%	25%
Natural gas distribution	0.8	55	15	4.9%	47%
Natural gas diversified	4.3	52	20	1.9%	54%
Newspaper & publishing	3.5	65	18	1.9%	37%
Office equipment & supplies	3.2	61	18	1.9%	34%
Oilfield services	3.7	34	38	0.5%	28%
Paper & forest products	4.1	61	16	2.7%	49%
Petroleum	13.2	56	19	2.3%	44%
Precision instrument	5.5	37	26	0.5%	27%
Recreation	1.7	33	17	1.3%	25%
Restaurant	2.3	25	13	0.8%	25%
Retail special lines	2.2	29	16	0.7%	17%
Retail store	21.3	51	19	1.0%	36%
Semiconductor	24.8	24	45	0.1%	13%
Steel	0.9	54	12	3.6%	31%
Telecom equipment	24.8	22	42	0.0%	15%
Telecom services	33.4	28	32	0.5%	40%
Average	10.3	42	21	1.5%	33%

This table reports the average values by industry for size, age, *P/E* ratio, dividend yield and fraction of debt. The number of firms in each industry is shown in Table 4. Variable definitions are in Table 5.

Peripherals industry to less than $1 billion in the Apparel and Textile industry. Average age ranges from 74 years in the Electric Equipment industry to 8 years in the Internet industry. The average P/E ratio is 45 for the growth-intensive Semiconductor industry, but is only 10 for the Auto Parts industry. The average dividend yield ranges from a high of 5.8% in the Electric Utility industry to virtually zero in the Telecom Equipment industry. The fraction of debt in corporate capital structures is highest in the Natural Gas Diversified industry and lowest in the Semiconductor industry.

Table 7 reports the industry variation in governance measures. For the full sample, inside ownership averages 13%, which is comparable to the prior studies reviewed in Table 3. Average inside ownership varies across industries. For example, the average value for the Cable TV and Entertainment industry is 36% while the average value for the Electric Utility industry is only 1%.

The second governance variable in Table 7 is the average number of directors. For the full sample, the average number of directors is ten. Firms in the Internet and Semiconductor industries have an average of seven directors, while firms in the Bank & Thrift industry have an average of 16 directors.

The data on the number of directors suggest a downward trend in board size. By way of comparison, Mace (1971, p. 10) reports an average board size of 15 directors in the early 1970s. Using data from the 1984 to 1991 time period, Yermack (1996, p. 191) reports an average board size of 12 directors.

4.3. *Industry variation in financial policy and corporate governance*

To determine whether there are regularities across industries in financial policy and corporate governance in the sample, the following three questions are addressed in turn:

1. Do financial policies vary by industry?
2. Does ownership vary by industry?
3. Does board size vary by industry?

4.3.1. *Do financial policies vary by industry?*

For a sample from the 1965 to 1985 period, Smith and Watts (1992) find that financial policies such as dividend payouts and capital structure vary systematically across industries as a function of investment opportunities. To assess the robustness of these results, similar analysis is performed on the current sample from the year 2000. The dependent variables for financial policy, average dividend yield and the average fraction of debt, are regressed on proxies for growth options, the *P/E* ratio and Age, and a variable that controls for company size.

Table 7. Average governance characteristics by industry

Industry	Inside ownership	Directors
Aerospace defense	7%	10.0
Air & trucking transport	18%	9.0
Apparel & textile	23%	9.7
Auto parts	10%	9.2
Bank & thrift	5%	16.0
Building materials	13%	9.7
Cable TV & entertainment	36%	10.5
Chemical	10%	10.2
Computer & peripherals	8%	8.5
Computer software & services	14%	7.7
Drug	11%	9.6
Electric utility	1%	11.2
Electrical equipment	9%	10.4
Electronics	15%	8.6
Financial services	9%	11.8
Food processing	19%	10.3
Grocery & drug store	12%	11.3
Household products	15%	11.0
Industrial services	20%	9.1
Insurance	14%	11.3
Internet	30%	7.2
Machinery	14%	9.0
Medical services	9%	9.9
Medical supplies	13%	8.9
Natural gas distribution	2%	10.0
Natural gas diversified	14%	11.5
Newspaper & publishing	35%	10.8
Office equipment & supplies	8%	9.6
Oilfield services	7%	9.2
Paper & forest products	8%	10.7
Petroleum	7%	10.8
Precision instrument	9%	8.2
Recreation	14%	8.6
Restaurant	14%	8.8
Retail special lines	21%	8.5
Retail Store	13%	11.6
Semiconductor	8%	7.1
Steel	11%	9.7
Telecom equipment	9%	8.4
Telecom services	16%	10.9
Average	13%	9.9

This table reports the average values by industry for inside ownership and directors. The number of firms in each industry is shown in Table 4. Variable definitions are in Table 5.

Table 8. Industry variation in financial policies

	Dependent variables	
Independent variables	Dividend yield coefficient (*p*-value)	Fraction debt coefficient (*p*-value)
Intercept	1.27 (0.09)	29.67 (0.0001)
P/E ratio	−0.053 (0.02)	−0.36 (0.09)
Age	0.034 (0.004)	0.28 (0.01)
Size	−0.007 (0.68)	−0.07 (0.66)
Adjusted R^2	0.47	0.36
N	40	40

This table reports regression analysis at the industry level of financial policy variables on proxies for growth options and size. Variables are defined in Table 5 and the underlying data are reported in Table 6.

The results of the analysis of financial policy are reported in Table 8. In the first column, Dividend Yield is found to be negatively related to the *P/E* ratio and positively related to Age. Hence, firms in older industries with fewer growth options are more likely to pay dividends than firms in younger, more growth-oriented industries. The control variable, Size, is not significantly related to dividend policy. The relation between dividend policy and growth options is consistent with Smith and Watts (1992).

The analysis of the Fraction of Debt in the capital structure produces similar results. Fraction of Debt is negatively related to the *P/E* ratio and positively related to Age. Firms in older industries with fewer growth options have a greater fraction of debt than firms in younger industries with more growth potential. These results are consistent with the model of Williamson (1988), who argues that the choice of debt versus equity responds systematically to asset characteristics.

The variation in financial policy reported in prior research and confirmed here for a recent sample of firms has important policy implications. Jensen (1986) provides a model in which debt provides an important monitoring device. Easterbrook (1984) formulates similar ideas as to the role of dividend payments. The evidence on the cross-sectional regularities in financial policy across industries, however, indicates that the monitoring role of debt and dividends cannot be expected to be the same for all firms.

4.3.2. *Does ownership vary by industry?*

Demsetz (1983) argues that inside ownership should vary with the underlying technological and managerial constraints faced by a firm. Demsetz and Lehn

Table 9. Industry variation in inside ownership

Independent variables	Dependent variable: Inside ownership coefficient (p-value)
Intercept	0.13 (0.000)
Utility	−0.11 (0.005)
Financial	−0.036 (0.26)
Media	0.23 (0.000)
Adjusted R^2	0.53
N	40

This table reports regression analysis at the industry level of insider ownership on proxies for regulation and amenity value. Variables are defined in Table 5. Ownership data by industry are reported in Table 7.

(1985) pursue this line of thought by contrasting the ownership in regulated industries such as utilities and banking and industries in the media sector with high amenity potential. Using data from 1980, they find that firms in regulated industries have relatively low ownership concentration, while firms in the media sector have relatively high ownership concentration.

To probe the robustness of these results, the analysis is replicated with the current sample from the year 2000. Table 9 reports regressions of the average percentage of shares owned by corporate insiders in an industry on dummy variables for the Utility, Financial, and Media sectors. Consistent with the prior research by Demsetz and Lehn, ownership concentration in the Utility sector is significantly lower than the representative industry. Unlike the results from 1980, ownership concentration in the Financial sector in 2000 is not significantly lower than other industries, which may stem from the deregulation of the banking industry in the 1990s (see, e.g., Crawford, Ezzell, & Miles, 1995). Also consistent with the findings of Demsetz and Lehn, the inside ownership in the media sector is significantly higher than the representative industry.

The robust finding of variation in inside ownership across industries is important for research on corporate governance. Motivated by work dating back to Berle and Means (1932), empirical analysis often estimates the effect of corporate ownership on performance. However, the regularities across industries point to the endogenous determinants of ownership sketched by Demsetz (1983) and raise cautions about naïve attempts to draw a causal relation from ownership to performance.

4.3.3. *Does board size vary by industry?*

A provocative result reported by Yermack (1996) is that the size of the board of directors appears to be inversely related to firm value. Such results support the call by Jensen (1993) for smaller corporate boards. Similar to the long history of research on corporate ownership, however, a question arises as to whether board size endogenously responds to the economic environment faced by a firm.

As an initial clue to the factors affecting board size, Table 10 sorts the average number of directors by industry in ascending order. This simple analysis suggests some regularities in average board size. The industries at the top of the table with the fewest number of directors tend to be young, growth-oriented sectors such as Internet, Semiconductor, and Computer Software. The industries at the bottom of the table tend to be from older sectors with less growth potential such as Bank & Thrift, Financial Services, and Retail Store.

To address the variation in board size across industries systematically, Table 11 regresses the average number of directors in an industry on the P/E ratio, Age, and Size. The average number of directors in an industry is inversely related to the P/E ratio, confirming that firms in industries with higher growth options have smaller boards. These results hold after controlling for the average Age and Size of firms in the industry.

These results have important implications for empirical research in corporate finance. The fact that industries with higher growth options have smaller boards suggests that care must be taken in regressing performance measures such as Tobin's q on board size. Since Tobin's q is affected by growth options, a simple OLS specification of the relation between q and board size might spuriously link board size and performance.

These results also have important policy implications. Jensen (1993, p. 865) argues that corporate boards larger than seven or eight people are less likely to function effectively. Using this benchmark, very few of the industries in Table 10 would be viewed as having effective boards. However, such a simple benchmark fails to consider whether the definition of "effective" might vary across the economic environment proxied by different industry classifications.

5. Summary and Suggestions for Future Research

The economic analysis of the organizational features and incentive effects of the corporation dates back to Adam Smith. The policy issues tied to the corporation also have a long history – for example, an article in the January 23, 1875, edition of the *Commercial and Financial Chronicle* addresses the duties and liabilities of corporate directors. Given this longstanding conceptual and policy interest, it is not surprising that there is a sizeable body of theoretical and empirical research on corporate governance.

Table 10. The average number of directors by industry

Industry	Directors
Semiconductor	7.1
Internet	7.2
Computer software & services	7.7
Precision instrument	8.2
Telecom equipment	8.4
Retail special lines	8.5
Computer & peripherals	8.5
Electronics	8.6
Recreation	8.6
Restaurant	8.8
Medical supplies	8.9
Air & trucking transport	9.0
Machinery	9.0
Industrial services	9.1
Oilfield services	9.2
Auto Parts	9.2
Office equipment & supplies	9.6
Drug	9.6
Steel	9.7
Apparel & textile	9.7
Building materials	9.7
Medical services	9.9
Aerospace defense	10.0
Natural gas distribution	10.0
Chemical	10.2
Food processing	10.3
Electrical equipment	10.4
Cable TV & entertainment	10.5
Paper & forest products	10.7
Petroleum	10.8
Newspaper & publishing	10.8
Telecom services	10.9
Household products	11.0
Electric utility	11.2
Insurance	11.3
Grocery & drug store	11.3
Natural gas diversified	11.5
Retail store	11.6
Financial services	11.8
Bank & thrift	16.0
Average	9.9

This table reports the average number of directors by industry in ascending order. Variables are defined in Table 5.

Table 11. Industry variation in the number of directors

Independent variables	Dependent variable Directors Coefficient (p-value)
Intercept	10.4 (0.000)
P/E ratio	−0.091 (0.008)
Age	0.019 (0.24)
Size	0.049 (0.07)
Adjusted R^2	0.22
N	40

This table reports regression analysis at the industry level of the number of directors on proxies for growth options and size. Variables are reported in Table 5 and the underlying data are reported in Tables 6 and 7.

A review of the theory and evidence indicates several related themes. First, corporate governance is multidimensional. Second, corporate governance is an endogenous response to a firm's economic environment. Third, the role of different governance mechanisms varies across industries.

New analysis of a sample of 1235 U.S. corporations from 40 different industries in the year 2000 confirms the empirical regularities reported in prior research. The financial policy tied to the capital markets varies with the growth potential of an industry. The average inside ownership in an industry is a function of regulation and amenity potential, consistent with the model of Demsetz and Lehn (1985). Average board size varies with the growth options and the average size of the firms in an industry. The central policy implication of the prior research and new supporting evidence is that one size does not fit all in corporate governance.

The regularities found in the empirical studies on corporate governance help to clarify what is meant by the query, does corporate governance matter? The predictable variation in governance across industry and firm characteristics indicates that governance is an important choice. At the same time, the lack of observed causal effects of a particular governance mechanism on firm value indicates the difficulty in piecemeal attempts at governance reform. As a whole, the empirical evidence on corporate governance is consistent with the theory underlying corporate finance as a whole – in their path-breaking work, Modigliani and Miller showed that ideas and products, rather than tinkering with financial policy, drive corporate value (Modigliani & Miller, 1958; Miller & Modigliani, 1961).

The analysis summarized in this paper has important implications for future work. One clear growth area for research in corporate governance is empirical modeling. Coles, Lemmon and Meschke (2003) suggest techniques to use in considering the relation between managerial ownership and corporate performance. Bhagat and Black (1999) look deeply into the various specifications of the relation between board independence and firm performance. Larcker, Richardson and Tuna (2004) consider the relation between a broad set of governance variables and measures of performance.

There are also several avenues along which to evaluate recent calls for governance reform. An obvious topic for future study is whether proposed changes in governance will lessen the fraud that has generated the ongoing policy debate. For example, Jensen (1993) has argued that smaller boards are a more effective monitor of corporate executives. To empirically study this proposal, one could follow the approach of Gerety and Lehn (1997) and estimate whether the firms cited for fraud in recent years had measurably larger boards than a control sample. In devising the control sample, the empirical evidence provided in Section 4 of this paper indicates that industry membership and growth options are important factors. More generally, the literature on corporate governance suggests that the analysis of a particular mechanism such as board size must also control for the interactions with other governance devices.

Similar analysis could consider a second proposal of Jensen (1993), namely, that the position of chairman of the board be separated from the position of chief executive officer. A simple question is whether the firms cited for fraud in recent years were more likely to have the chairman also act as the CEO. Complicating such analysis is the fact that a large majority of firms have the same person in both positions. In the sample for this current study, for example, the same person is both CEO and chairman of the board in 71% of the firms. More generally, such analysis would have to control for both the costs and benefits of separating the chair and CEO that have been modeled by Brickley, Coles and Jarrell (1997).

The cross-sectional regularities in corporate governance also indicate that a fruitful path for future research would be to inquire as to the interest groups that would be expected to benefit from or be harmed by the enacted and proposed changes in governance. Stigler's (1964) analysis of the onset of federal securities regulation in the 1930s found differential effects based on firm size. Watts and Zimmerman (1978) report similar evidence on the effect of changes in accounting standards. Future work could study a recent sample to contrast the effects of the current governance reform on small and large firms as well as new and old industries.

Related to the analysis of the differential effects of governance reform, future research could also consider the possible unintended consequences of the current governance reform. Simon (1989), for example, notes that one possibly unintended effect of the creation of federal securities regulation was to push smaller, relatively riskier firms to the unregulated over-the-counter market. A study of more recent securities reform by Beatty and Kadiyala

(2003) indicates that the Penny Stock Reform Act of 1990 may have actually lowered rather than increased the quality of speculative stock issues. Future research might study the extent to which the current governance reform affects the rate of listings and de-listings on major stock exchanges as well as the performance of firms for which any regulatory changes impose a binding constraint.

As a whole, the topic of corporate offers a wide variety of avenues for further inquiry. The ongoing proposals for corporate governance reform only heighten both the potential and the importance of further theoretical and empirical research.

Acknowledgments

I thank Mike Maloney and seminar participants at Claremont McKenna College for comments on a prior draft.

References

Agrawal, A., & Knoeber, C. R. (1996). Firm performance and mechanisms to control agency problems between managers and shareholders. *Journal of Financial and Quantitative Analysis, 31*(September), 377–397.

Alchian, A. A. (1950). Uncertainty, evolution and economic theory. *Journal of Political Economy, 58*(June), 211–221.

Alchian, A. A. (1977a). Some economics of property rights. In Alchian A. A. (Ed.), *Economic Forces at Work* (pp. 127–149). Indianapolis, IN: Liberty Press.

Alchian, A. A. (1977b). Corporate management and property rights. In Alchian A. A. (Ed.), *Economic Forces at Work* (pp. 227–257). Indianapolis, IN: Liberty Press.

Alchian, A. A., & Demsetz, H. (1972). Production, information costs and economic organization. *American Economic Review, 62*(December), 777–795.

Andrade, G., Mitchell, M., & Stafford, E. (2001). New evidence and perspectives on mergers. *Journal of Economic Perspectives, 15*(Spring), 103–120.

Beatty, R., & Kadiyala, P. (2003). Impact of the Penny Stock Reform Act of 1990 on the initial public offering market. *Journal of Law and Economics, 46*(October), 517–541.

Becht, M., Bolton, P., & Roell, A. (2002). Corporate Governance and Control. Working paper. European Corporate Governance Institute, Brussels, Belgium.

Berle, A. A., & Means, G. S. (1932). *The Modern Corporation and Private Property*. New York: Macmillan.

Bhagat, S., & Black, B. (1999). The uncertain relation between board composition and firm performance. *Business Lawyer, 54*(May), 921–963.

Brickley, J. A., Coles, J. L., & Jarrell, G. (1997). Leadership structure: Separating the CEO and chairman of the board. *Journal of Corporate Finance, 3*(June), 189–220.

Cho, M.-H. (1998). Ownership structure, investment, and the corporate value: An empirical analysis. *Journal of Financial Economics, 47*(January), 103–121.

Coase, R. H. (1937). The nature of the firm. *Economica, 4*(November), 386–405.

Coase, R. H. (1960). The problem of social cost. *Journal of Law and Economics, 3*(October), 1–44.

Coles, J. L., Lemmon, M. L., & Meschke, J. F. (2003). Structural models and endogeneity in corporate finance: The link between managerial ownership and corporate performance. Working paper, Arizona State University, Tempe, AZ and University of Utah, Salt Lake City, UT.

Crawford, A. J., Ezzell, J. R., & Miles, J. A. (1995). Bank CEO pay-performance relations and the effects of deregulation. *Journal of Business, 68*(April), 231–256.

Demsetz, H. (1983). The structure of ownership and the theory of the firm. *Journal of Law and Economics, 26*(June), 375–390.

Demsetz, H., & Lehn, K. (1985). The structure of corporate ownership: Causes and consequences. *Journal of Political Economy, 93*(December), 1155–1177.

Demsetz, H., & Villalonga, B. (2001). Ownership structure and corporate performance. *Journal of Corporate Finance, 7*(September), 209–233.

Easterbrook, F. H. (1984). Two agency-cost explanations of dividends. *American Economic Review, 74*(September), 650–659.

Fama, E. F. (1980). Agency problems and the theory of the firm. *Journal of Political Economy, 88*(April), 288–307.

Fama, E. F., & Jensen, M. C. (1983). Separation of ownership and control. *Journal of Law and Economics, 26*(June), 301–325.

Garvey, G. T., & Swan, P. L. (1994). The economics of corporate governance: Beyond the Marshalian firm. *Journal of Corporate Finance, 1*(August), 139–174.

Gerety, M., & Lehn, K. (1997). The causes and consequences of accounting Fraud. *Managerial and Decision Economics, 18*(November/December), 587–599.

Gillan, S. L., Hartzell, J. C., & Starks, L. T. (2003). Explaining corporate governance: Boards, Bylaws, and Charter provisions. Working paper, University of Delaware, Newark, DE and University of Texas, Austin, TX.

Hermalin, B. E., & Weisbach, M. S. (1998). Endogenously chosen boards of directors and their monitoring of the CEO. *American Economic Review, 88*(March), 96–118.

Himmelberg, C. P., Hubbard, R. G., & Palia, D. (1999). Understanding the determinants of managerial ownership and the link between ownership and performance. *Journal of Financial Economics, 53*(September), 353–384.

Jensen, M. C. (1986). Agency costs of free cash flow, corporate finance, and takeovers. *American Economic Review Papers and Proceedings, 76*(May), 323–329.

Jensen, M. C. (1993). The modern industrial revolution, exit, and the failure of internal control systems. *Journal of Finance, 48*(July), 831–880.

Jensen, M. C., & Meckling, W. H. (1976). Theory of the firm: Managerial behavior, agency costs and ownership structure. *Journal of Financial Economics, 3*(October), 305–360.

Jensen, M. C., & Meckling, W. H. (1979). Rights and production functions: An application to labor-managed firms and codetermination. *Journal of Business, 52*(October), 469–506.

Kamerschen, D. R. (1968). The influence of ownership and control on profit rates. *American Economic Review, 58*(June), 432–447.

Katz, W. G. (1960). Responsibility and the modern corporation. *Journal of Law and Economics, 3*(October), 75–85.

Klein, P. (2004). Buffett says coke board critics "Silly". *Reuters* (May 2).

Kole, S. R. (1995). Measuring managerial equity ownership: A Comparison of sources of ownership data. *Journal of Corporate Finance, 1*(April), 413–435.

Kole, S. R., & Lehn, K. M. (1999). Deregulation and the adaptation of governance structure: The case of the U.S. Airline Industry. *Journal of Financial Economics, 52*(April), 79–117.

La Porta, R., Lopez-de-Silanes, F., Shleifer, A., & Vishny, R. W. (1998). Law and finance. *Journal of Political Economy, 106*(December), 1113–1155.

Larcker, D. F., Richardson, S. A., & Tuna, R. (2004). Does corporate governance really matter? Working paper, University of Pennsylvania, Philadelphia, PA.

Lehn, K., Patro, S., & Zhao, M. (2003). Determinants of the size and structure of corporate boards, 1935–2000. Working paper, University of Pittsburgh, Pittsburgh, PA.

Lowenstein, R. (2003). A Boss for a Boss. *New York Times* (December 14).

Mace, M. L. (1971). *Directors: Myth and Reality*. Harvard Business School: Boston.

Manne, H. G. (1965). Mergers and the market for corporate control. *Journal of Political Economy, 73*(April), 110–120.

McConnell, J. J., & Servaes, H. (1990). Additional evidence on equity ownership and corporate value. *Journal of Financial Economics, 27*(October), 595–612.

Megginson, W. L., & Netter, J. M. (2001). From state to market: A survey of empirical studies of privatization. *Journal of Economic Literature, 39*(June), 321–389.

Miller, M. H., & Modigliani, F. (1961). Dividend policy, growth, and the valuation of shares. *Journal of Business, 34*(October), 411–433.

Mitchell, M. L., & Lehn, K. (1990). Do bad bidders become good targets? *Journal of Political Economy, 98*(April), 372–398.

Mitchell, M. L., & Mulherin, J. H. (1996). The impact of industry shocks on takeover and restructuring activity. *Journal of Financial Economics, 41*(June), 193–229.

Modigliani, F., & Miller, M. H. (1958). The cost of capital, corporation finance, and the theory of investment. *American Economic Review, 48*(June), 261–297.

Monsen, J., Chiu, J. S., & Cooley, D. E. (1968). The effect of separation of ownership and control on the performance of the large firm. *Quarterly Journal of Economics, 82*(August), 435–451.

Morck, R., Shleifer, A., & Vishny, R. W. (1988). Management ownership and market valuation: An empirical analysis. *Journal of Financial Economics, 20*(January/March), 293–315.

Mulherin, J. H. (Ed.) (2004). *Mergers and Corporate Governance*. Edward Elgar: Cheltenham, UK and Northampton, MA, USA.

Mulherin, J. H., & Boone, A. L. (2000). Comparing acquisitions and divestitures. *Journal of Corporate Finance, 6*(July), 117–139.

Mulherin, J. H., Netter, J. M., & Stegemoller, M. (2003). Privatization and the market for corporate control. Working paper, Claremont McKenna University, Claremont, CA and University of Georgia, Athens, GA.

Mulherin, J. H., & Poulsen, A. B. (1998). Proxy contests and corporate change: Implications for shareholder wealth. *Journal of Financial Economics, 47*(March), 279–313.

Palmer, J. (1973). The profit-performance effects of the separation of ownership from control in large U. S. industrial corporations. *Bell Journal of Economics and Management Science, 4*(Spring), 293–303.

Ross, S. A., Westerfield, R. W., & Jaffe, J. (2005). *Corporate Finance*, 7th ed. McGraw-Hill/Irwin: Boston.

Shleifer, A., & Vishny, R. W. (1997). A survey of corporate governance. *Journal of Finance, 52*(June), 737–783.

Simon, C. J. (1989). The effect of the 1933 securities act on investor information and the performance of new issues. *American Economic Review, 79*(June), 295–318.

Smith, A. ([1776] 1991). *On the Nature and Causes of the Wealth of Nations*. Prometheus Books: Buffalo, NY.

Smith, C. W., & Watts, R. L. (1992). The Investment opportunity set and corporate financing, dividend, and compensation policies. *Journal of Financial Economics, 32*(December), 263–292.

Sorensen, R. (1974). The separation of ownership and control and firm performance: An empirical analysis. *Southern Economic Journal, 40*(July), 145–148.

Stano, M. (1976). Monopoly power, ownership control, and corporate performance. *Bell Journal of Economics and Management Science, 7*(Autumn), 672–679.

Stigler, G. J. (1958). The economies of scale. *Journal of Law and Economics, 1*(October), 54–71.

Stigler, G. J. (1964). Public regulation of securities markets. *Journal of Business, 37*(April), 117–142.

Stigler, G. J., & Friedland, C. (1983). The literature of economics: The case of berle and means. *Journal of Law and Economics, 26*(June), 237–268.

Watts, R. L., & Zimmerman, J. L. (1978). Towards a positive theory of the determination of accounting standards. *Accounting Review, 53*(January), 112–134.

Weston, J. F., Mitchell, M. L., & Mulherin, J. H. (2004). *Takeovers, Restructuring, and Corporate Governance* (4th ed.). Pearson Prentice Hall: Upper Saddle River, NJ.

Williamson, O. E. (1988). Corporate finance and corporate governance. *Journal of Finance, 43*(July), 567–591.

Winston, C. (1998). U. S. industry adjustment to economic deregulation. *Journal of Economic Perspectives, 12*(Summer), 89–110.

Yermack, D. (1996). Higher market valuation of companies with a small board of directors. *Journal of Financial Economics, 40*(February), 185–211.

Public Choice (2005) **124:** 205–222
DOI: 10.1007/s11127-005-4762-z

The public choice of educational choice*

LAWRENCE W. KENNY
Department of Economics, University of Florida, Gainesville, FL 32611-7140, USA
(E-mail: larry.kenny@cba.ufl.edu)

Accepted March 2005

Abstract. The very small literature explaining (i) how citizens have voted in two California voucher referenda, (ii) how legislators have voted on voucher bills in the State of Florida and the US Congress, and (iii) the variation across states in charter school provisions is summarized. New empirical evidence documenting the cross-state variation in the success of voucher referenda and voucher bills is examined. Voucher bill characteristics and state characteristics play important roles. Voucher bills have been passed only in the more conservative Republican states, and almost all of the successful voucher programs have been targeted at large, struggling school districts.

1. Introduction

Eighty percent of the US population lives in a metropolitan area, and in most of these metro areas families have some choice of school districts across which to sort, as Tiebout (1956) envisioned. In a sample of 161 metro areas in 1990, the number of separate school districts ranged from one to 117 (Husted & Kenny, 2002). Eighty percent of these metropolitan areas had at least five school districts, 63% had at least ten school districts, 31% had at least 20 school districts and 21% had at least 30 of them. Having more districts produces a better matching of desired school quality with offered school quality and makes it easier for parents to judge whether some school districts are inefficient. Homeowners in underperforming school districts, facing potential capital losses, are expected to take steps to improve the quality of the local public schools (Fischel, 2001). There is indeed evidence that the public schools are more efficient (i.e., test scores are higher, holding various inputs into learning constant) in metropolitan areas where there are more school districts. But, as in the private sector, not many "firms" are needed to produce a fully competitive educational market. Zanzig (1997) finds that no more than five districts per county were needed to reap the full efficiency benefits of competition among school districts.

*Christine Piette was a tremendous help in finding and documenting roll call votes in legislatures and referenda on educational choice. I have benefitted from comments by Bill Bomberger, David Brasington, David Denslow, David Figlio, David Sappington, and Paul Sotkiewicz.

Even though there clearly is some Tiebout-competition among public school districts in many metropolitan areas, some economists claim that public education in the United States suffers from insufficient competition, reducing incentives on the part of local school boards, principals and teachers to deploy available resources cost-effectively and causing the public schools to perform more poorly than otherwise. Vouchers have been proposed to foster more competition between public and private schools. Magnet schools, charter schools and affording parents and students a choice of schools have all been touted as means to bring about more competition among public schools within individual school districts. But, surprisingly, there has been little concern about the limited competition among school districts in states that restrict the formation of school districts.[1] There have been few calls for more public school districts.[2]

Most of the research by economists on educational choice has been on the effects of vouchers, charter schools and the like on school performance. There have been very few studies of the factors that explain the observed geographical variation in the level of political support for educational choice. Brunner, Sonstelie, and Thayer (2001) studied precinct returns from Los Angeles County in California's 1993 referendum on vouchers (Prop. 174), and Brunner and Sonstelie (2003) utilized individual responses to survey questions assessing voucher support for California's 2000 referendum on the same issue (Prop. 38). Gokcekus, Phillips, and Tower (2004) examined the 2001 vote on amendment 57 to H 1 in the US House of Representatives that would have allowed federal Title IV funds for disadvantaged children to be used for financing private school vouchers. In addition, there are several unpublished student papers that explain (i) voting in the Florida legislature on a bill that bundled vouchers with several other educational "reforms" (Gonzalez, 2003; McDade, 2003) and (ii) why some states allow charter schools and others do not (Alvarez, 2003).[3]

In this paper, I summarize the findings of this small literature as background for describing and explaining the pattern of overall success of voucher proposals. Ideology is found to play an important role. Conservatives expect that the additional competition between public and private schools generated by voucher programs will produce more efficient public schools, and they welcome some shift of the educational function from the public sector to the private sector. The analysis shows that Republicans, especially conservative Republicans, provide the strongest support for vouchers and charter schools. Voucher features also matter. Successful voucher programs do not give vouchers to parents whose children are already enrolled in private schools and generally are targeted to specific large, struggling urban school districts. There also is evidence that a voucher proposal fares better in precincts with fewer teachers, and that charter schools are more likely to be allowed in states with weak teachers' unions.

2. Vouchers

2.1. *Background and evidence in the literature*

What are the factors that affect voter and legislator support for vouchers? As Brunner and Sonstelie (2003) note, families with school-age children are a minority in the typical statewide referendum on vouchers. Other voters, who are single or in households with no children present, are thus pivotal. Under what circumstances do vouchers make these other voters better off? Brunner et al. (2001) and Brunner and Sonstelie (2003) stress the voucher's impact on the housing market. Houses in neighborhoods with "good" public schools command a premium.[4] Since a voucher reduces the cost of private alternatives to good public schools, property owners who live in districts with good schools face capital losses if vouchers are approved. Brunner and Sonstelie (2003) found with survey data that support for vouchers fell among homeowners without children as perceived public school quality rose, while for renters with no children (and no potential for capital gains or losses), perceived school quality had no impact on support for the voucher. Brunner et al. obtained similar results with precinct voting data. These findings are consistent with the authors' capital gain/loss scenario where the consequences of approving voucher proposals are more salient for homeowners.

A traditional voucher providing $X to parents who enroll their children in a private school defrays only part of the cost of private schooling in many cases and may be used by any family choosing the private-school option. This is effectively a transfer of wealth to parents whose children already attend a private school. As expected, Brunner et al. (2001) find greater support for traditional vouchers in precincts where private schools enroll larger percentages of school-age children.

Private schools offer religious or moral training that is not available in the public schools and provide higher quality schooling than may be obtained in public schools due to limited public school options or restrictions imposed by state government. Private schools thus tend to service religious and rich families (Hamilton & Macauley, 1991; Schmidt, 1992). By reducing the cost of attending private school, vouchers are expected to lead to greater utilization of that option by religious and wealthy families. This helps to explain why the Catholic Church has been an active supporter of vouchers in some voucher referenda (e.g., Michigan's Prop. 1 in 2000). Surprisingly, there has been no statistical analysis of the effect of religious composition on voucher sentiments. Support for vouchers also is expected to come from relatively rich families that would take advantage of the then-cheaper private school alternative. But both California voucher studies find that support falls as income rises and that race has no consistent effect on support for these proposals.

In the traditional voucher system, the voucher can be used by any family sending a child to private school. Families with children already in private school will take advantage of vouchers, which raises taxes and makes other families worse off. But this traditional voucher is worth much less than the amount typically spent per pupil in the public schools. As a result, the cost savings for each child who leaves public school to attend private school offsets the loss associated with payments to children already in private school, and taxes could fall if enough students abandon public school. There seems to have been considerable uncertainty about how many students would take advantage of vouchers, thus making it difficult to predict the net impact of the voucher on taxes (Brunner & Sonstelie, 2003, pp. 241–242). There was even more uncertainty surrounding Michigan's proposal H, which did not specify the dollar value of the voucher and did not offer a financing mechanism as an alternative to the property taxation the proposal would have eliminated. Fiscal uncertainty is expected to lead many risk-averse households to support the status quo by voting against vouchers.

Most of the more recent voucher proposals deal with the potentially adverse impact on taxes by limiting vouchers to students in failing public schools, which guarantees that families that already have children in private school cannot receive vouchers. A second recent provision limiting vouchers to poor families also reduces the overlap with those already in private school. Some recent voucher proposals also are more generous, offering private-school vouchers that approximate per-pupil public expenditure if the private schools agree to not charge any additional tuition. This facilitates utilization of vouchers by poor families. These targeted voucher programs should be supported by the poor or minority families that would be expected to benefit from them.

Although many would label schools with very low test scores as failing, some of these schools may be doing the best they can with students whose parents are themselves poorly educated, uninvolved with their children's education, or both. A more appropriate measure of whether a school is inefficient would take into account the raw student material the school has to work with. South Carolina, for example, divides its schools into deciles based on the fraction of students who qualify for a free or reduced-price school lunch program. School are then graded on the basis of performance within their decile group. In South Carolina's "value added" system, poorly performing schools can be found in every income stratum, and consequently support for vouchers would not be confined to the poor and minorities. It is clear that any uncertainty over how "failing" will be defined will reduce support for vouchers.

The Florida voucher was restricted to students in failing public schools.[5] Florida legislators appear to have expected "failing" to be equated to low test scores, which generally are found in poor communities. Gonzalez (2003) and McDade (2003) show that legislators from rich counties were less likely to vote for vouchers than legislators representing poor counties. McDade finds that Republicans from counties with high test scores were more likely to break party ranks and vote against vouchers, whereas Democrats from counties with low test scores were more likely to defy their party's principles by voting for vouchers.

Amendment 57 to H 1, considered by the US House of Representatives in 2001, would have allowed funds appropriated under Title IV of the Innovative Grants for Disadvantaged Students program to be used to finance vouchers for students attending low performing schools. Poor minority families should have benefitted from this proposal, and Gokcekus et al. (2004) find that support for the amendment was greater in districts with higher percentages of African-Americans, but was unrelated to district income.

Public schools have been found to be less effective in areas with little competition among public school districts (Zanzig, 1997) and in states that leave voters with little latitude to determine education spending or that meddle in local decisions (Husted & Kenny, 2000). There should be more support for vouchers among those who are served by inefficient public schools, but this hypothesis has not yet been tested.

Certification requirements for public school teachers have protected them from easy entry into teaching by private sector workers, and teachers' unions often have done away with performance-based incentives and established work restrictions that make teaching easier. Vouchers would cause some public school teachers to be thrust into the private non-unionized sector, where wages are lower, there are no certification requirements, merit-pay systems are more common, and there are no union-imposed work restrictions. As a result, public school teachers are staunch opponents of vouchers. Brunner et al. (2001) report less support for the voucher in precincts with larger percentages of the workforce employed in education services (i.e., public school teachers and administrators). Gokcekus et al. (2004) find that legislators receiving contributions from teacher PACs were much less likely to vote for vouchers.

Ideology plays an important role in the debate over vouchers. Republicans and conservatives tend to support vouchers because they believe that more competition would make education more efficient and that private schools are likely to be more effective in carrying out their educational missions than public schools. Democrats and liberals, on the other hand, tend to oppose vouchers because they have a stronger faith in the public sector and are aligned politically with teachers' unions. Empirically, there is greater support for vouchers in precincts in which larger fractions of voters are registered as Republicans (Brunner et al., 2001), among conservative voters (Brunner & Sonstelie, 2003), and among Republican legislators (Gokcekus et al., 2004).

Let us now examine and attempt to explain the variation across states in voter support for voucher proposals in referenda as well as the success of legislative roll-call votes on voucher proposals. Referenda or bills to allow public funding of religious schools (Oregon 4 in 1972, Maine LD 182 in 2003) are not analyzed because such proposals dealt only with the separation of church and state. Michigan's proposal H in 1978 also is not included in the dataset because that voucher proposal was tied to eliminating property tax funding of public schools. A "peripheral" vote on vouchers for special education (Hawaii HB 1678 in 2001) is not analyzed either.

2.2. *Referenda on vouchers*

In the past four decades there have been ten statewide referenda on public support for private schools. These are listed in Table 1. The entries there include proposals to provide transportation for private school students, to prohibit public funds from being used to support private schools, and to establish voucher programs. Some proposals were quite vague, while others were very

Table 1. Referenda results on vouchers

State	Year	Referendum	Vote share (%)	Description
Nebraska	1966	6	43	Transportation for private school students
Michigan	1970	C	43	(Vote against prohibiting) public funds for private schools
Nebraska	1970	12	42	Tuition reimbursement for private school students (up to one-third of per-pupil public school costs)
Maryland	1972	18	45	State scholarship program for students in approved private schools
Maryland	1974	14	43	Transportation for private school students, among other provisions
Colorado	1992	7	33	Vouchers worth at least 50% of per-pupil public school costs, redeemable at any public or private school
California	1993	174	30	$2,600 voucher for private school students; at least 50% of per-pupil public school costs
Washington	1996	173	36	$3,400 voucher for private school students
California	2000	38	29	Voucher for private school students, worth the greatest of $ 4,000, 50% of US per-pupil public school costs, or 50% of California per-pupil costs
Michigan	2002	1	31	Vouchers for private school students in districts with low high-school graduation rates and for families in other districts approving voucher use

specific. Only one proposal, Michigan proposal 1 in 2000, contemplated a targeted voucher program. It would have required that a small number of school districts with low high-school graduation rates (30 out of 555 districts) offer vouchers and would have allowed other districts to offer vouchers if there was sufficient sentiment for vouchers.[6]

None of these referenda, even Michigan's targeted voucher proposal, produced a majority in favor of public support for private schools. The greatest support came in Maryland's proposal 18 in 1972, in which 45% favored establishing a voucher. There was stronger support for public funding of private schools in the late 1960s and early 1970s than in the 1990s. Proposals for vouchers and other forms of support garnered 42% to 45% of the vote in the early period, but only 29% to 36% of the vote in the past decade. This evidence is consistent with newly formed teachers' unions being less powerful than the established teachers' unions are now. Unreported regressions provide no support for other hypotheses that public funding of private schools gets more votes in conservative states or in states with larger shares of students in private school.

2.3. *Roll-call votes on vouchers in legislatures*

Table 2 examines the success in Congress and in state legislatures of various bills or amendments that would establish vouchers. The votes are grouped according to their success – panel A: winning a majority in both legislative chambers; panel B: garnering a majority in one chamber; and panel C: failing to get a majority in the one chamber in which there was a roll call vote. State governments have enacted vouchers in Colorado, Florida, Ohio, and Wisconsin, and Congress has approved vouchers for the District of Columbia.

Vouchers were first approved in 1989 in Wisconsin, when the state legislature authorized a voucher program for poor families in the City of Milwaukee. The bill restricted the number of voucher slots and required that no more than 49% of a private school's enrollment consist of pupils using vouchers. Over the years, the latter restriction was lifted and the number of voucher slots has steadily increased.

In 1995, Ohio passed a voucher program for low-income families in Cleveland as part of the biennial budget bill. The bill provided for a voucher worth $2,250 and required that parents pay 10% to 25% of the private school's tuition charge. The Ohio Supreme Court ruled in 1999 that attaching the voucher program to the biennial budget bill violated the state's single-subject rule, and the state legislature rectified this situation by passing a distinct voucher bill one month later.

Florida was the first state to pass a bill authorizing vouchers statewide. This measure was passed in 1999, the first year in which the Republicans controlled the governor's office and both chambers of the state legislature. Vouchers were

Table 2. Legislative roll call votes on vouchers

State	Year	Bill No.	Outcome	% Republican House	% Republican Senate	Chief Executive	Description
			a. Bills passed in both chambers				
Colorado	2003	HB 03 1160	H 35–29 S 18–17 *enacted*	57	51	R	11 districts with 8+ schools with poor grades poor residents <6% of students
DC	1995	HR 2546[a] amendment 891	H 241–177 S 56–44 *filibuster*	55	54	D	poor residents only residents of DC
DC	2003	HR 2765 amendment 368	H 205–203 S no roll call *enacted*	53	52	R	poor residents only residents of DC
Florida	1999	H 751[b]	H 70–48 S 25–15 *enacted*	53	58	R	failing schools
Ohio	1995	HB 117[c]	H 82–16 S 29–3 *enacted*	57	61	R	poor residents only residents of Cleveland
Ohio	1999	HB 282	H 87–11 S 31–2 *enacted*	61	63	R	poor residents only residents of Cleveland
Wisconsin	1989	AB 601	H 62–35 part of Senate's biennial budget bill *enacted*	43	39	R	poor residents only residents of Milwaukee <3% of students
			b. Bills passed in one chamber				
Arizona	1999	HB 2279	H 31–27 S no vote	63	60	R	poor residents
New Hampshire	1998	SB 456	H no vote S 16–8	64	63	D	any families in districts (up to five) allowing vouchers
New Hampshire	1999	HB 633	H 172–171 S no vote	63	63	D	school test scores in bottom one-third poor residents <5% of school's students

(*Continued on next page*)

Table 2. (*Continued*)

State	Year	Bill No.	Outcome	% Republican House	% Republican Senate	Chief Executive	Description
Wyoming	2002	sf0002 s2040	H no vote S 16–14	77	67	R	200 sixth grade students selected by state superintendent (two-year pilot study)
c. Bills failing in both chambers							
Georgia	1999	SB 68	S 23–31	43	39	D	poor residents in failing schools
Kansas	1995	HB 2217	H 23–98	64	68	R	all families
Louisiana	1999	SB 964	S 14–22	26	36	R	first to eighth grade students in failing schools
New Hampshire	1999	HB 701	H 78–283	63	63	D	all families; 10% of per-pupil costs
Wyoming	2000	sf0002 s2036	S 13–16	72	70	R	100 third-grade students selected by state superintendent two-year pilot study
Wyoming	2001	sf0001 s2010	S 12–18	77	67	R	100 seventh-grade students selected by state superintendent one-year pilot study
US	2001	HR 1 amendment 57	H 155–273	51	50	R	failing schools use of Title IV funds to finance vouchers for disadvantaged students

[a]There were other items in the amendment dealing with reforming public schools in the District of Columbia.
[b]The bill also addressed making schools more accountable, improving student learning, raising standards, improving training for educators, improving school safety and reducing truancy.
[c]Part of the biennial budget bill.

bundled with a number of other educational “reforms” in Florida’s “A+ Plan for Education” plan. Students attending a school that had received an “F” in two of the last four years were eligible for a voucher worth at least $4,000.

Colorado passed a voucher bill in 2003 that provided for vouchers in 11 (out of 180) districts with at least eight schools characterized as “low” or “unsatisfactory” in the 2001–2002 school year; vouchers equal to 75%–85% of the district’s per-pupil revenues would be available only to children eligible for a free or reduced-price school lunch. The 11 targeted districts are large urban districts in the Denver, Colorado Springs and Pueblo metropolitan areas. Participation was capped at 1% of the district’s enrollment in 2004–2005, rising to 6% in 2007–2008. The Colorado Supreme Court ruled in 2004 that the voucher bill was unconstitutional because the program was partially funded with local tax dollars, stripping school boards of their authority.

Bills granting vouchers to poorer residents of the District of Columbia have twice gotten a majority in both chambers of Congress. In 1995, amendment 891 to H.R. 2546 passed in the House by a vote margin of 241 yeas to 177 nays. The amendment provided for vouchers and a number of other “reforms” for the D.C. public schools. The bill was filibustered in the Senate. A cloture vote got a majority (56 votes), but not enough to end the filibuster. In 2003, a voucher amendment (368) to H.R. 2765 that established a voucher worth up to $ 7,500 was more successful. The amendment passed the House in a very close vote (205 to 203). The final bill was approved by the Senate and signed by President Bush.

Panel B shows that voucher bills passed the lower chambers in Arizona and New Hampshire, and won majorities in the upper chambers in New Hampshire and Wyoming. In both instances, however, the bills were bottled up in the legislature’s other chamber and never made it to the floor for a vote.

Voucher success depended in part on the proposal’s specific features. It was noted earlier that allowing families with children already in private school to receive vouchers creates uncertainty about whether the voucher program will raise taxes. All of the voucher programs that passed deal with this by restricting vouchers to students in poor families, to failing schools, or both. Several of the less successful voucher proposals did not have these limitations. In Kansas’s HB 2217 bill in 1995 and two of the three New Hampshire bills, any family could utilize a voucher to send their child to private school.

Wisconsin and Colorado dealt with uncertainty about the demand for vouchers and the related adjustment costs by limiting voucher participation and allowing that limit to increase slowly over time. One of the New Hampshire bills that passed one chamber also limited voucher eligibility. But there is a danger in limiting participation too much. Other bills may have failed because there were almost no prospective beneficiaries to lobby for the bill’s passage. For the three pilot study bills considered in Wyoming, the state superintendent would be given the authority to select 100 to 200 student participants. Given that restriction, there were few obvious participants and thus no well-defined decisive coalition of beneficiaries. In 1999, New Hampshire's lower chamber failed to pass HB 701, which provided for a voucher equal to 10% of local per-pupil public school spending. This was the least generous voucher proposal that went to a roll-call vote.

Many very large school districts appear to be inefficient. This may be because there is little effective competition facing districts covering large geographic areas or because there is less parental monitoring of large school districts due to low incentives to be politically active. There should be more support for vouchers that would help students in large inefficient schools, and that is indeed so. Florida's voucher program is the only one to be approved that is not specifically targeted to large, struggling urban school districts.[7] Ohio's voucher program is limited to Cleveland, and Wisconsin's is restricted to Milwaukee. Colorado's is limited to 11 large urban districts with eight or more schools receiving poor evaluations. Congress barely approved a voucher program for the District of Columbia in 2003, but a proposal to allow the use of Title IV funds to finance vouchers for disadvantaged students in schools nationwide received only 36% of the votes cast in the House only two years earlier. The greater success of geographically targeted vouchers also can be explained by strong teacher opposition emerging only in the districts of representatives where the public schools will be directly affected by the proposal.

Given the sharp differences between political parties in support for vouchers, it is not surprising that most voucher activity has occurred in states in which the Republicans controlled both chambers of the legislature. Republicans dominated the legislature in each instance in which one chamber passed a voucher law, and in six of the seven instances in which both chambers voted for vouchers. The only exception is the 1989 bill to establish vouchers in Milwaukee, where a voucher program was approved despite Democratic majorities in Wisconsin's house and senate. And five of the seven failed floor votes on vouchers occurred in states with Republican majorities in the state legislature. Finally, note that every legislatively successful voucher law was signed by a Republican governor or president.

Although virtually all of the roll-call votes on vouchers took place in states in which the Republicans controlled the state legislature, voucher proposals nevertheless were successful in only a minority of Republican-controlled states. Thus, Republican control of state government appears to be an almost-necessary but not a sufficient condition for vouchers to have some success. An explanation of voucher success must start with Republican states, which comprise the set of states for which vouchers have some prospect of approval. A state is included in the set of "Republican" states if at some point in the election cycles of 1990–2000 the Republicans controlled state government, with a Republican governor and Republican majorities in the state house and senate. Eighteen states meet this criterion.[8] These states accounted for all but two of the votes listed Table 2. It is not surprising that the only roll-call votes not occurring in states defined as "Republican" here took place in Georgia and Louisiana, states where Democrats are more conservative politically than usual. A voucher proposal did not garner a majority in either vote.

Two variables measure voucher success. PASS is a dummy variable that equals one for the four states that enacted vouchers (Colorado, Florida, Ohio and Wisconsin) and equals zero otherwise. Alternatively, 1–2 CHAMBERS equals one for these states as well as for the three other states in which voucher proposals garnered a majority in only one legislative chamber (Arizona, New Hampshire, Wyoming); this variable also equals zero otherwise. Which factors make some "Republican" states more favorable to vouchers than others?

Conservative Republicans are hypothesized to be more likely to support vouchers than moderate Republicans because the conservatives generally have greater faith in markets and other private institutions. Americans for Democratic Action (ADA) has for decades assessed the voting records of members of the US Congress. Its widely used measure of political ideology equals the percentage of a legislator's votes that agree with the liberal position taken by the ADA on key bills selected by the ADA. The ideology of a state's legislators is measured here by the average ADA score for the state's Republican US senators in 1979–1997.[9] In Table 3 it can be seen that voucher programs were established only in states in which Republicans were relatively conservative. In fact, even though average state ADA scores for Republican US Senators were as high as 48.3 (Pennsylvania), Republican ADA scores were no higher than 12.3 in the states that enacted vouchers. This was also the case for the seven states in which vouchers cleared at least one legislative chamber.

Private schools emerge to satisfy a demand for religious instruction or in response to dissatisfaction with the public schools. Thus, states with larger percentages of students enrolled in private school (PRIVATE SCHOOL ENROLLMENT) are expected to view vouchers more favorably. A larger private

Table 3. Political ideology and voucher success

	Pass		1–2 Chambers	
US senate republican ADA score	No (0)	Yes (1)	No (0)	Yes (1)
0–10.0	4	2 (33%)	3	3 (50%)
10.1–20.0	5	2 (29%)	3	4 (57%)
20.1–30.0	2	0 (0%)	2	0 (0%)
30.1–40.0	1	0 (0%)	1	0 (0%)
40.1–50.0	2	0 (0%)	2	0 (0%)
Total	14	4	11	7

Table 4. Private school enrollment and voucher success

	Pass		1–2 Chambers	
Private school enrollment	No (0)	Yes (1)	No (0)	Yes (1)
0.001–0.040	3	0 (0%)	2	1 (33%)
0.041–0.080	4	0 (0%)	3	1 (25%)
0.081–0.120	4	2 (33%)	3	3 (50%)
0.121–0.160	1	1 (50%)	1	1 (50%)
0.161–0.200	2	1 (33%)	2	1 (33%)
Total	14	4	11	7

school enrollment also can reflect a higher population density, which makes it easier for private schools to take advantage of economies of scale (Husted & Kenny, 2002). The relationship between private school enrollment and voucher success is summarized in Table 4. The hypothesis is supported when success is measured in terms of a voucher plan being enacted. In none of the states that enacted vouchers did fewer than 8% of students attend private schools, and between a third and a half of states in the categories with higher private school enrollment enacted voucher programs. On the other hand, there is little apparent relationship between private school enrollment and success in getting a voucher bill through at least one chamber of the legislature.

Most of the successful voucher proposals have targeted large failing school districts. This strategy obviously is impossible if there are no large school districts in the state to target. BIG CITY is a dummy variable that equals one if the largest city in the state had at least 400,000 people in 1990 (Arizona, Colorado, Florida, Illinois, Michigan, Ohio, Pennsylvania and Wisconsin); it equals zero otherwise. BIG CITY's relation with voucher success is shown in Table 5. All of the states that enacted voucher plans had a city with a population of at least 400,000. The presence of a large city also has a strong impact on the other measure of voucher success, 1–2 CHAMBERS. A voucher proposal passed at least one chamber in only 20% of the states with no big city and in 63% of states with one.

Table 5. Large cities and voucher success

	Pass		1–2 Chambers	
Big city	No (0)	Yes (1)	No (0)	Yes (1)
No (0)	10	0 (0%)	8	2 (20%)
Yes (1)	4	4 (50%)	3	5 (63%)
Total	14	4	11	7

Table 6. Linear probability regressions explaining voucher success[a]

Independent variables	Pass (1)	Pass (2)	1–2 Chambers (3)	1–2 Chambers (4)
US senate republican ADA score	−0.0172 (2.32)	−0.0204 (2.46)	−0.0187 (1.93)	−0.0225 (2.13)
Big city	0.439 (2.35)		0.525 (2.14)	
Private school enrollment	2.556 (1.17)	5.408 (2.63)	−0.094 (0.03)	3.317 (1.26)
Intercept	0.067 (0.43)	0.040 (0.21)	0.477 (2.23)	0.445 (1.87)
Adjusted R^2	0.438	0.269	0.298	0.130
Root mean squared error	0.321	0.366	0.420	0.468
N	18	18	18	18

[a]Absolute values of *t*-statistics in parentheses.

Linear probability regressions using these three variables to explain voucher success are reported in Table 6. The regressions using all three variables explain 44% of the variation in PASS and 30% of the variation in 1–2 CHAMBERS. BIG CITY is excluded from the second and fourth regressions, which causes a sharp drop in the adjusted R^2s. The null hypothesis of no overall significance is rejected in the first three regressions, but not the fourth.

As expected, the most conservative "Republican" states are the most likely to establish voucher programs and to pass voucher proposals in at least one chamber. That is, voucher support falls as the average ADA score for the state's US Republican senators increases. A one standard deviation (13 point) rise in the average ADA score among Republican states is estimated to reduce the probability of adoption of vouchers by 0.22 to 0.27, and to reduce the probability of passing at least one chamber by 0.24 to 0.29.

Targeting vouchers to poor children in large struggling school districts makes vouchers more acceptable, but this can be done only in states with large cities. The BIG CITY dummy variable has the predicted positive sign and is statistically significant. States with at least one city with more than 400,000 people are estimated to have a 0.44 higher probability of enacting vouchers, and a 0.53 greater probability of a voucher bill passing at least one legislative chamber.

The fraction of school-age children attending private school has the hypothesized positive sign in three of the four regressions, but the variable is significant only in the voucher passage regression that excludes BIG CITY.

In that regression, a one standard deviation rise in PRIVATE SCHOOL ENROLLMENT (0.05) is estimated to lead to a 0.27 increase in the probability that a state establishes a voucher.

3. Charter Schools

Charter schools operate within the public school system but are not shackled by some of the regulations that are claimed to make public schools less efficient. Charter schools have spread rapidly since Minnesota became the first state to authorize them in 1991. Forty-five states now have charter schools, which account for 1.5% of public school enrollment nationwide.

Alvarez (2003) explains the cross-state pattern of charter school approval as well as the differing strengths of charter school laws. Economies of scale for alternatives to traditional public schools, such as private schools and charter schools, are easier to realize in densely populated jurisdictions and in large metropolitan areas (Husted & Kenny, 2002). As the share of the population living in metro areas rises, charter schools should be more feasible and Alvarez indeed finds that states with high urban population percentages are more likely to allow charter schools. States with larger Republican majorities in the state house also are more likely to authorize charter schools and to have stronger charter school laws. Not surprisingly, charter schools are less likely to be approved in states with strong teachers' unions.

Wong and Shen (2004) studied the adoption of 16 charter-school law provisions in 39 states that have allowed charter schools. Their empirical results are not very revealing insofar as only one independent variable typically is found to be statistically significant in each of the 16 logit regressions they report.

4. Conclusion

Political ideology plays a powerful role in explaining the success of educational choice proposals. Conservative and Republican voters are more likely to support vouchers in referenda. Similarly, Republican legislators tend to view vouchers more favorably than Democrat legislators. With very few exceptions, voucher proposals have come to a vote in the state legislature only in "Republican" states, defined herein as states where Republicans have controlled both the executive and legislative branches of government sometime in the past decade. But voucher bills passed at least one chamber in only seven of the 18 states identified as "Republican" states. Differences in ideology within the Republican Party explain some of differences in legislative voting on voucher proposals across Republican states. Empirical analysis reveals that voucher proposals have had more success in conservative Republican states than in moderate Republican states. Ideology played the same role in determining observed political support for charter schools. As expected, Republican control of the state legislature increased the likelihood of success of bills authorizing charter schools as well as in strengthening charter school laws.

All but one of the voucher plans that have been enacted have targeted vouchers at large urban school districts, where schools appear to be less efficient. The availability of a large school district to target helps explain voucher success in Republican states. Republican states with large cities have been more likely to approve voucher plans than Republican states with no large cities. Additional analysis is needed to fully understand why proposals that target vouchers to large school districts have been so much more successful than other voucher proposals.

Under traditional voucher plans, in which vouchers are available to all children in private school, there is fiscal uncertainty. Taxes rise if few students switch to private school and fall if many students do. Recent voucher proposals have eliminated this risk by limiting vouchers to poor families, to families with children in failing schools, or both, and consequently have had more success than traditional voucher proposals. The traditional voucher also transfers wealth to households with children already attending private school. As such, traditional voucher proposals fare better in precincts with proportionately higher private-school enrollments.

Homeowners living in districts served by good public schools, facing capital losses if vouchers pass, rationally will oppose vouchers. Studies of California voucher proposals support this prediction.

As expected, legislators representing low-income and minority constituents standing to benefit from newer proposals that limit vouchers to the poor or to students in failing schools are more likely to support vouchers. But poor voters surprisingly also are more likely to support traditional vouchers, which should benefit the rich. Further empirical analysis is needed to unravel the effect of income on support for vouchers.

Teachers' unions, which emerged in the 1960s, have been powerful foes of educational choice. These organizations appear to have been much less effective in opposing vouchers in the early 1970s than they have been recently. Voucher proposals typically have garnered less support in precincts with more teachers and from legislators receiving contributions from teachers' unions. Furthermore, states with strong teachers' unions are less likely to authorize the creation of charter schools.

The research described herein has been confined to educational choice in the United States. Vouchers and charter schools of various forms are allowed in Belgium, Canada, Chile, Columbia, France, Ireland, Japan, the Netherlands and Sweden. Studies explaining why vouchers and alternatives to public schools are found in some countries but not others would be a valuable addition to this literature.

Notes

1. Hawaii has one statewide district, and six states (Florida, Louisiana, Maryland, Nevada, Virginia, West Virginia) mandate countywide school districts. In several other states the number of school districts exceeds the number of counties only slightly.
2. Over the years, some Florida legislators have expressed an interest in allowing multiple county school districts, but a bill authorizing this has never progressed to a floor vote.
3. Sandy (1992) utilized survey responses from individuals who voted in Michigan's referendum H in 1978, which would have established vouchers of unspecified value and eliminated the use of property taxes to fund public schools. The bundling of these two issues makes it difficult to interpret his results, which accordingly are not summarized below.
4. Note that the *Serrano* decision mandated that spending per pupil be the same in each California public school district, eliminating the usual link between district wealth and spending.
5. Florida's history of assessing schools is illuminating. Initially schools were evaluated on the basis of raw test scores. Subsequently, schools were judged on their "value added". This change appears to have caused considerable confusion (Figlio, 2004).
6. The proposal also required testing of teachers in their academic subjects areas both in public schools and in private schools redeeming tuition vouchers.
7. Nevertheless note that Florida has seven of the 21 largest school districts in the country.
8. These are Arizona, Colorado, Florida, Idaho, Illinois, Iowa, Kansas, Michigan, Montana, New Hampshire, New Jersey, North Dakota, Ohio, Pennsylvania, South Dakota, Utah, Wisconsin and Wyoming.
9. These data are taken from Francis and Kenny (2000, pp. 88–89).

References

Alvarez, D. T. (2003). Determinants of charter law adoption and law strength across states. Undergraduate honors thesis, University of Florida, Gainesville, FL.

Brunner, E., Sonstelie, J., & Thayer, M. (2001). Capitalization and the voucher: An analysis of precinct returns from california's proposition 174. *Journal of Urban Economics, 50*(3), 517–536.

Brunner, E., & Sonstelie, J. (2003). Homeowners, property values, and the political economy of the school voucher. *Journal of Urban Economics, 54*(2), 239–257.

Figlio, D. N. (2004). What's in a grade? School report cards and the housing market. *American Economic Review, 94*(3), 591–604.

Fischel, W. A. (2001). The homevoter hypothesis: How home values influence local government taxation, school finance, and land-use policies. Harvard University Press: Cambridge.

Francis, W. L., & Kenny, L. W. (2000). *Up the Political Ladder: Career Paths in U.S. Politics.* Sage: Thousand Oaks, CA.

Gokcekus, E., Phillips, J. J., & Tower, E. (2004). School choice: Money, race, and congressional voting on vouchers. *Public Choice, 119*(3–4), 241–254.

Gonzalez, G. (2003). Florida HB 751. Undergraduate paper, University of Florida, Gainesville, FL.

Hamilton, B. W. & Macauley, M. K. (1991). Determinants and consequences of private-public school choice. *Journal of Urban Economics, 29*(3), 282–294.

Husted, T. A. & Kenny, L. W. (2000). Evidence on the impact of state government on primary and secondary education and the equity-efficiency trade-off. *Journal of Law and Economics, 43*(1), 285–308.

Husted, T. A. & Kenny, L. W. (2002). The legacy of *serrano*: The impact of mandated equal spending on private school enrollment. *Southern Economic Journal, 68*(3), 566–583.

McDade, C. E. (2003). Analysis of the Florida house of representatives vote on the issue of school vouchers. Undergraduate paper, University of Florida, Gainesville, FL.

Sandy, J. (1992). Evaluating the public support for educational vouchers: A case study. *Economics of Education Review, 11*(3), 249–256.

Schmidt, A. B. (1992). Private school enrollment in metropolitan areas. *Public Finance Quarterly, 20*(3), 298–320.

Tiebout, C. (1956). A pure theory of local government expenditures. *Journal of Political Economy, 64*(1), 16–24.

Wong, F. K., & Shen, F. X. (2004). Political economy of charter school funding formulas: Exploring state-to-state variations. In DeMoss, K. & Wong, F.K. (eds.), *Money, Politics, and Law: Intersections and Conflicts in the Provision of Educational Opportunity, 2004 Yearbook of the American Education Association,* 169–196. Eye on Education: Larchmont, NY.

Zanzig, B. R. (1997). Measuring the impact of competition in local government education markets on the cognitive achievement of students. *Economics of Education Review, 16*(4), 431–441.

Public Choice (2005) **124:** 223–236
DOI: 10.1007/s11127-005-4763-y

Public choice and tort reform

PAUL H. RUBIN
Department of Economics, Emory University, Atlanta, GA 30322-2240 USA
(E-mail: prubin@emory.edu)

Accepted March 2005

Abstract. The common law originally was thought to be immune to rent seeking. More recently, scholars have recognized that attorneys are engaged in exactly that activity. Rent seeking by the legal profession has greatly expanded the scope of US tort law, and generated efforts to reverse its expansion. Organized groups (attorneys, businesses and doctors) are active on both sides of the issue and the partisans have numerous tools available for advancing their agendas, such as litigating, lobbying for favorable rules and attempting to elect sympathetic legislators and judges. All of this creates an ideal setting for public choice analysis.

1. Introduction

Law and economics scholarship initially contended that the common law is efficient. However, there are two problems with that contention. (For a review of the history of efficiency analysis in law and economics, see Rubin, 2004.) First, in spite of valiant attempts to model the law's evolution toward efficiency, no plausible mechanism, Darwinian or otherwise, exists for generating that desirable property. Second, while there is evidence of "macro" efficiency, in the sense that the common law is more efficient than various forms of civil law, the arguments for "micro" efficiency (i.e., efficiency of particular doctrines) are more problematic. In particular, it is very hard to make a case for the efficiency of modern American tort law.[1]

More recent scholarship argues that much of the modern law of torts has been shaped by special-interest lobbying efforts and rent seeking by the trial lawyers (Epstein, 1988; Rubin & Bailey, 1994). Businesses and other groups oppose these efforts. Thus, the setting is ideal for a public choice analysis of the issues. Moreover, the analysis can be particularly rich because the stakes are high and there are many players involved with many tools to use in attempting to influence policy outcomes. The partisans encompass groups having somewhat different interests, and so can be studied as coalitions. In addition to the normal methods of political influence familiar to public choice scholars, such as lobbying and legislative voting, parties seeking change in the tort law can use litigation strategies to advance their agendas. The possibilities for wielding influence also include efforts to elect sympathetic legislators and judges. Additionally, issues of federalism are relevant since US tort law is a product of state and federal legal systems. Tort reform is an important political issue, and if public choice scholars can help understand the sources of existing tort law and of the impetus for reform, they may be able to make important contributions to the policy debate.

In what follows, I first provide a brief introduction to tort law. Both the size and the scope of the potential legal liability faced by tortfeasors have increased greatly in the past fifty years. The most significant change bringing this expansion about was moving from contract to tort in product liability claims; I discuss this move and some of the other changes in the law that occurred as a result. I then discuss the players in the tort-reform game. These are essentially organized groups of attorneys on one side (operating mainly through the American Trial Lawyers Association) and organized groups of businesses and medical doctors on the other. I then discuss the tools available to these interest groups in supporting or opposing tort reform. I conclude with a summary, stressing possibilities for future research.

2. Tort Law[2]

There are several reasons for public choice scholars to study tort reform. The issue is important. The tort system is estimated to cost $233 billion nowadays, a sum the represents 2.2% of US GDP. Administrative costs account for 54% of the total and legal fees for about 33%. (All data are for 2002, as reported in US Council of Economic Advisers, 2004). Additionally, the law of torts engages a number of important policy issues. It is agreed by most law and economics scholars who study the tort system that it has serious problems (Landes & Posner, 1987 are two exceptions). Moreover, the actual cost of the system now in place is substantially greater than its money cost. Many other decisions are affected by the relative price changes caused by expansive tort liability. For example, the prices of many products are increased, and this may lead some consumers to avoid purchasing them. Some of the products are risk-reducing (e.g., medical care, pharmaceuticals), and so it is not even clear that tort liability leads to overall reductions in risk (Calfee & Rubin, 1992). Moreover, by undermining contract, the tort system weakens the rule of law and leads to increased uncertainty and perhaps reduced investment.

Traditionally, tort law governed accidents between "strangers" – parties with no prior relationship. In the past, tort law generally was relegated to a legal backwater, both in terms of practice and in terms of scholarship. Until relatively recently, automobile accidents dominated attorneys' tort practice workloads, and the practitioners were derided as "ambulance chasers". Accidents on the job were covered by workers' compensation, a statutory no-fault system with a schedule of well-defined payments (Fishback & Kantor, 1998).That is, employees automatically collected a fixed amount of compensation for injuries sustained in the workplace (depending on type and severity), with no need to prove fault or negligence. For what is now covered by product liability law (and approximately so for medical malpractice), contractual terms governed. In practice this meant that there generally was no possibility of recovery for product-related injuries; the health-care professions were liable for medical malpractice, but liability was limited.[3]

The most important change leading to rising costs of product liability and malpractice was the replacement of contractual liability with tort liability. Since about 1960, following a case involving the Chrysler Corporation,[4] the courts have in general been unwilling to enforce contracts between buyers and sellers involving compensation for harms caused by accidents. No matter what provisions the parties may want to make to govern the consequences of an accident, the courts will decide and impose their own terms. For example, the parties may want to agree that if there is an accident, the producer of the product will pay only for the customer's lost earnings and his actual medical costs, and will not pay anything for so-called pain and suffering. But if a product-related injury occurs, this voluntary agreement will have no effect. The courts will decide what level and type of damage payments from the manufacturer to the purchaser are appropriate. Judges have used several related legal concepts to justify their unwillingness to enforce voluntary contracts. They may say that the parties have "unequal bargaining power", so that the contract becomes one of "adhesion" and therefore "unconscionable" or "against the public interest". These legal justifications for eliminating voluntary contract ignore the roles of markets and competition in establishing terms. This may be because in their professional lives lawyers look at contracts as protecting parties, and do not grasp the importance of market forces.

Following this major shift in the status of voluntary contracts, numerous subsidiary policy changes led to increased tort liability. These changes involved both standards for liability and also damage payments in the event of an accident. Although most lawyers believe that the change from contract to tort was desirable, economists who study the issue are coming to believe that greater reliance on contract would enhance the law's efficiency (Rubin, 1993; US Congressional Budget Office, 2003; US Council of Economic Advisers, 2004).

I now discuss some of the areas in which tort law has expanded since the move from contract to tort.

2.1. *Liability standards*

One basic distinction in liability standards is between *strict liability* and *negligence*. Under strict liability, the injurer is liable for any harm, no matter what efforts have been made to prevent it. Under negligence, the injurer is liable only if he did not take the proper amount of care to prevent the accident, where "proper" is defined by the legal standard of care. Negligence regimes also differ with respect to the obligation of the victim. In a regime of *contributory negligence*, any responsibility on the part of the victim to causing an accident (for example, product misuse) will release the injurer from any liability, even if the injurer also was negligent. In a regime of *comparative negligence* (which is universal in the United States today), if both parties are at fault the victim is compensated in proportion to the share of responsibility for the accident caused by the injurer's negligence. It is an accepted result in the economic analysis of law that if the standard for determining negligence is based on efficient (cost-justified) levels of care, then any of the negligence rules lead to optimal precautions by both victims and injurers (see, for example, Posner, 2003 or Shavell, 2004). The rules differ only in determining compensation in the event that both parties are negligent.

Tort analysts find it useful to distinguish between *manufacturing defects* and *design defects*. A manufacturing defect occurs when a particular product does not meet its own production specifications. If, for example, the steering wheel in a new car should break during normal driving, this is a manufacturing defect. Most analysts agree that strict liability for manufacturing defects may be appropriate, and in any case such defects are relatively rare and therefore do not add greatly to the costs of the tort system. Under a strict liability standard, the manufacturer is fully liable for any harm associated with the defect. There is nothing a consumer can do to avoid these defects (since they occur in the manufacturing process). Manufacturers decide how much to spend on inspection and quality control. The costs of determining whether a defect exists are relatively low. Thus, a strict liability standard for this class of error would likely evolve in a free market. Indeed, there is evidence that the original proponents of strict liability for product-caused injuries had exactly this class of defects in mind.

Design defects are quite different. Design defects are said to occur when the courts rule that it would have been possible for the manufacturer to design the product differently and so make it safer. For example, a finder of fact may decide that an automobile manufacturer should have put the vehicle's gas tank in a different location. Such defects apply to all units of some product, not merely to faulty units, so that possibilities for litigation are substantial. A major expansion in product liability occurred when the courts extended strict liability from manufacturing defects to design defects. This extension requires courts and juries to second-guess product designers and determine whether a safer alternative was available when the product was on the drawing board. Such second-guessing is problematic (what did the manufacturer know, and when did he know it?), so that litigating such issues is very expensive. Some of the major problems identified with the current tort system are due to the extension of something like strict liability to design defects.[5]

Another major class of modern liability cases involves a "failure to warn". Originally, the law was written so that product warnings would insulate manufacturers from liability. However, the doctrine has been turned on its head, and manufacturers are often found liable for failure to warn in circumstances where consumers have misused the product in dangerous and unpredictable ways. Viscusi (1991) has shown that product liability's significant expansion has been causally related both to the expansion of liability for failure to warn and to the extension of strict liability to manufacturing defects.

2.2. *Damage payments*

The sizes of damage payments paid to injured parties also have increased dramatically. It is useful to divide damage payments into three classes. *Pecuniary damages* compensate consumers for actual out-of-pocket expenses. This class of damages comprises about 22% of total tort damages (US Council of Economic Advisers, 2004, p. 209). The major categories here are medical costs and lost wages. *Nonpecuniary damages* compensate consumers for other, nonmoney losses. The most important class of nonpecuniary payments is for pain and suffering. This class comprises 24% of total damages. Payments for *hedonic* losses, or lost pleasure of life, a relatively new and controversial class of payments in the tort system, are also nonpecuniary in character.[6]

In analyzing damage payments for product liability accidents, we must keep in mind that consumers themselves pay for whatever damage payments they ultimately receive. Damage payments are like insurance: consumers pay premiums in the form of higher prices for goods and services and then receive compensation if injured by them. Many consumers find it worthwhile to insure themselves against medical costs and lost wages; it is nevertheless appropriate for injurers to pay compensation for this class of losses, although some coordination between payments from injurers and payments from insurers in the form of "subrogation" would be useful. (Under subrogation, a person's first-party insurer pays the injured party, but then collects from the injurer.)

If given a choice, consumers never buy insurance against pain and suffering. There are sound theoretical explanations for this. Essentially, this class of harms does not increase the marginal utility of wealth, and so does not provide a profitable opportunity for insurers since the value of such policies is less than their actuarial cost (Calfee & Rubin, 1992). Because the administrative costs of operating the tort system are higher than the costs of operating any other insurance system, consumers would be even more unwilling to pay for compensation for pain and suffering through the tort system than through a system of direct first-party insurance.

Punitive damages are a more difficult issue. There are some behaviors of firms that normal tort damages will not adequately deter. Firms will sometimes make efforts to hide their wrongful behavior. If they succeed, then there is insufficient deterrence. Therefore, multiplied damages can be useful in preventing such efforts at concealment. The optimal damage multiplier should be the inverse of the probability of detection (Rubin, Calfee & Grady, 1997; Polinsky & Shavell, 1998).

2.3. *Jurisdiction*

The United States is governed by a federal system, and most tort law is state law. This creates several issues of interest. First is the issue of whether a particular tort case will be tried in state or federal court. In general, plaintiffs prefer state court and defendants prefer federal court. For class actions, this issue is the subject of a major lobbying campaign by proponents of tort reform.[7] A second issue involves the venue in which a case will be tried. Some states and some counties are friendlier to plaintiffs than others. Plaintiff-friendliness depends on matters such as the income and race of residents (who are potential jurors) and whether judges are elected or appointed (Tabarrok & Helland, 1999; Helland & Tabarrok, 2003). Tort law can serve as a means of transferring wealth from the citizens of one state to those of another: the stockholders of companies accused of committing torts typically live in all states and the headquarters of defendant firms often are located in states other than the one where the cases against them are tried. This wealth-transfer potential gives state judges (particularly elected judges) strong incentives to rule in favor of plaintiffs. Thus, although matters of private law traditionally have been state law, there are arguments for treating tort law as a federal matter (Rubin, Calfee & Grady, 1997).

A related issue is the way in which "choice of law" issues are handled. This deals with situations in which more than one body of law could govern; for example, a citizen of Colorado harms a citizen of Arizona in Michigan. State courts have exhibited an ever greater willingness to hear cases involving their own citizens in matters where there is some jurisdictional ambiguity (O'Hara & Ribstein, 2000). The growing use of "long-arm" jurisdiction has added to the expansion in tort liability.

Plaintiffs generally decide where to file cases, and so choose the jurisdiction. The locus of a trial is important for two reasons. First, damage awards are more likely and larger in some jurisdictions, so plaintiffs naturally want cases heard in those places, while defendants do not. Second, the process of jurisdictional choice by plaintiffs can itself have important implications for the law's contours as plaintiffs chose friendly jurisdictions where they win favorable verdicts that establish precedents for the courts in other jurisdictions (Fon & Parisi, 2003). For students of tort reform, the fact that tort law is formulated at the state level provides rich datasets for hypothesis testing (see, for example, Landes & Posner, 1987; Curran, 1992; Rubin & Bailey, 1994; Rubin, Curran & Curran, 2001; Helland & Tabarrok, 2003).

2.4. *Other issues*

A number of other important issues surround the tort law. One is the role of class actions. A class-action lawsuit is a method of aggregating many small claims. Since litigation is expensive, the legal system will provide no recourse for injured parties suffering small losses. A class action can solve this problem by combining these small claims in one case and so creating economies of scale in litigation. If the underlying law is efficient, then class actions can be an efficient adjunct to the litigation system. However, if the underlying law is itself inefficient, then this form of lawsuit will serve to exacerbate the problems in the system. Since there is no real "client" in many class-action lawsuits, there are few checks on attorneys' fees, and so these lawsuits can be very profitable for lawyers. There is also a hybrid called "joined claims", in which the litigation addresses many small claims simultaneously and also addresses individual claims; this is the form of lawsuit used in the asbestos litigation (White, 2004).

There are other factors generating incomes for lawyers. These include particular classes of litigation. Asbestos has been a big money-maker for attorneys; lawyers have made (as of 2004) $41 billion ($21 billion for defendants' lawyers and $20 billion for plaintiffs' lawyers) and are projected ultimately to earn $118 billion altogether (White, 2004).[8] Tobacco litigation (pursued by private attorneys in conjunction with state attorneys general) has generated $13 billion in fess to be paid out over 25 years (ibid.). As discussed below, fees of this magnitude have significant implications for the political behavior of the parties in tort reform.

3. The Players

The major players in the tort reform game are the lawyers (opposed to tort reform) and businesses and sometimes doctors (in favor). The protagonists are organized interest groups, whose relative strengths have been assessed by Epstein (1988) and by Rubin and Bailey (1994).[9] The lawyers are in the best position because they merely must oppose any and all forms of tort reform. Moreover, lawyers representing both plaintiffs and defendants favor expansive tort systems (Olson, 2003); for example, as mentioned above, lawyers for the defense have earned more from asbestos litigation than have plaintiffs' lawyers.[10] (Of course, defense lawyers must be more circumspect in their advocacy since their clients generally favor tort reform.)

A major player on the side of the lawyers is the American Trial Lawyers Association (ATLA).[11] It is aligned with the Democratic Party and other left-leaning groups, and one of its members, John Edwards, was the Democratic nominee for Vice President in 2004. Association members contribute money and sometimes time and other resources to elect political candidates supportive of their views. In many respects the ATLA is an ordinary, albeit powerful, interest group. As discussed below, however, it has an additional tool to use in influencing policy besides those available to all interest groups: it is able to litigate to establish favorable precedents. In the litigation process, the ATLA provides various private goods to nonmember lawyers (e.g., documents received from defendants, information about courtroom techniques, data and methods of litigation), which would induce them to join the association (Rubin & Bailey, 1994). A particularly important but insufficiently studied set of ATLA allies comprise members of the "consumer movement", including various "public interest research groups" (PIRGs) and other organizations associated with Ralph Nader.

Numerous business groups are involved on the side of tort reform. For example, the US Chamber of Commerce and its Institute of Legal Reform are very active.[12] The American Tort Reform Association (ATRA) also is an active player.[13]

Business groups are less monolithic and have more difficulty in organizing and promoting their policy agendas than the trial attorneys. This is for several reasons. Issues in particular product liability cases are somewhat idiosyncratic: was the gas tank in a particular model of automobile in the right place? There are also standard free-rider problems in organization. The stakes are not always the same for all businesses. Epstein (1988) points out, for example, that machine tool companies will have an interest in coordinating workers' compensation programs with tort law; pharmaceutical companies will not care about this issue, but will care about whether approval of a new chemical entity by the Food and Drug Administration is a defense against tort liability, an issue of no particular interest to chemical companies. However, Epstein's point may be a bit overdrawn. There are some issues of interest to all businesses. These include the locus of lawsuits (with businesses favoring federal rather than state jurisdiction), procedural rules, such as limits on class actions and on the amounts and forms of damage payments. These are among the issues that have been at the forefront of the battles between the plaintiffs' bar and manufacturers.

For research purposes it is useful to note that business-related organizations provide substantial amounts of information valuable for students of tort reform and public choice. The aforementioned Institute of Legal Reform, for instance, has released a study based on a survey of company general counsels rating states in terms of their tort systems.[14] The ATRA identifies "judicial hellholes",[15] counties in which tort litigation is particularly harmful to defendant companies, as well as state-by-state lists of successful tort reform initiatives. It might appear that this information is biased since it is generated by interest groups actively involved on one side of the tort reform process. However, if one is studying the effects of tort liability on business decisions, or the distribution of business political contributions to judicial candidates, then the perception of business organizations is a relevant datum, and these reports do supply useful information on business perceptions. The ATLA's website also provides information on tort reform from the perspective of the plaintiffs' attorneys.

4. Tools

The study of tort reform should be especially interesting to students of public choice because the players have many strategies and methods of influence available to them, and the interplay among the various ways the players have of advancing their agendas is a worthy subject of study. This is best seen by reviewing the history of tort law and tort reform. As discussed above, there has been a major expansion in tort liability, marked by numerous changes in the law and in legal standards, since the 1950s. Rubin, Curran and Curran (2001) argue that in general lawyers have a comparative advantage in using litigation as a method of expanding liability. They examined the sources of some of the changes leading to expansion of liability, such as rejection of privity and adoption of strict liability, and found that these policy changes did indeed come about mainly through the litigation process. That is, in all of the cases examined by Rubin et al. extensions of tort liability resulted from judicial decisions in state courts.[16] For a similar analysis, see Osborne (2002).

Moreover, there is evidence that some innovations (specifically, the elimination of privity) occurred faster in states with more attorneys per capita (Rubin & Bailey, 1994). Rubin and Bailey also describe in detail the process employed by the ATLA in litigating for the purpose of generating favorable precedents which have expanded the scope of tort law. Essentially, lawyers pooled their information through the auspices of the ATLA. This information-pooling both increased the likelihood that a particular case would be won and helped to generate verdicts that would be helpful to other lawyers working on similar matters. Lawyers also have the ability to select cases that are more likely to establish favorable precedents.

Groups supporting tort reform generally have responded by employing more normal tools of political advocacy, using campaign contributions and lobbying in working to convince state legislators and the US Congress to pass tort reform measures. To illustrate, Rubin, Curran and Curran (2001) find that adoption of workers' compensation and limits on strict liability occurred as a result of statutory changes. Attorneys then appealed some reforms to courts (often state supreme courts) in the attempt, often successful, to have the reforms declared unconstitutional. Schwartz, Behrens and Lorber (2000) supply a nice discussion of various tactics in the legislation-litigation campaign from the viewpoint of tort reform advocates. More recently, as tort lawyers have become richer, they have also begun to use the lobbying process; this has been less well studied. The trial lawyers have thus far used this strategy mainly defensively, primarily to stop legislative tort reform. (For an interesting anecdotal discussion, see Olson, 2003, Chapter 9.) An example can be found in a bill introduced in the US Congress to reform class-action litigation in various ways (S. 2062, titled the Class Action Fairness Act), which has not passed the Senate. Anecdotal evidence indicates that the failure of this bill was due to lobbying efforts of lawyers, but the issue has not been studied carefully.

On the other hand, proponents of tort reform have been able to use the litigation process to influence some aspects of policy implementation. Specifically, several Supreme Court decisions have had the effect of limiting punitive damage awards. The most recent case is *Campbell*,[17] in which the Court indicated that in most circumstances punitive damages cannot be more than nine times larger than actual damages (a "single-digit" multiplier). Viscusi (2004) indicates that this decision is likely to reduce the level of punitive damages. Supporters of tort reform also have succeeded in requiring higher scientific qualifications for experts in lawsuits.[18] Additionally, groups with strong stakes in the outcome of the tort reform debate undertake efforts to influence the selection of judges at both the state and federal levels. For federal judges as well as for states where judges are appointed, interest groups can influence the judicial selection process indirectly by contributing to the campaigns of politicians they think will nominate people to the bench compatible with their policy preferences.

Because the relevant interest groups have so many tools available to them, the nature of political equilibrium is not clear. When one party loses in a particular forum, it can shift the locus of combat to another venue. Thus, as described above, groups have gone from litigation to lobbying to political action aimed at judicial appointments in order to advance their agendas. Moreover, parties on both sides of the tort reform issue have used the complete toolset, although it would seem that lawyers have a comparative advantage in litigation and businesses in lobbying. Both sides have used the political process to try to elect candidates who will pass laws or appoint judges sympathetic to their positions; it is not clear where the competitive advantage lies in this method of legal change. In states where judgeships are elective offices, both sides also have invested resources in contenders with compatible views. The lawyers have been dong this for a long time, but recently business group have adopted this electoral strategy as well.

5. Summary and Possible Avenues of Future Research

Although the tort reform debate is important, the literature bringing a public choice perspective to bear on the issue is small; relatively little has been written. This means that research in this area can have a big payoff; it is possible to contribute significantly to scientific understanding of the policy issues and perhaps to influence the terms of the debate as well. Moreover, because tort law is mostly state law, there is a good deal of variation available for empirical study.

There are many interesting questions to be examined. I have mentioned some of them in this essay, but I will provide a more complete list here.

1. Political coalitions operate on both sides of the tort reform debate. These coalitions are themselves worthy of study through the lens of public choice. How do they overcome free-rider problems? Are private, Olsonian goods (Olson, 1965) provided to group members? Do the particular policy areas chosen as targets for reform efforts have to do with the coalitional nature of the parties? For example, much litigation by the proponents of reform has dealt with damage payments; is this because it is an important issue in its own right or because it is a concern common to all potential defendants and so an issue on which it is easier to reach agreement?
2. The political links among the coalitions active in the tort reform debate could be studied. The trial lawyers, who oppose reform, seem to be aligned with the Democratic Party, and the groups favoring reform are more likely to be Republicans. The relation between the trial lawyers and the forces behind the "consumer movement", including various "public interest research groups" (PIRGs) and other Naderite organizations, is particularly interesting, but has not been examined carefully examined.
3. Although there has been some analysis of the ATLA and of business groups, I am not aware of any public choice analysis of medical doctors as actors in the tort reform debate. That neglect merits remedy. Doctors may straddle the relevant coalitions and parties, favoring Democrats on some issues, such as increased health-care spending, and Republicans on others, including tort reform. These divergent interests may help explain why doctors appear to be less effective than other groups in pushing tort reform, but this is subject to study.
4. Since many state court judges are elected, it would be possible to study campaign contributions and campaign spending by interested parties in such electoral contests. Since the decisions the courts in one state can affect corporations in all states, we would expect out-of-state interests to involve themselves in judicial elections, particularly in states that are viewed as "tort hellholes". This issue has not been examined in the literature.[19]
5. Some states have enacted tort reform measures. The determinants of whether or not a state passes such legislation as well as the form such legislation takes could be more carefully studied. Possible explanatory variables include the number of attorneys in a state, measures of business presence as well as other standard economic and public choice predictors, such as income per capita and party control of the state's executive and legislative

branches. Empirical analyses of the determinants of the elimination of privity by states (Landes & Posner, 1987; Bailey & Rubin, 1994) and of the adoption of comparative negligence (Curran, 1992) have been undertaken, but other policy changes have not yet been studied systematically.

6. The partisans of tort reform on both sides of the debate have many potential means of influence available, including litigation, lobbying, contributions to judicial campaigns and contributions to politicians who will vote for favorable legislation or appoint judges sympathetic to one side or the other. How do the partisans decide which tool to use in particular circumstances? Are attorneys, for instance, more likely to contribute to political campaigns in states where judges are appointed or where they are elected?
7. It would be useful to study the pattern of votes in the US House of Representatives and the US Senate on tort reform bills. Additionally, the US Senate holds confirmation hearings on federal judges, and its committee and floor votes on judicial nominations could be studied. The impact of political campaign contributions and lobbying activities by advocacy groups and other interested parties (such as the plaintiffs' bar) on tort reform legislation also merits examination.
8. Many legislators at both the federal and state levels are attorneys. Owing to potential conflicts of interest, attorneys dealing with tort reform issues as legislators offer an interesting area for the study of agency problems in a representative democracy. To what extent do these attorneys represent themselves and to what extent do they represent their constituents? That is, do lawyer-legislators vote differently on tort reform issues than non-attorneys who represent otherwise similar districts or states? Including a dummy variable in a voting equation, indicating whether a legislator is an attorney or not, would be a way to examine this issue empirically.

In sum, there are important and interesting questions relating to tort reform awaiting public choice scholars. Theoretical tools are available for analyzing these issues. Rich datasets for testing hypotheses are available for collection. Tort reform is a fruitful area for research.

Notes

1. Tort law has several components. Much of it is automobile accident law, which is mostly efficient and of little interest. As it is generally applied, "tort reform" deals with product liability and medical malpractice law, and that is how I use the term in what follows.
2. This section is based in part on Rubin (1995).
3. The governing legal doctrine was "privity", which insulated manufacturers from liability because there was no direct relationship between manufacturers and injured customers. Of course, manufacturers could have assumed liability if they had chosen, so the limit was essentially a matter of contract.

4. Henningsen v. Bloomfield Motors, 32 N.J. 358, 161 a. 2d 69 (1960).
5. Although product liability is said to be a regime of "strict liability", the term is not used in legal parlance in the same way it is used by economists. For example, a plaintiff must show that some alternative, safer product design was feasible; in a pure world of strict liability, this would not be necessary.
6. This class of damages, based on econometric studies of "willingness to pay", actually was invented by an economist. The courts have not been very friendly to the theory of hedonic damages, however.
7. S. 2062, the Class Action Fairness Act, discussed at http://www.legalreformnow.com/newsroom/display_release.cfm?ID=98. Also see below.
8. Many plaintiffs in the asbestos cases are workers who installed asbestos long ago. However, these workers are suing the manufacturers of asbestos, not their own employers, and so the damage limits in workman's compensation do not bind. This type of lawsuit represents an important category of current product liability litigation.
9. Insurance companies have more mixed motives. In the short run, they lose from expansive tort liability, but in the long run greater liability exposure leads to greater sales of insurance.
10. For completeness, it must be mentioned that some economists (including the author) have also made money as experts in such litigation.
11. The ATLA's website can be accessed at http://www.atla.org.
12. See http://www.legalreformnow.com.
13. See http://www.atra.org.
14. The study can be accessed at http://www.legalreformnow.com/study030804.cfm.
15. Available at http://www.atra.org/reports/hellholes/.
16. The analysis of comparative negligence was more complicated, but still consistent with the arguments here.
17. State Farm Mutual Automobile Insurance Co. v. Campbell et al., S.Ct. 1513 (2003).
18. Daubert v. Merrell Dow Pharmaceuticals, Inc., 113 S.Ct. 2786 (1993).
19. Soyong Chong and I are in the process of conducting such an examination.

References

Calfee, J. E., & Rubin, P. H. (1992). Some implications of damage payments for nonpecuniary losses. *Journal of Legal Studies, 21*(2), 371–411.

Curran, C. (1992). The spread of the comparative negligence rule throughout the United States. *International Review of Law and Economics, 12*(3), 317–332.

Epstein, R. A. (1988). The political economy of product liability reform. *American Economic Review Papers and Proceedings, 78*(2), 311–315.

Fishback, P. V., & Kantor, S. E. (1998). The adoption of workers' compensation in the United States, 1900–1930. *Journal of Law and Economics, 41*(2), 305–341.

Fon, V., & Parisi, F. (2003). Litigation and the evolution of legal remedies: A dynamic model. *Public Choice, 116*(3–4), 419–433.

Helland, E., & Tabarrok, A. (2003). Race, poverty, and American tort awards: Evidence from three data sets. *Journal of Legal Studies, 32*(1), 27–58.

Landes, W. M., & Posner, R. A. (1987). *The Economic Structure of Tort Law*. Harvard University Press: Cambridge.

O'Hara, E., & Ribstein, L. (2000). From politics to efficiency in choice of law. *University of Chicago Law Review, 67*(Fall), 1151–1233.

Olson, M. (1965). *The Logic of Collective Action: Public Goods and the Theory of Groups*. Harvard University Press: Cambridge.

Olson, W. (2003). *The Rule of Lawyers: How the New Litigation Elite Threatens America's Rule of Law*. St. Martin's Press: New York.

Osborne, E. (2002). What's yours is mine: A rent-seeking theory of the common law. *Public Choice, 111*(3–4), 399–415.

Polinsky, A. M., & Shavell, S. (1998). Punitive damages: An economic analysis. *Harvard Law Review, 111*(4), 869–962.

Posner, R. A. (2003). *Economic Analysis of Law*, 6th ed. Aspen Publishers: New York.

Rubin, P. H. (1993). *Tort Reform by Contract*. American Enterprise Institute: Washington, DC.

Rubin, P. H. (1995). Fundamental reform of tort law. *Regulation, 1995*(4), 26–33.

Rubin, P. H. (2005). Micro and macro legal efficiency: Supply and demand. *Supreme Court Economic Review, 13*, 19–34.

Rubin, P. H., & Bailey, M. J. (1994). The role of lawyers in changing the law. *Journal of Legal Studies, 23*(2), 807–831.

Rubin, P. H., Calfee, J., & Grady, M. (1997). *BMW v. Gore*: Mitigating the punitive economics of punitive damages. *Supreme Court Economic Review, 5*(1), 179–216.

Rubin, P. H., Curran, C., & Curran, J. F. (2001). Litigation versus legislation: Forum shopping by rent seekers. *Public Choice, 107*(3–4), 295–310.

Schwartz, V., Behrens, M. A., & Lorber, L. (2000). Tort reform past, present and future: Solving old problems and dealing with "New Style" litigation. *William Mitchell Law Review, 27*(1), 237–269.

Shavell, S. (2004). *Foundations of Economic Analysis of Law*. Harvard University Press: Cambridge, MA.

Tabarrok, A., & Helland, E. (1999). Court politics: The political economy of tort awards. *Journal of Law and Economics, 62*(April), 157–188.

US Congressional Budget Office (2003). *The Economics of U. S. Tort Liability: A Primer*. US Congressional Budget Office: Washington, DC.

US Council of Economic Advisers (2004). *Economic Report of the President*. US Council of Economic Advisers: Washington, DC.

Viscusi, W. K. (1991). The dimensions of the product liability crisis. *Journal of Legal Studies, 20*(1), 147–177.

Viscusi, W. K. (2004). The blockbuster punitive damage awards. *Emory Law Journal, 53*(3), 1404–1456.

White, M. (2004). Asbestos and the future of mass torts. *Journal of Economic Perspectives, 18*(2), 183–204.

Public Choice (2005) **124:** 237–247
DOI: 10.1007/s11127-005-4765-9

The unfinished business of public choice

WILLIAM F. SHUGHART II[1,*] and ROBERT D. TOLLISON[2]
[1]*Department of Economics, The University of Mississippi, P.O. Box 1848, University, MS 38677-1848, USA;* [2]*John E. Walker Department of Economics, Clemson University, 222 Sirrine Hall, Clemson, SC 29634, USA (*Author for correspondence, E-mail: shughart@olemiss.edu)*

Accepted March 2005

Abstract. Over the past fifty years, the public choice research program has generated important insights into collective decision-making processes, especially as they operate within the political institutions of Europe and North America. Despite a half-century of progress, a great deal of unfinished business remains on the public choice research agenda. In the course of assessing the current state of the literature, as represented in the contributions to this special issue of *Public Choice*, this essay identifies some of the unanswered questions.

1. Introduction

The contributors to this volume were invited to utilize current events in their particular areas of expertise as points of departure for assessing the extant public choice literature and for speculating on the direction it might take in the new century. They were asked to think expansively in laying out public choice frameworks for analyzing how democratic governments have responded (or might respond) to some of the major policy challenges that have surfaced in the recent past. We think our authors have fulfilled their assigned missions of demonstrating the energy and continued relevance of the public choice research program.

There is much left to be done, however. In this essay, we briefly summarize what has gone before. Relying on the set of topics addressed in this volume as a foundation for discussion, we identify some of the unanswered questions. Our list of unfinished business is idiosyncratic; other researchers active in the field undoubtedly would want to expand or contract it. Our intention here merely is to generate enthusiasm among the next generation of public choice scholars for carrying the field's research program forward.

2. Unfinished Business

One of the key insights of public choice, grounded in the seminal work of Buchanan and Tullock (1962), is that constitutional rules impose the only effective constraints on democratic policy processes. Among other things, the constitution divides the domains of collective choice and private choice and, within the former, establishes the institutional framework within which collective choices will be made. That framework includes such matters as the universality of the franchise, the qualifications for holding public office, the size and composition of the legislature, the powers of the chief executive, the voting majority required to elect officeholders and to approve legislation, and so on. Once the constitution is in place, the game of ordinary, day-to-day, "in-period" politics plays out in a setting where voters are rationally ignorant, incumbent politicians have substantial advantages over challengers, and well-organized interest groups actively compete for special favors. No man is safe when the legislature is in session, as the old saying goes. The only things not up for grabs are those things constitutionally removed from the collective-choice domain, such as the freedoms of religion, speech and peaceable assembly guaranteed by the First Amendment ("Congress shall make no law...").

Owing to the logic of collective action (Olson, 1965), the business of government, especially government in geographically based representative democracies like the United States, is mostly about wealth redistribution. Pressure groups lobby for the many benefits the state can supply – subsidies, tax relief, protection from competitive market forces – and self-interested politicians, who rely on these groups for campaign contributions and other forms of support to ensure election or reelection to office, rationally cater to their demands. Because the taxpaying public, who will be called upon to finance the benefits conferred on politically favored groups, is unorganized, is less effective in delivering political support and, hence, plays only a subsidiary role in politicians' electoral strategies, it predictably gets short shrift in the wealth-transfer process.

In explaining why the welfare state continues to expand notwithstanding collectivism's loss of intellectual respectability, we can now add James Buchanan's insight about the appeal of "parental socialism" to the familiar story of interest-group politics. As the baby-boom generation ages, the elderly have become a powerful political force.[1] They are well-organized (under the auspices of the American Association of Retired Persons) and represent significant voting blocs in Florida and other electorally important "battleground states". As a result, it should come as no surprise that senior citizens have lobbied successfully for a new taxpayer-financed prescription drug benefit; nor is it much in doubt that their demands will be decisive in shaping "reform" of the Medicaid and Social Security programs necessary to avert looming bankruptcy.[2] Horror stories about elderly Americans having to choose between paying for food and paying for needed medications aside, seniors as a group comprise the wealthiest segment of the US population. Government-mediated transfers to them therefore fail a social benefit-cost test and would not command majority support in the absence of the realities of rent-seeking and interest-group politics.

Surely Buchanan is right, though, that an entitlement mentality, grounded in a shared willingness to trade freedom for dependency on the state, is an important factor underlying the demands of senior citizens and other interest groups for ever greater government involvement in health care and similar aspects of daily life once the provinces of personal responsibility. The emergence of the modern culture of dependency can be traced to the Great Depression. Public clamoring for relief from conditions of mass unemployment and falling incomes fueled unprecedented expansions in the size and scope of the public sectors in the United States and elsewhere. Although public choice economists have begun studying the depression era in depth and, in particular, assembling evidence on the electoral strategies that guided the Roosevelt administration's responses to the economic crisis (Wright, 1974; Anderson & Tollison, 1991; Couch & Shughart, 1998), they have not yet been able to explain satisfactorily the Supreme Court's dramatic reversal in 1935, when it began overturning well-established constitutional protections for economic liberties and thereby set the American welfare state on its modern growth path (Shughart, 2004).

That episode, marked as it was by the Supreme Court's apparent submission to political pressure emanating both from the White House and the Congress, points to a number of unresolved issues on the public choice research agenda. One of them has to do with the institutional characteristics of the judiciary itself: are judges truly "independent" of the other branches of government, or are they instead merely the enforcers of contracts between interest groups and the legislature? If judicial independence is a desirable property, are life tenure for judges and protection from having their pay reduced while serving in office necessary or sufficient for fostering it? On the other hand, if judges are not entirely independent of the political process, what are the mechanisms by which their decisions are swayed? Does influence on the judiciary operate primarily through the nomination and appointment process, through the budgetary process, or by some other means? Some headway has been made here (for a review of the relevant literature, see Anderson, 2001), but the behavior of the "third branch" is still something of a black box.

Nineteen thirty-five's infamous "switch in time that saved nine" launched a period of judicial activism that established new "rights" nowhere found in the Constitution written by the Founding Fathers in 1787. The view that the constitution is an organic, living document adaptable as necessary to accommodate changing circumstances of time and place quickly entered the mainstream of American legal thinking. Judicial activism raises important questions about the durability of constitutional rules and the very purposes served by having a constitution in the first place. If the constitution is not immune to rent-seeking or to the interpretative whims of a "progressive" judiciary, then the distinctive role it plays in the public choice paradigm requires reevaluation. An implication of Buchanan's essay, although not one with which he would necessarily agree, is that one cannot look to the constitution for relief from the consequences of the polity's fear of freedom and the avoidance of personal responsibility it entails. Relief will be found instead in run-of-the-mill political processes: it will materialize only at some future time when the fiscal burden required to support the welfare state's continued expansion becomes unacceptably heavy.

Charles Rowley's entry supplies even stronger reason to question the pride of place assigned to constitutions in public choice thinking. From Abraham Lincoln to George W. Bush, according to him, the economic liberties spelled out in the parchment crafted at Philadelphia have failed to withstand invasion by ambitious chief executives exercising claimed emergency war powers. Time and time again, constitutional provisions safeguarding humankind's most basic natural rights, including freedoms of speech, of the press, and of peaceable assembly, have been breached in the name of national security. Suppressing the enemies of the state, be they foreign or, as at Waco and Ruby Ridge, domestic, provides convenient cover for governmental overreaching. Just as the accounting frauds perpetrated in the 1990s by aggressive corporate managers justify serious reevaluation of the efficient markets hypothesis, the steady erosion of liberal principles superintended by saber-rattling presidents, actions aided and abetted by complaisant legislatures and judges, demand the attention of constitutional political economists.

Faith in democracy's capacity to elicit the "will of the people" is widespread, but wholly unfounded, as emphasized in Michael Munger's contribution to this volume. Spreading democracy to all corners of the globe nevertheless has become a priority of western foreign policymakers. A mindset equating the holding of elections with political freedom has guided American planning for post-war Afghanistan and Iraq. With western encouragement, the new governments formed in Russia and many of the former Soviet republics scheduled elections early in their transitions away from communist dictatorship. Opportunistically propagating the electoral process in a few nations is seen as a way of building a critical mass of free societies that quickly will diffuse to other parts of Central Asia, the Middle East and beyond, as people still living under autocratic regimes see democracy's virtues and demand voices in the affairs of government.

Arguably, however, the precedence given to holding elections puts the cart before the horse. Given the defects in collective choice processes – their vulnerabilities to faction, their potential to produce tyrannies of the majority or of the minority, their susceptibility to manipulation by agenda-setters and strategic voting – Munger reasons that it is critical for the institutional underpinnings of a liberal democracy to be created first. Those institutional underpinnings can only be supplied by a constitution that delimits the domain of collective choice, provides protections for basic civil liberties, defines property rights and establishes the rule of law.

The new century will witness that process playing out in reverse. It would be useful for public choice scholars to study the development of political institutions in settings where democracy has no historical roots, populations are ethnically and religiously diverse, and elections precede the writing and ratification of constitutions. Will the institutions established safeguard the rights of minorities, or will they instead be designed to protect the interests of the officials holding positions in pre-constitutional provisional governments and their supporting coalitions? Are the institutions more likely to shift state power to the center or will they be federalist, with relatively weak central governments and a great deal of local political autonomy? Comparisons with the transitions to democracy in post-Second World War Germany and Japan, whose constitutions were imposed by the victorious allied powers, might be helpful. Munger's point that democracy should be the last, not the first, priority for developing and transitioning nations merits thoughtful consideration.

A similar conclusion is reached in Dennis Mueller's essay, which emphasizes the importance of constitutional rules in constraining and shaping political outcomes, but which also demonstrates that, at least as it has played out in the European Union (EU) and the former Soviet socialist republics, the activity of constitution writing is itself vulnerable to special-interest influence. A constitution consistent with classical liberal principles is especially in doubt when the individuals who are likely to hold public office under a new constitution are allowed to participate in its drafting, thereby violating what Mueller calls the "first law of constitution writing". The strong Russian presidency desired by Boris Yeltsin at the constitution-writing stage begat Vladimir Putin. The drafters of the proposed EU constitution, chosen from among the continent's political elites, crafted a document that, by way of comparison with the one written at Philadelphia, is excessively long and overly complex. A major challenge for public choice scholarship in general and for students of constitutional political economy in particular is to model the political institutions and political processes that emerge in settings where the constitutional rules of the game are written by players themselves.

In addition, constitution-making in the European Union is shifting power toward Brussels at the same time that the reemergence of ethnic and national identities, suppressed by authoritarian governments for much of the twentieth century, has set centrifugal forces in motion in many other parts of the globe. Is there a public choice explanation for the two divergent paths being taken by peoples in the new century, one toward separatism and the other toward supranational governance? What are the implications of Europe's growing political integration (and of the continuing expansion of the EU's membership list) for the lives of ordinary citizens? Will harmonization and coordination produce more market-friendly policies and more liberal governance than in the past or, by short-circuiting intergovernmental competition, move the continent in an entirely different direction?

As the events in the Ukraine at year-end 2004 illustrate, electoral fraud stalks the democratic process, and not only in nascent democracies or in Third-World countries whose rulers have invited former president Jimmy Carter to "observe" polling on Election Day. Charges of vote-buying and vote-stealing have surfaced in nearly every contested US election; Lyndon Johnson's first senate campaign, John Kennedy's razor-thin victory over Richard Nixon in the 1960 presidential race and, of course, the 2000 Bush-Gore contest rank among the most well-known electoral controversies of modern times. Anecdotal evidence from the United States suggests that election "irregularities" are by and large a matter of Democratic Party politicking, possibly perpetuating the legacies of the big-city "machines" that dominated the American political landscape during the nineteenth century and most of the twentieth. It would be illuminating for public choice scholars to study the causes and consequences of electoral corruption. Is the Democratic Party's apparent propensity for engaging in vote-buying and other less than savory electoral practices explained by the characteristics of the constituencies it tends to serve, or is it simply a result of the fact that, owing to that party's historical dominance of local politics, most state and county election officials are Democrats? More fundamentally, is vote-fraud in fact mainly a Democratic Party problem, or are the Republicans equally guilty, as Rutherford B. Hayes's controversial defeat of Samuel Tilden in 1876 exemplifies, and as public choice reasoning might suggest?

Many of the same questions could be asked about political corruption in general. Why are some government regimes, be they local, state or national, more corrupt than others? The public choice literature is beginning to turn its attention to the analysis of the corruption problem, but there are many questions still to be answered. Is public corruption more prevalent where the salaries of public office are low and, hence, corruption might be contained by paying politicians "efficiency wages"? Is corruption more likely to be exposed when the existing political equilibrium has been disturbed by a regime change, and the newcomers to public office stop making payoffs to the previous regime's supporters (who predictably become whistleblowers) in order to redirect government contracts and other forms of governmental largesse to their own supporting coalitions? Is political corruption on the rise, perhaps because governmental growth has enlarged the rent-extraction potential of holding of public office, or is the incidence of corruption today commensurate with that of the past? If corruption is becoming more prevalent, causality may operate in the reverse: what role, if any, does misconduct on the part of public officials play in explaining the growth of government?

As we noted in our introductory essay, the era of big government returned with a vengeance during the early years of the new century. One possible explanation for this is that President Bush's narrow victory in the 2000 presidential contest, combined with a razor-thin Republican majority in the US

Senate, led him to reward supporters in key states by, for example, imposing steel tariffs and shoring up agricultural price supports, and to embark on a domestic spending spree in order to position himself and his party for electoral gains in 2004. Running the tape of history backwards, FDR oversaw massive increases in federal government spending after being swept into office with substantial popular and electoral vote margins in 1932. Juxtaposing these two very different episodes provokes several potentially interesting public choice questions. Other things being the same, are fat or thin victories more conducive to spending growth? Does electoral closeness help explain the ensuing time paths of the principal tools of public finance, taxes, borrowing and money creation? Do close elections or their opposite lead to more foreign conflict?

Given the substantial increases in the size and scope of the public sector over the past four years, why has there been little or no public discussion of the merits of constraining the federal government's fiscal choices? Constitutional limits on spending, taxes and debt were at the forefront of policy debates during the Reagan years, when budget deficits and the federal debt last reached historically high levels. Yet, fiscal discipline, along with the most effective way of ensuring it, has thus far been a non-issue in the new century. Is the absence of public dialogue in 9/11's wake simply additional evidence supporting the ratchet hypothesis of governmental growth discussed in Randall Holcombe's contribution to this volume?

One obvious engine of government growth is the pork barrel spending that predictably emerges in a geographically based representative democracy. A politician representing a geographically defined district or state in the legislature has strong incentives to support programs and policies whose benefits are narrowly focused on his own constituents and whose costs are distributed broadly across the taxpaying public, most of whom reside (and vote) elsewhere. Logrolling bargains with like-minded legislators representing other districts and states help ensure majority support for "Christmas tree" appropriations bills generously trimmed with socially unjustified pork-barrel projects, none of which would pass if voted on alone.

As far as serving as a basis of political representation, geography has no special properties recommending it, however. "Surely where a man lives is the least important thing about him. Constituencies might be formed by dividing people by occupation ... or by age ... or even alphabetically. Or they might not be divided [at all], every member [of the legislature] elected at large..." (Heinlein [1966], 1994, p. 301). Would New York City be better off if, as William F. Buckley, Jr. once said, it was governed by the first 100 people listed in the phonebook than by the politicians then holding office? The positive and normative properties of alternatives to geographically based representation are worthy of additional study.

So, too, is direct democracy. John Matsusaka identifies three reasons why that institution is flourishing, namely, rising educational attainment among the electorate, falling costs of voter access to policy-relevant information and loss of confidence in legislative processes. One could add another item to the list: reductions in the cost of voting itself. Polls are now open longer in most precincts, rules for obtaining absentee ballots have become more generous, and the number of jurisdictions permitting "early voting" in advance of Election Day is growing. To what extent do variations in the costs associated with the act of voting help explain the pattern of direct democracy's diffusion across US states and across nations?

While the twenty-first century was still wearing diapers, the political class congratulated itself for having passed the Bipartisan Campaign Finance Reform Act (McCain-Feingold), having successfully sold it as one of the most effective actions ever taken to control the climbing costs of political campaigns. Faith in the democratic process would soon be restored as the sinister influence of special interests faded away. But, as Thomas Stratmann documents in his essay, the 2004 US presidential election was the most expensive in history, not counting the tens of millions spent to produce "issue" ads that, although sponsored by groups not affiliated formally with any campaign organization, clearly endorsed the policy position of one particular, if unmentioned, candidate. Were these issue ads merely an "unintended consequence" of McCain-Feingold? What motives underlie proposals to reform existing campaign finance laws? Who wins and who loses when limits are imposed on campaign contributions, or if the financing of political campaigns is shifted from the private to the public sector? Public choice is uniquely positioned to inform debate on these important questions.

Corporate governance is a collective action problem, and it is therefore somewhat surprising that public choice scholars have not devoted much attention to the issues it raises. Are participation rates by shareholders in elections deciding matters directly impacting their wealth – the membership of the board of directors, proposed changes in corporate bylaws, and so on – higher or lower than participation rates in democratic elections? Do participation rates vary systematically according to the total number of a corporation's shareholders or the distribution of equity ownership positions across them? Given that shareholders, like voters, typically are large in number, have well-diversified investment portfolios (and therefore have only small claims on any one corporation's profit stream), and tend to be rationally ignorant, the institutions and mechanisms of corporate control are paramount in helping close the principal-agent gap between the owners and managers of corporations, as Harold Mulherin emphasizes in this volume. What lessons does the literature of corporate governance hold for public choice thinking on the relative effectiveness of the various institutions and processes of democratic governance in aligning the interests of politicians, bureaucrats and voters?

Todd Sandler's essay documents some of the important light the economic model of rational choice has shed on the behavior of terrorist groups and on the efficacy of various strategies designed to counter them. How do terrorist groups form? How do they overcome the free-rider problems that plague collective action? Are promises of paradise sufficient to motivate martyrdom, or do less otherworldly selective incentives, such as guarantees of financial rewards to martyrs' families, tend to be more salient? Is "profiling" an effective way of identifying terrorists? Does ordinary politics explain the distribution of funds appropriated in the name of homeland security to harden potential terrorist targets?

Two of our contributors have focused attention on the interest group activity that shapes the policy process in the important areas of school choice and tort reform. Do ideas matter in these or any other policy issue that engages public debate, or are the outcomes simply determined by the partisans' relative political strengths? One possible test in the area of tort reform would involve examining the decisions of federal judges before and after participating in a program created by Henry Manne to educate them in the principles of economics, or by comparing participants with non-participants. Do judges schooled in the economic way of thinking tend to be less generous in awarding damages for pain and suffering? Are their decisions less likely to be overturned on appeal? Milton Friedman, the originator of the school voucher idea, is an articulate spokesman for the benefits of parental choice. But some of the resources of the Milton and Rose Friedman Foundation also have been mobilized to support the activities of voucher proponents around the country. Good ideas may be necessary ingredients in policy change, but perhaps they are not sufficient.

The most important unanswered question on the public choice agenda for the new century is among the oldest: why do people vote? Owing to the law of $1/N$, no one person's vote has more than a vanishingly small chance of being decisive ex ante. Ex post, disputed elections ultimately will be resolved by the sitting legislature or by the courts. The logic of collective action seems to rule out the possibility that votes are cast for instrumental reasons, with an eye toward influencing an election's outcome. But if individuals instead vote for consumption reasons or merely to express their preferences at the polls, what are the implications for public policy formation? How do we get from an assumption that voters are motivated to participate in elections merely to fulfill their civic responsibilities, but in the act of voting nevertheless confer property rights on political officeholders, to hard-edged public policies reflecting the parochial concerns of politicians, bureaucrats and special-interest groups? Can an answer to that question be found in the costliness of modern political campaigns, in conjunction with gerrymandered constituencies and other barriers to entry that insulate incumbents from challengers? Is electoral participation better explained at the level of the group, with group leaders motivating turnout by providing selective incentives to their rank-and-file memberships, than it is at the level of the individual voter? If so, how do these groups form in the first place? Do they tend to coalesce around a single, hot-button issue or a charismatic candidate? How do they maintain their identities and their cohesion over the election cycle, and how do they forge links with potential political allies?

Many other items could be added to the public choice research agenda for the new century. Although an active Japanese Public Choice Society has existed for many years, the field has barely scratched the surface in studying political institutions and political behavior external to western traditions. Study of transitions from centrally planned to market-based economies and from authoritarian regimes to liberal constitutional republics should not default to the Harvard-Berkeley-Stanford axis. More work is needed even within western democracies on such issues as explaining the political forces that trigger privatization and deregulation, understanding how political campaigns are financed and how candidates spend their campaign war-chests, how litigation impacts economic growth, how interest groups allocate their resources between lobbying the legislature and lobbying the judiciary (and how the consequences of rent-seeking through these two institutions might differ), and so on.

We have purposely focused on the potential areas of future research provoked by reading the contributions to this volume; our intention is not to convey the impression that there are no other interesting public choice questions remaining to be asked or answered.

3. Conclusion

The preceding catalog of unfinished business on the public choice research agenda undoubtedly is incomplete and in some cases guilty of confounding positive and normative issues. Read against the backdrop of the essays contributed to this volume, however, the explanatory power of public choice reasoning is undeniable. The field has come far over the past fifty years, but the end of the road is not yet in sight. Public choice is alive and well. Its theories and analytical methods have passed the intellectual market test; they promise to continue to illuminate the political responses to the policy challenges of the new century, including those that none of us can now foresee.

Let us say that modern microeconomics was invented not by the French engineers, but by Alfred Marshall in the late nineteenth century. Nearly 75 years would pass before Ronald Coase (1960) added an exclamation point to the corpus of Marshallian price theory. *The Calculus of Consent* was published in 1962. As the twenty-first century begins, public choice is still awaiting its own exclamation point.

Notes

1. On the other hand, Olson's (1965) "law of the few" predicts that, as a group, the elderly will become less politically effective as their numbers increase. Italy might serve as a useful

natural laboratory for testing Olson's prediction: by 2050, that nation is expected to have fewer taxpayers than pensioners (Rajan & Zingales, 2004, p. 106).

2. During the 1990s, Singapore adopted a reform measure not yet on the table in the United States or Europe. Legislation enacted there grants parents the right to sue children who fail to support them in old age (Rajan & Zingales, 2004, p. 106).

References

Anderson, G. M. (2001). The judiciary. In W. F. Shughart II & L. Razzolini (Eds.), *The Elgar Companion to Public Choice* (pp. 293–309). Edward Elgar: Cheltenham, UK and Northampton, MA, USA.

Anderson, G. M., & Tollison, R. D. (1991). Congressional influence and patterns of new deal spending, 1933–1939. *Journal of Law and Economics, 34*(April), 161–175.

Buchanan, J. M., & Tullock, G. (1962). *The Calculus of Consent: Logical Foundations of Constitutional Democracy*. Ann Arbor: University of Michigan Press.

Coase, R. H. (1960). The problem of social cost. *Journal of Law and Economics, 3*(October), 1–44.

Couch, J. F., & Shughart, W. F. II (1998).*The Political Economy of the New Deal*. Edward Elgar: Cheltenham, UK and Northampton, MA, USA.

Heinlein, R. A. ([1966] 1994). *The Moon is a Harsh Mistress*. New York: Tom Doherty Associates.

Olson, M. (1965). *The Logic of Collective Action: Public Goods and the Theory of Groups*. Cambridge: Harvard University Press.

Rajan, R. G., & Zingales, L. (2004). Making capitalism work for everyone. *Journal of Applied Corporate Finance, 16*(4), 101–108.

Shughart, W. F. II (2004). Bending before the storm: The U.S. supreme court in economic crisis, 1935–1937. *Independent Review, 9*(Summer), 55–83.

Wright, G. (1974). The political economy of new deal spending: An econometric analysis. *Review of Economics and Statistics, 56*(February), 30–38.

MIX
Papier aus verantwortungsvollen Quellen
Paper from responsible sources
FSC® C105338

If you have any concerns about our products,
you can contact us on
ProductSafety@springernature.com

In case Publisher is established outside the EU,
the EU authorized representative is:
Springer Nature Customer Service Center GmbH
Europaplatz 3, 69115 Heidelberg, Germany

Printed by Libri Plureos GmbH
in Hamburg, Germany